Right Where We Belong

Right Where We Belong

HOW REFUGEE TEACHERS AND STUDENTS

ARE CHANGING THE FUTURE

OF EDUCATION

Sarah Dryden-Peterson

HARVARD UNIVERSITY PRESS

Cambridge, Massachusetts

London, England

2022

First printing

Library of Congress Cataloging-in-Publication Data
Names: Dryden-Peterson, Sarah, author.
Title: Right where we belong : how refugee teachers and students are changing
the future of education / Sarah Dryden-Peterson.
Description: Cambridge, Massachusetts : Harvard University Press, 2022. |
Includes bibliographical references and index.
Identifiers: LCCN 2021039651 | ISBN 9780674267992 (hardcover)
Subjects: LCSH: Refugee children—Education. | Refugees—Education. |
Educational innovations. | Teacher-student relationships.
Classification: LCC LC3663 .D78 2022 | DDC 371.826/914—dc23
LC record available at https://lccn.loc.gov/2021039651

For teachers and students,
who are seeking sanctuary, creating home,
and building futures.

For Scott, Khaya, and Mara,
who love deeply, laugh contagiously,
and learn together, always.

Contents

A Note on Word Choice

Some of the people you will get to know in this book embrace the word "refugee." And some reject it. As with all labels, embracing or rejecting depends on how the term is used, in particular how it is co-opted to disempower and to exclude. I use the word "refugee" to embrace the ideas of seeking refuge, of locating sanctuary, and of creating possibilities of belonging.

Abbreviations

ALP	Accelerated Learning Program
CRC	Convention on the Rights of the Child
DRC	Democratic Republic of Congo
EFA	Education for All
KCSE	Kenya Certificate of Secondary Education
MDG	Millennium Development Goals
MEHE	Ministry of Education and Higher Education (Lebanon)
NGO	Non-Governmental Organization
SDG	Sustainable Development Goals
UN	United Nations
UNESCO	United Nations Educational, Scientific and Cultural Organization
UNHCR	United Nations High Commissioner for Refugees
UNICEF	United Nations Children's Fund
UNRPR	United Nations Relief for Palestine Refugees
UNRWA	United Nations Relief and Works Agency for Palestine Refugees in the Near East

Prologue

Our Futures

Currently 26.4 million people live as refugees, the equivalent of Australia or Texas or Delhi or Shanghai. In 2019 alone, 2.4 million people were newly displaced. That is 6,500 people each day, fleeing across a border to seek refuge. Almost half of these refugees are children.[1] The number of refugees globally is growing, and all of our children's chances of experiencing unwanted displacement as a result of conflict and climate change are also increasing.

Home for many refugees who are newly displaced is Syria, Venezuela, or Myanmar. They join millions more whose exile has spanned multiple decades from forty years of conflict in Afghanistan, twenty-five years in Democratic Republic of Congo, and thirty years in Somalia. These countries are not alone. In each year since 1990, between forty and sixty-eight countries, making up 46 to 79 percent of the world's population, have had armed conflict within and between their borders.[2] Conflict and resulting displacement are widespread and global experiences.

Once displaced, refugees now live in exile without a permanent home for between ten and twenty years, three times as long as in the early

1990s.[3] While political solutions and peace remain elusive, millions of refugee children globally risk spending their entire childhoods as if in suspended animation, as if their futures are on hold. They are less likely to go to school.[4] They are less likely to finish school. They are less likely to learn. And they are less likely to feel like they can contribute to their communities.

What would it take to ensure that all refugee young people have access to learning that enables them to feel a sense of belonging and prepares them to help build more peaceful and equitable futures?

I have spent the last fifteen years focused on this question. It is the kind of question that is not easily answered with a single study. I needed to shift the nature of the boundaries that we usually place around research studies. I needed to look across countries; across time; and across political, social, and economic contexts. To align with refugees' lives, experiences, and education that do not fit neatly within these boxes, and in line with emerging transnational social science, I "follow the inquiry" across the artificial lines that typically bound research designs, sites, and samples.

The question has thus led me to sit among students in history classrooms for a year just after the end of apartheid in South Africa; to interviews with Somali newcomer and White long-time resident high school students in the United States; to three years of observations and interviews in open-air community spaces turned into schools by refugees for refugees in Uganda; to transnational communications with students and teachers in refugee-only public schools in isolated camps in Kenya; to work on new United Nations global refugee education strategies in Geneva and from my desk in Boston; to interviews with Afghan, Haitian, South Sudanese, and Zimbabwean refugees rethinking curriculum in their conflict and postconflict homes; to classrooms and cafés and WhatsApp messages, learning from Syrian young people supporting each other to live, and to learn, in Lebanon. Not all of these contexts fit neatly into the legal and political boxes of who is and is not a refugee. While I explore the ways in which legality and politics circumscribe refugees' experiences and their education, my question has led me to adjacent experiences. Other settings of mass migration, marginalization, and political change illuminate processes of conflict mitigation and negotiation of belonging in classrooms, communities, and countries, directly relevant to refugee education.

The research for this book includes fifteen years of ethnographic observation and more than 600 interviews in twenty-three countries (see Map 1, page 8, for the contexts discussed). I have been teacher, observer, interviewer, and advisor. Each position has allowed me—and forced me—to think through divergent perspectives on and experiences with the challenges and the opportunities of refugee education within each specific context and across them all. Long-term research, focused on individuals' experiences, their thinking and decision-making processes, illuminates ways in which particular histories, specific political and social relationships among refugees and nationals, and distinct laws and resources shape the lives of refugees in each context. These particularities act as a caution against universalizing. At the same time, the methods that I have developed in the studies that make up this book center on what can be learned when we resist our inclinations to place boundaries, often artificial ones, around what we study and how, when instead we follow where the questions lead and trace connections between places, among people, and over time (see Map 2, page 24, for locations and movements of selected participants). As I looked across country contexts, across time, and across individuals' and communities' experiences, patterns emerged across particularities that open new ways of thinking about the kinds of education that enable young people to learn, to feel a sense of belonging, and to be prepared to help build more peaceful and equitable futures. The examples I have chosen to include in this book are ones that illuminate these broader patterns and allow a deep probing of the mechanisms of *how* refugee young people and their teachers are creating these kinds of learning, belonging, and future-building (see the Appendix for detailed methodology).

The story that emerges is both discouraging and hopeful. Refugees bump up against ever-changing limits on where they can seek refuge and how long they can stay. Amid this uncertainty, refugee children often find themselves unwelcome in schools and taught to defer even imagining their futures. Yet, despite increasingly polarized and isolationist border politics and migration policies, refugee children and their teachers show us that it is hard, but not impossible, to thrive in uncertainty and build new futures by remaking what and how we learn. The optimism in this story runs quite counter to narratives of individual suffering and broken systems that characterize most of what is written about refugees. This optimism derives from the people who do the work of refugee education daily: refugee teachers and young people who experience these inequities at every turn, consider replicating the status quo as no option at all, and become forerunners in navigating uncertainty and reconceptualizing new futures.

In Chapter 1, you will get to know one of these teachers, Jacques, also a father, a husband, and a refugee from Democratic Republic of Congo. Jacques started a school in Kampala, Uganda, when, in the early 2000s, refugees were not permitted to live in Kampala and refugee children did not have formal access to school. Jacques and the hundreds of other teachers of refugees whom I have observed and learned from ask really good questions. They ask themselves and their students to imagine the kind of life they are seeking in a new country. They ask themselves and their students to question who has power over what and how they learn. They ask themselves and their students to figure out what the purposes of education are and, together, how to make schools into places to act on those purposes. They ask themselves and their students what kind of learning is valuable to them and how to create it. And they ask themselves and their students how they can support each other to imagine and build better futures.

Refugee teachers and students show us, empirically, a new vision for refugee education. They also contribute new conceptual tools for this re-visioning of education, related to experiences of systemic marginalization in schools, demands for justice in the content and structures of learning, and the creation of belonging in classrooms, schools, and communities. They show us that refugee young people need education that enables them to connect their pasts, their presents, and their futures—a wish for education perhaps not dissimilar from parents in any part of the world, those forced to flee conflict, those marginalized in the place they call home, and those much more privileged. And they show us that orienting refugee education toward equity and belonging requires engagement with teachers and schools and also with laws, policies, and institutions that structure migration and economic, social, and political opportunities.

The organization of the book follows a similar logic: weaving together where we are now in refugee education, how we got here, and where we go from here; and purposefully panning in and panning out, weaving together micro and macro, small-scale interactions and their connections with global and national institutions. I focus in on classrooms and relationships among teachers and students. And I step back to the laws, policies, and politics that govern global mobility and that circumscribe who has access to what opportunities and where. I show how patterns of educational practice in refugee education, in schools and classrooms, often replicate the hegemonic structures that govern international development, humanitarianism, and geopolitics. I also show what people—particularly refugee teachers and students—are doing about these systematic exclusions to remake the future of education.

The themes of each chapter reflect this vision and these practices— "Teacher," "Sanctuary," "Power," "Purpose," "Learning," and "Belonging." Each theme resonates both within each context and across them. The arc of them, the way I have ordered them, also reflects the ways teachers and students come to weave together past, present, and future, so that the momentum of the book moves primarily from past to present to future, while also showing the spiral of these three temporalities throughout. In "Teacher," the longitudinal experiences of Jacques, as refugee and as teacher, give shape to the sequential questions that students and teachers pose to themselves and each other as they experience learning and teaching in exile. When forced to leave home, what can protect us ("Sanctuary")? Who decides what we learn, and with what consequence for our futures ("Power")? How are our education and our future opportunities connected ("Purpose")? What kind of learning can prepare us—all of us—to take up and create opportunities ("Learning")? How can we fight the inequities that limit these opportunities, changing how each of us see ourselves in connection to others and redesigning our institutions to reflect that ("Belonging")?

Across places and times, I have found that it is teachers like Jacques and their students who are the generative and forward-looking leaders *doing* this work. They learn how to accept uncertainty and adapt to change. Rather than forward the unrealistic notion that all will soon return to "normal," they embrace unfamiliar contexts and develop lifelong capacities to navigate new situations. They also learn how to examine historical and current inequities and take action to disrupt them. Understanding the root causes of the conflicts and inequities that shape refugee young people's experiences becomes core and not tangential to education in these spaces, reducing the dissonance between school learning and students' identities and daily lives. They learn as well how to build relationships across lines of difference and to remake spaces of exclusion into ones of belonging. Despite rigid and exclusionary boundaries on legal and political sanctuary imposed by states, some teachers and students create relationships in schools that are filled with listening and care, that foster stability, and that cultivate connections of interdependence. Across these kinds of learning is a focus on the future: embracing a future of uncertainty and learning to thrive within it; envisioning a future that disrupts current inequities to create opportunities for social, economic, and political participation; and modeling a future of interconnectedness, rooted in intentionally cultivated relationships.

In these relationships, often in opposition to larger social and political forces, teachers and their refugee students blur boundaries of belonging that had felt unwelcoming and immoveable and experience how their individual and collective interests are entwined. They demonstrate how a major rethinking of refugee education in terms of institutions and state governance and also in terms of relationships and future-building can enable a renegotiation of who belongs and a reimagination of how we are interdependent. These new ways of thinking are relevant not only for refugees but also for many of our young people globally, especially those who experience marginalization and for whom uncertainty is the only context in which they have ever experienced education, in schools and education systems that fail to deliver the future-building opportunities they promise. In an increasingly divided world, we need the examples and insights of refugee teachers and young people on how to reimagine education so that all children are prepared to address ever-more-common uncertainties and inequities—exacerbated by war, climate change, pandemics—and to build peaceful and equitable futures.

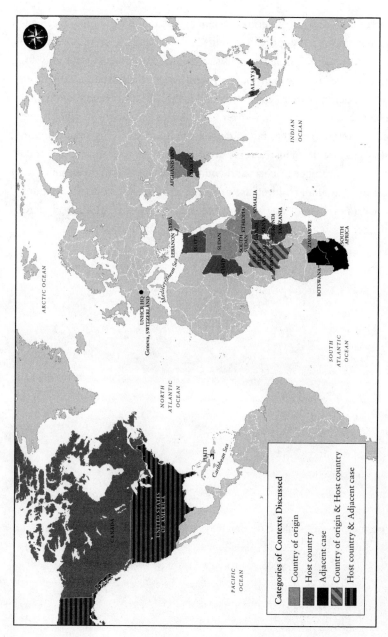

Map 1. Contexts Discussed

1

Teacher

Jacques sits on the edge of the only chair in his one-room home.[1] It has thick, well-worn armrests and the once-overstuffed blue cushion on the seat sags a little while a bright yellow embroidered doily is draped carefully across the top, behind Jacques's head. It is almost seven o'clock in the morning and, in the equatorial country of Uganda, that means the sun has just risen, no matter the time of year. The room is dark, though. There are no windows in its concrete walls and the lacy, white curtain that covers the one narrow doorway to the outside has not yet begun its fluttering dance in the so far calm and windless morning.

This is the one time of day that Jacques is alone, that his guard is down, that his mind is quiet. His children, Julie and Nicolas, are in the back of the house, in the little laneway that separates this row of concrete homes from the next and the next. In the rainy season, the laneway fills to become a creek of dirty, sewage-like water with swarms of malarial mosquitoes. This time of year, at this time of morning, it is filled with soapy, laughing children from around the neighborhood, splashing water from brightly colored plastic basins onto their skin, still warm from sleep, wriggling with the chill of the cold water. The lucky ones, those for whom a day of learning stretches ahead of them, know that every inch of their bodies must be clean before they put on their perfectly washed and pressed school uniforms. Julie and Nicolas are among the lucky ones.

Jacques's wife, Marie, is on the front stoop. She is bent at the waist, deeply attentive to a large tin pot balanced on a charcoal stove. There are no handles on the pot, only a skinny rim, which she holds steady with her almost heat-resistant hands. Marie has been up for hours. The morning porridge has been made, served, and consumed. But the midday meal cannot wait. *Matoke*, a Ugandan staple that her family, in their new home, has only just learned to like, takes hours to cook. She has already peeled these hard, green bananas with a knife and set them to boil in a pot of water lined with shiny, pliable banana leaves. She stands up every once in a while to get away from the heat of the stove and, each time, adjusts the red, green, and yellow swath of cloth that is tied tightly around her waist and that falls straight downward to cover her almost to the ankles.

Jacques enjoys these few minutes on his own. The family's one-room home is by night a crowded bedroom and by day a crowded living area. There is no wasted space. Dishes and cooking supplies, neatly stacked, line one side of the room. Mattresses, already put away at this early hour, are tucked behind the cabinet. A small shelf, behind the chair where Jacques sits, holds their most prized possessions: photos from home, and books.

Julie, age six, comes into the room and, with a slight shiver from the predawn air, walks over to sit down next to her father, to share in his warmth. Jacques knows that Julie never likes to be far from his side. She gazes up at him and smiles. He smiles back down at her and squeezes her gently.

A few years ago, Julie had hair full of braids, with red and white plastic beads that clicked when she moved her head, which she did often for the love of the sound. A schoolgirl now, Julie must have short, cropped hair, defined by the school as part of the uniform. She can look serious in the semi-darkness, but her sparkling and playful eyes belie that impression.

"Julie," Jacques says, in Kiswahili, "can you fetch me the Bible, in English."

It takes Julie only a split second to jump from her seat, gracefully place herself in the narrow space between her father's chair and the bookshelf, and pick out the correct one among the many: not the French one, not the Kiswahili one, not the Luganda one, but the English one, as her father had asked.

Jacques smiles when Julie hands him the Bible. "Thank you," he says, in English this time.

"You are most welcome," Julie pipes back in the sing-song way she has learned to say these English words at school.

Language is a constant reminder to Jacques that this is not his home. Home is DRC. Home is the Kihunde language. Home is the family he has not seen in five years. Jacques is a refugee in Uganda. Home is a place where he could build his future.

For Jacques, though, home is also what he makes for his children no matter where they are. "You cannot leave the future of your children for others to take care of," he says.

"They do not know that we are refugees," Jacques explains about his children, sadly yet with a matter-of-fact tone. "Nicolas," who is three, "knows that he is Congolese, he knows that he comes from Goma. He knows that his grandmother and grandfather are in Goma. Julie knows that also. They do not think they are Ugandans." Jacques pauses, but then quickly continues. "But they do not think we are refugees."

Yet not a day goes by when Jacques is not reminded that *he* is a refugee. The Jacques of home, the husband to Marie, the father to Julie and Nicolas, does not dare enter the streets of Kampala—Uganda's capital— as himself.

When he walks away from the neighbors who know him, he becomes a different person. Small in stature, in the streets of Kampala, Jacques becomes small in presence. His body stiff and rigid, he weaves between the crowds of people shining shoes, selling tomatoes, on their way to somewhere. His own eyes are always focused on a destination, never on a face. The broad smile that is always present when he is in the company of family and friends disappears. So changed is his look and disposition that he becomes unrecognizable.

And that is his goal. Jacques was a human rights activist in Congo. His work began as a personal protest against the persecution of his minority Bahunde ethnic group in his home districts of Walikale and Massisi. As the conflict in Congo grew, he became involved with an NGO named L'Action pour la Défense des Droits de l'Homme au Congo (Action for the Defense of Human Rights in Congo), which fought, visibly and in many districts, for the rights of civilians. But government forces on one side and rebel militia on the other are both powerful in eastern Congo, and it is civilians like Jacques in the middle who bear the burdens of the conflict. Over four million people have been killed in Congo since 1998, more than in any other part of the world.[2] While this massive conflict has seemed to escape attention outside Congo, the human rights activities of a small group could not escape the attention of the authorities.

In a letter dated December 26, 1999, the Direction Générale de la Sécurité Interieure (General Directorate of Internal Security) ordered the immediate arrest of anyone associated with the human rights group with which Jacques worked. Two days later, he was imprisoned and later tortured, only to escape on January 17, 2000, when a fire spread through the prison and all of the guards fled to protect themselves. The International Committee of the Red Cross helped Jacques and Marie, who was pregnant with Julie, to reach the Ugandan border.

When he arrived in Uganda in late January 2000, Jacques was one of 236,100 refugees there. Overwhelmingly, these refugees had fled Sudan, which was then enduring a decades-old civil war, but there were also growing numbers of people who had come from DRC and a few from Somalia.[3] Uganda's refugee policies at this time fell under the Control of Alien Refugees Act (CARA), an outdated legal framework that predated Uganda's 1976 ratification of the 1951 Refugee Convention.[4]

The Act determined where in Uganda refugees had to live. It severely restricted refugees' freedom of movement and mandated that they live in rural and isolated refugee camps, known in Uganda by the magnanimous words yet no less constraining concept of "refugee settlements." As Zachary Lomo, then the director of the Refugee Law Project of Makerere University in Kampala, described, "Legal mechanisms are in place in terms of opening the door and allowing them [refugees] in [to Uganda], but once they were in, their lives were chained. They used all forms of chains . . . [saying] 'You are only a refugee if you accept my terms.' . . . The Control of Alien Refugees Act actually creates criminals of those refugees who leave the refugee settlement. . . . All of this affected the ability of the refugee to exploit their own abilities. . . . The whole refugee system is control-based to satisfy the ego of the 'helper.'"[5] With control over where and how refugees could live in Uganda, these global and national "helpers" defined parameters for any possible new home in exile. Though the Act was not consistently or strictly applied, assertion of control over where and how refugees lived—rather than practices of protection of their rights—was a key component of refugee policy in Uganda at the time of Jacques's exile.[6]

Jacques did not know the specifics of this Act, but these specifics circumscribed every action he took from the moment he arrived in Uganda. Before Jacques could even enter the office of InterAid, the NGO mandated to assist refugees in Kampala, his way was blocked by a big sign on the door that stated "It is government policy that all asylum seekers must register at entry points in the north. You are, therefore, all asked to return to the north and register there."[7] The "north" was more than five hundred kilometers away and the cost of getting there was far more than Jacques and Marie had to their name. They stayed in Kampala. They were seeking refuge, but they could not register for the protections of refugees, which they would receive only within the distant settlements.

After five months in Kampala—Jacques remembers the exact date and time, June 22, 2000 at 10 A.M.—he was stopped at the Kibuye roundabout. This roundabout acts as a kind of guard post for Kampala. With five roads that come together at this very point from in and out of the city, the traffic is always stopped: bumper to bumper, mirror to mirror, with drivers able to reach out and touch each other. In this jam of invisibility, it is usually easy to pass through it from one side to the other, unnoticed. But as unrecognizable as Jacques is as Jacques, he is immediately identifiable to any Ugandan as a foreigner, a refugee, or, in the derogatory slang he heard so often, *"MuZaïri,"* a word literally meaning from the former Zaïre but said with a tone that signaled to Jacques "you are not welcome here."

Jacques was stopped at Kibuye by two men, one in a Ugandan police uniform and one in civilian clothes. Knowing well his own body's reaction to fear, Jacques was not surprised when he felt beads of sweat begin to form at the nape of his neck and his heart begin its side-to-side dance. He recognized the man in civilian clothes as an information agent from the Rassemblement Congolais pour la Démocratie-Goma (RCD-Goma), the main rebel group operating in his home of eastern DRC that was fighting to overthrow Congo's then president, Laurent-Désiré Kabila. It was RCD-Goma that had arrested the members of Jacques's human rights group. The government of Uganda had been working with the RCD-Goma in eastern Congo, trading military support for the right to exploit Congo's rich mineral resources, in particular diamonds and the tantalite used to make cell phones. Now, with so many refugees from Congo in exile in Uganda, this collaboration extended into Ugandan territory.[8] Human Rights Watch documented the danger in which this placed refugees: "Refugees from the territories of the DRC controlled by Uganda until October 2002 are under the control of the same authorities responsible for their original persecution [in Uganda]. Human rights activists and other prominent community leaders are frequently followed by security services of the RCD-Goma, and sometimes threatened. The situation is so difficult for some refugees that they are terrified to leave their shelters."[9]

Luckily, the RCD-Goma agent did not recognize Jacques as a human rights activist wanted by Congolese authorities, only as a Congolese man.

After two hours of questioning and having his documents confiscated, Jacques was released. Heading straight to the Kampala offices of the United Nations High Commissioner for Refugees (UNHCR), the international agency responsible for refugee protection, Jacques related his experience.

The UNHCR protection officer had a simple answer. He told Jacques, "You are a civilian in enemy territory. The only place we can protect you is in the refugee camp. You must go there immediately."

"Allez au camp [go to the camp]" had not yet become the familiar refrain for Jacques that it would be years later, when he would come to think of it as UNHCR's throw-your-hands-up-in-the-air solution to every refugee's problems. He did not yet know what the camp had in store, only that he was not safe in Kampala. So he and Marie packed their few belongings and, with newborn Julie, made the day-long journey to the Kyangwali refugee settlement in western Uganda.

Jacques knew the refugee camp was in a rural area and that he would need to take up, for the first time in his life, subsistence agriculture. "I had never held a hoe!" he exclaimed. Even so, he had what he called "hope in his heart" that he would find safety and that his family would be *tran-quille,* the French word that, said aloud, sounds exactly like what it is supposed to mean: calm, quiet, serene, peaceful.

In the camp, though, Jacques encountered the very same RCD-Goma combatants, now attempting to pass as refugees. Jacques was so fearful that he did not want to leave his small, mud-walled home. He was terrified of being killed in the middle of this camp and abandoning his family to a fate he could not bring himself to imagine. Eight months later, he and his family packed up again, left the refugee camp, and moved back to Kampala. Jacques and his family were part of a growing number of refugees—now over 60 percent globally—who settle in cities, defying the persistent stereotype that refugees, by definition, live in camps.[10] He preferred the fear of living undocumented in a place that would allow him to practice his profession over the fear of having to subsist where he had to dig and cultivate, unsuccessfully and in fear, to feed his family.

Jacques is a teacher. It is his vocation, or what he often describes as his "calling." He completed secondary school in DRC in what was called the "pedagogy" track. Most teachers in DRC have only this level of education, and Jacques still shakes his head when he thinks of how little he knew when he first began teaching: "Just barely more than my pupils," he said. What Jacques did have was a disposition that had been cultivated in him by several of his own teachers, including his father who was a teacher himself and also known as a peacemaker in their community. Jacques felt a keen responsibility to teach children, wherever he might find them. Eastern DRC is a place of dense forests and widely dispersed villages, and he knew that he might find himself in a situation where all he had were a group of children and the shelter of a tree as his classroom. No matter the difficulty, no matter how distant from a world of school buildings, Jacques would teach these children. When he arrived in Kampala, he found himself, he said, "as someone who is in the forest." A dense urban forest, in which groups of children, especially refugee children, were not even privy to the shelter of a tree.

In Kampala, without so much as a bunch of matoke to feed his own family, Jacques dedicated himself to building a school. "What prompted me [to start this school]," he said, was that "there were many refugee children who did not go to school. They passed their days in the street." Jacques's idea of "building" a school was not so much to construct a physical structure but rather to gather a corps of teachers who would inspire learning in Kampala's refugee children. "A school is not the building. It is the teachers," Jacques often says. He wrote down his goal for the school, in red ink, on a plain white sheet of paper, in a file that he carried around with him everywhere: *"Assurer une éducation de base à nos enfants et leurs préparer à leur vie future* [Ensure for our children a basic education to prepare them for their future lives]."

Jacques's physical school depended on what he could arrange. Once it was a room in a church leader's home, where the children, who sought refuge there, rolled up their sleeping mats and blankets each morning to make space to sit (2000–2002). Then it was a cavernous, windowless, doorless space of a church under construction, where children of all ages placed benches on the dusty floor, stacked one high for seats, two high for desks (2002–2004). Then, a local school where refugee children shared space with Ugandan national children (2005–2006). Then, a brand-new, stand-alone classroom, built with boards and dirt, paid for with funds from the French Embassy (2007–2009). And, finally, the refurbishment and extension of that classroom into a full school with concrete walls and floors and a tin roof, with funding from UNHCR and registered with the Uganda Ministry of Education and Sports (2010 to the present).

At nine o'clock on a sunny Monday morning in October 2002, I met Jacques at his school. I had heard about him at InterAid, the same NGO where Jacques had found the unwelcome sign and the directive to go to the camps. I was sitting in a waiting room crowded with refugees who, like Jacques, did not have the resources to "return to the north to register" for their rights. I sat next to an older Congolese man. When I greeted him in French, his eyes lit up. "But, Madame, you speak French?" he asked me incredulously. I explained that I was Canadian, and he explained that even within these large organizations dedicated to serving refugees, English was the language of choice, of power, and of getting things done. The *mʒungus*, he said, speak only English. I knew by this time that I was a mzungu, a Kiswahili word that translates to "one who wanders" but is used widely in East Africa to refer to foreigners, usually White foreigners. While French was perhaps this man's fourth or fifth language, it was the language of his education, and it reminded him of home. He was so happy to speak it that I sat listening to him as he waited to speak with an NGO staff member, for almost three hours. He was then told that they could not see him that day and that he would have to come back. "This is normal," he told me in full-voiced French, not afraid that someone in the office would understand what he said. "Refugees' time is not valued." "What has been valuable to me," he continued, "has been speaking with you." He had introduced himself to me as Innocent, but I never saw him again. Yet he had also given me a lasting gift. He told me about a man he called "the refugee teacher."

The next day, I went to Najjanankumbi, the area of Kampala where Innocent told me I would find "the refugee teacher." I asked the shopkeepers of the two small stalls filled with neatly stacked tomatoes and buckets of beans if they knew where I might find a school for refugee children from Congo. At the third stall, a wizened old woman shrugged her shoulders and gave me a quizzical look, but she then pointed to a man sitting on the back of a motorcycle and told me, "He is from Zaïre." Seeing himself pointed out, the man jumped off his motorcycle and approached me. Before he had time to greet me, I spoke to him in French. Like Innocent, his eyes lit up. I asked him about the school. Of course he knew where it was, he said, and he would take me there right away.

We walked for several kilometers, off the main road, and finally up a steep and deeply rutted dirt path. It was the time of year of the flying ants, *enswa*, and together we walked through swirling clouds of these white insects and of children, home because they were unable to afford the hidden costs of school, who were catching and eating this once-a-year treat.[11] Amid the glistening, green banana leaves, and the tall piles of trash, and the shreds of plastic bags fluttering in the wind, we found the school and "the refugee teacher." We approached the door, a hole in the concrete wall. In each of the four corners of this otherwise hollow building, I saw children, sitting in neat rows, listening intently to their teachers, raising their hands, talking with each other. Without walls or dividers, the teachers and students had, with their focus on each other, created small-feeling classrooms in this wide-open space.

Jacques, obviously the head teacher, approached the doorway to greet his uninvited guests, while a teacher from the far classroom corner stepped in to teach Jacques's class. After we spoke for several minutes, Jacques politely told me that while he was very interested in knowing more about my work, his students were waiting for him. He invited me to return to the school the next day, after class time, when he would have more time to talk.

Every other person I had met in Uganda had been quick to drop what they were doing to talk to me. I was aware of the assumptions and expectations embodied in my White skin. But Jacques was clear: his loyalty was to his students and his priority was their learning, despite the thick powers of race and class that surrounded us.

Over the next ten years, Jacques consistently demonstrated this deep care for his students and acted unwaveringly to inspire their learning, to "prepare them for their future lives," as he had once written in red ink on that plain sheet of white paper. In addition to his father, Jacques remembers two teachers important in his own life. The first was an old man by the name of Léonard who answered every question his students asked. The second was Sidonie, a young woman from his community who also "was [a] neighbor." Jacques explained how she fed all the children who lived nearby when they were hungry, and he recalled the loving way she had carried him once when his legs were too short and he could not walk through the deep mud.

I could see these two teachers in Jacques as he interacted with his students. Jacques called every student by name. He made sure to hear the voice of each student during every lesson. This personalized attention is rare in refugee classrooms, as it is in the classrooms of his DRC home and across many low- and middle-income countries, where there are often more than one hundred students in a single class.[12] Instead of writing a list of vocabulary words on the sole fragment of chalkboard he had, Jacques wrote "*J'apprends du vocabulaire* [I learn vocabulary]," placing each student in the role of active learner. At the end of each lesson, Jacques said to his students, "*Merci beaucoup pour aujourd'hui* [thank you for today]." When I visited students' homes with him, he was welcomed as a respected teacher and as a friend.

Through his teaching and interactions like these, Jacques explained that he had two goals for his students. First, that they learn to be part of life in Uganda for now and, second, that they learn what they need to know to prepare themselves for their futures. But where and what would these futures be? This is the question Jacques was preoccupied with, for himself and for his students.

For himself, Jacques's preferred future was to return home to DRC. "In one's own village," that is where one really feels at home, he said. It is a place where the future can be imaginable. But in the context of ongoing war and "no rule of law," where "you could be killed no matter when for no matter what reason," any sort of predictable future of return is not possible.

Jacques had come to the conclusion that home, then, is what he can build for himself, his students, and his children wherever they are. When you become a refugee, "you must begin to *live* here," Jacques said, pointing to the ground beneath him to emphasize that here is where one is, "from the moment you arrive." With this in mind, he had multiple futures mapped out for his students. As he made plans for the school, he wrote in his notebook, in French, "The students who benefit from our teaching are the future citizens and workers should they return to their countries of origin and can thus contribute to the development of the world. On the other hand, once integrated into Ugandan society, they could also contribute to the development of Uganda."

Since the future does not yet exist, unknowable futures are ubiquitous for all children, not only for refugees like Jacques's students.[13] Yet uncertainty is magnified for refugee young people, as what can seem like unanswerable questions about where the future will be and how to best prepare for it are permanent features of their lives. Refugees may enter exile as children, but they remain in exile as adults in almost every case. In 2004, I met a Somali man in the Nakivale refugee settlement who had grown up in that place and was now raising his own family there. "My name is Uganda," he said metaphorically.[14] Exile was all he had known.

Refugees are defined by the 1951 Refugee Convention and 1967 Protocol Relating to the Status of Refugees as those who are outside their countries of nationality "owing to well-founded fear of being persecuted for reasons of race, religion, nationality, membership of a particular social group or political opinion."[15] These legal definitions can hide the complex and devastating human consequences of flight, the leaving behind of property and livelihoods, as well as family members and networks of belonging, and plans and imaginings of a future.

Despite the increasing number of refugees and the current heightened awareness of their situations across Europe and North America, forced migration is an old and recurring experience. Between 1501 and 1867, 12.5 million Africans were kidnapped, forced to migrate, and enslaved.[16] More than 40 million people were displaced across Europe by the end of World War II.[17] Independence movements across Africa saw more than 850,000 people become refugees in the single year of 1965. Between March and May of 1971, more than 100,000 people per day entered India from East Pakistan, now Bangladesh; by the end of 1971, there were 10 million refugees in India. In July 1994, one million refugees crossed from Rwanda into what was then Zaïre, 15,000 each hour on one particular day.[18]

The conflicts that force people from their homes are often cyclical, adding to the uncertainty that refugees experience. When Jacques arrived in Uganda in 2000, South Sudan was eleven years away from gaining its independence. Subsumed within Sudan, the South Sudanese had experienced two prolonged civil wars in the second half of the twentieth century, each lasting two decades.[19] In 2000, 212,156 Sudanese refugees were living in Uganda.[20] After the signing of the Comprehensive Peace Agreement in 2005, much of the violence in what was to become South Sudan ceased, and refugees returned "home." Yet these now-former refugees, many of whom had never before been outside of Uganda, "returned" home to "a shattered infrastructure . . . generations of youth who have never had the opportunity to attend school . . . and insecurity in many parts of the country."[21] In December 2013, tensions in South Sudan between political and ethnic factions aligned with the president, Salva Kiir, and the former vice president, Riek Machar, erupted in renewed widespread violence. Just prior, the number of South Sudanese refugees in Uganda had been reduced by almost 200,000, with just 22,483 remaining.[22] Yet, since then, the South Sudanese states of Upper Nile, Jonglei, and Unity have been engulfed in conflict. By June 2020, there were more than 2.2 million South Sudanese refugees, 1.4 million of them in Uganda.[23]

Like Jacques, most refugees imagine and plan that their exile will be short-lived, that they will return to their homes within a matter of months, at most a year or two. The reality is that, like Jacques, they will remain refugees for large swaths of their lives and, even if they do return home, as for so many South Sudanese, that return of which they dream may be shockingly temporary. Langston Hughes asks in his poem *Harlem*, "What happens to a dream deferred?" and suggests that it might "dry up," "fester," or explode."[24]

When Jacques arrived in Kampala, gathered together refugee children and teachers, and brought them into a community of learning, his actions were out of a conviction that "a dream deferred" was not an option. At that time, this was a radical idea. Prevailing thought by the global and national "helpers" was that education for refugees was nothing but a holding ground, to create a more stable present but to defer the creation of a future. With little more than a nod toward the right to education for all, the focus was on school as a way to return refugee children, temporarily, to "normalcy," whatever it is that might be normal or desirable about the experiences these children had amid conflict and exile.[25]

Jacques's actions and the school he created represented a different vision for refugee education. Centered in countering the underlying inequities and the violence that his students had experienced, education was not about a return to some idealistic "normalcy." Jacques understood the kind of future the children who came every day to sit on hard wooden benches in the cavernous space of a dirt-floored church stood to inherit if he—as their teacher—did not help them to cultivate the capacities to disrupt the status quo and to create the future anew.

2

Sanctuary

When Abdi was a child, his sanctuary was his mother's strong, loving arms. She was born in Ogaden, which the maps in his school said was Ethiopia but which his father had grown up to think of as part of Somalia.

"Am I Ethiopian?" Abdi remembers asking himself. "Am I Somali?" Abdi didn't know. But both, he felt as a young boy, seemed to be bad words, spat at him in the streets and at his school by other children.

As a little boy, he did not understand why.

He remembers, though, the stories he heard in whispered tones. Struggles over land that dated back centuries between Somali and Ethiopian kingdoms. Borders drawn hastily by colonial powers, doing a lot more dividing than uniting.

Abdi remembers other stories that were told to him in less hushed tones, ones that held possibilities for him creating a future different to this past that was filled with division and exclusion. In 2003, when I met him, as a refugee in Kampala, Uganda, he described thinking back to a

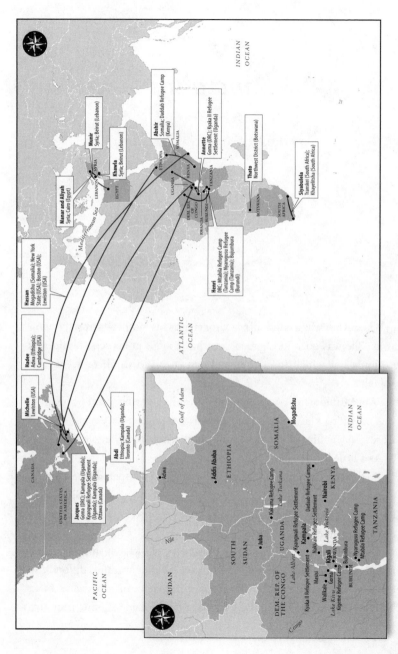

Map 2. Locations and Movements of Selected Protagonists

story he had once been told about a sultan, a girl, and a sheep's gullet (a gullet is the passageway for food between the mouth and the stomach). Once upon a time, the story went, there was a sultan, a clever one.[1] He set a challenge for his people to answer this question: what part of the sheep can divide people or unite them? This was a test all of them wanted to take up, as they all wanted to be honored by the sultan as a wise man. Each man returned to his compound, thinking and talking to one another about the possible answer. What part could it be? Perhaps it is a fat and juicy part, thought one, setting aside a leg. Perhaps it is the prized liver, thought another. One man thought more than most. He was the poorest man in the kingdom, when measured by the livestock he possessed. Yet in children, he was the richest. How could he bring part of one of his few sheep to the sultan, he wondered, when this meat might keep his children healthy and strong? His eldest daughter, ever attentive to the questions of her father, looked to the horizon and over the hills of the kingdom. Quietly, she removed the sheep's gullet and handed it to her father. Her father was shocked. How could this unusable part of the sheep be the answer to the wise sultan's challenge? But the father trusted his daughter, and together the two of them brought the gullet to the sultan. He waited for the sultan's laughter at his ignorance, for his rage at his disrespect. But none came. His daughter had chosen wisely. To the sultan she said, "I had my father bring you a sheep's gullet because it is truly a symbol of what unites or divides us. There are those in this world who have much and those who have little. When people do not share, they become enemies. But when they share with one another they can live in peace. The gullet delivers shared food to a hungry stomach. When no food is shared it is empty. It can be a symbol of greed or generosity. Greed or generosity, in turn, divide people or unite them."[2]

For Abdi, the girl in this story described a place he did not recognize but that he wanted to know. In his life at home in Ethiopia and in exile in Uganda, Abdi saw very little sharing. He had seen very many hungry stomachs. When he was a teenager, he watched his parents die for what others thought they were, not what he knew them to be.

The question that the sultan posed to his people was one that Abdi confronted daily: what unites us and divides us? In the sheep's gullet, the wise girl found a metaphor that could convey to the people of her home the importance of sharing and of bridging the divide between greed and generosity to create peace. What are the possibilities for living this metaphor in our daily lives?

At the time I met him, home for Abdi was a small shed, at the back of an office building in Kampala. It was simply where he lived and had for more than nine years. The floor was cold, his thin mattress providing little protection. But Abdi was a refugee, living in Kampala, and his experience had shown him that this was the sanctuary a refugee could hope for. He wrote poetry about this life of a refugee in the "dark night" of his backyard shed: "I have no place to go, I'm just like / The air blowing around, no stay . . ."[3] and "I said that I'm an unhcr mandate refugee / The officer said, "what is that?" / And started beating me with a stick."[4]

Abdi had a letter from UNHCR: "This is to certify that the above-named person whose photograph appears below is a refugee known to this office. Any assistance rendered to him will be highly appreciated."[5] He pointed to the bottom of the letter. An expiration date. For Abdi, it confirmed what he already knew: sanctuary expires.

On a fall day in 2005, Abdi invited me to share Ethiopian food with him.[6] This food, he explained, represented for him the continued connection he felt to the strong, loving arms of his late mother, even living as he did more than twelve thousand kilometers away. We were in Toronto, Canada, a few blocks from my own childhood home, from the strong and loving arms of my mother. Abdi lived in Toronto now, resettled, unlike 99 percent of refugees, by UNHCR to a place that might, finally, be the sanctuary he had been seeking since he was a child: a sanctuary with no expiry date.

Abdi had his own apartment and a real mattress off the floor. He wore stylish cargo pants and carried a backpack, on his back rather than on his front, something he would never dare to do in Kampala for fear of being robbed.

"Do you feel free here?" I asked him.

Abdi thought for a long time. "Yes," he said, finally, slowly and still uncertainly. "Yes."

"Can you see the future now?" I asked the question hesitantly, knowing that he had been looking for months, without success, for a job, knowing too that without this shared meal, this would be one of yet another long night of a hungry stomach.

Abdi took another piece of *injera*, the staple Ethiopian flatbread, and lowered his eyes. "I don't know," he said, almost unheard.

We sat quiet for some time.

"Do you remember?" Abdi asked. "Do you remember the song you taught in that English class?"

I smiled, remembering, but I thought he was changing the subject. It was "Blowin' in the Wind," Bob Dylan's civil rights protest song with its melodic origins in the African American antislavery spiritual "No More Auction Block." The English class Abdi remembered was in Kampala. It was made up of a group of refugee women from DRC who, like Jacques, were trying to make their lives in the city. They had approached me with a letter, signed by sixty-two people, asking me to teach an English class. They wanted to be able to interact with neighbors and possibly find jobs in Kampala. So I began the class and was teacher to forty women, most of whom had small babies strapped to their backs.

One day in March 2003, I decided to shift the habitual rhythm of the class from practice dialogues, and the learning of vocabulary through these dialogues, to learning a song. At one moment, the women were sitting, learning the words to the song and their meaning, one word at a time: ". . . how many years can some people exist / Before they're allowed to be free? . . . The answer, my friend, is blowin' in the wind."[7] At the next, as the words began to come together and their meaning became clear, the women rose and started to sing.[8]

Sitting in Toronto, Abdi tells me he never thought he would see a room full of refugees singing. "What was there for a refugee to sing about?" he said.

I remember seeing Abdi that day in Kampala, only as we belted out the last few words of the song. His body, half hidden by the banister, his face peering through the triangle between the ceiling and the stairs, above the room where we were singing. He looked like a kid, peering down into a nighttime grown-up's world, wanting to remain invisible long enough so that his presence would not change what was going on.

"It gave me hope," he said quietly these two years later in Toronto. I realized he was not changing the subject. Seeing the future depended on hope.

As a child, I thought "blowin' in the wind" meant that everyone could figure out the answers to the questions the song asked: ". . . how many times can a man turn his head / Pretending he just doesn't see? . . . how many ears must one man have / Before he can hear people cry? . . . how many deaths will it take till he knows / That too many people have died?"[9] After all, the wind belonged to all of us, was around all of us. We just needed to listen.

With a sanctuary that felt always on the verge of expiring, Abdi could not begin to see answers to these questions and could not imagine the future. Like he said in his own poem, written two weeks after he learned "Blowin' in the Wind" from the women in my class, he is "just like / The air blowing around, no stay. . . ."

Locating Sanctuary

Everyone has the right to seek and to enjoy in other countries
asylum from persecution.

—ARTICLE 14, UNIVERSAL DECLARATION OF HUMAN RIGHTS

In July 1951, in Geneva, Switzerland, twenty-six countries signed the Convention Relating to the Status of Refugees.[10] Building on the 1948

Universal Declaration of Human Rights and the right to seek asylum from persecution, this Refugee Convention was part of a massive undertaking to redefine global responsibility in the wake of World War II, during which more than forty million people had been displaced.[11] The 1951 Refugee Convention defines the status and rights of a refugee when they are outside their country of nationality due to this persecution.[12] In 1967, an additional protocol to accompany the Refugee Convention expanded the initial focus, which had been on Europe and post–World War II displacement, in order to apply the provisions, regardless of geography or time.[13] These two documents continue to provide the framework to determine who is a refugee and who is not. One hundred and forty-five countries are now signatory to the Refugee Convention, and 146 to the accompanying protocol.[14]

What constitutes a "well-founded fear of being persecuted" along any of the dimensions articulated in the Refugee Convention—"race, religion, nationality, membership of a particular social group or political opinion"—is defined by the country of possible sanctuary, each by itself. When Jacques arrived in Uganda in 2000, he was granted *prima facie* refugee status, like all others fleeing eastern DRC at that time. Prima facie, literally from the Latin "at first look" or in the law "accepted as correct until proven otherwise," means that a country grants refugee status to all refugees from a particular country. In 1956, Hungarians arriving in Austria after the failed revolution were granted this form of refugee status. Years later, between the fall of Saigon and the final Vietnam peace accord, any Vietnamese individual arriving in a neighboring Asian country was also prima facie a refugee.[15] But after the peace accord, anyone fleeing Vietnam was required by countries in which they arrived to pursue refugee status through a different process: Refugee Status Determination (RSD). No longer was such a person considered prima facie a refugee but instead needed to make their individual case as to what the well-founded fear of persecution was that required a country to provide sanctuary.

As an Ethiopian national, Abdi spent years in limbo, seeking asylum in Uganda through this RSD process. While counter to the 1951 Refugee

Convention, global and national refugee policies at this time, including in Uganda, had become restrictive on the geography of sanctuary. Policies on refugee status aimed at limiting "secondary movement", emphasized a first country of possible asylum over a safe country of asylum.[16] Because Uganda and Ethiopia do not share a border, a would-be refugee from Ethiopia would need to have money enough to fly from Addis Ababa to Entebbe to make Uganda the first country of possible asylum. For poor Ethiopians not able to travel by plane, instead often on foot with the occasional ride from a generous truck or bus driver, the first country would not be Uganda. Having reached Uganda through what was then Sudan—not a safe place of asylum, given its decades-long civil war—Abdi could obtain asylum in Uganda only if an RSD process determined extenuating circumstances for him, which, only years later, it did.

Refugee status granted through prima facie or RSD processes is country-dependent and also event- and time-dependent, with the outcome uncertain for any individual seeking asylum in a particular country at a particular moment in time. Hannah Arendt, reflecting on the post–World War II European refugee crisis, noted that rights were "supposed to be independent of all governments."[17] Yet as Abdi was being beaten with a stick by a Ugandan police officer, or as Jacques was being detained against his will by Congolese rebel leaders in Kampala, they lived what Arendt had written: "The moment human beings lacked their own government and had to fall back upon their minimum rights, no authority was left to protect them and no institution was willing to guarantee them."[18] In this way, the "loss of *national rights* was identical with the loss of *human rights*" as these rights, although "supposedly *inalienable*, proved to be *unenforceable*."[19]

Human rights are rules for normative behavior, and when, where, and how they are enforced is central to locating sanctuary. In theory, international laws and instruments such as the Universal Declaration of Human Rights legitimate the rights of individuals beyond a particular country or a set of institutions.[20] Yet the enforcement of these rights generally continues to be the domain of each country, as Abdi experienced in Uganda. And, like other international laws, the provisions of human rights associated with the Refugee Convention and Protocol are limited in their enforceability within sovereign states and hold weight primarily through moral authority or the powers of economic and political interests and pressures. In the post–World War II period, there was a general optimism about the possibilities of reconciling universal human rights with the institutions of enforcement within countries.[21] In Uganda in 2002, Abdi's optimism was tempered by the daily tensions he experienced between the global promise of his right to asylum and its limited realization in this country of possible sanctuary.

For Abdi, tensions around the enforcement of his rights differed by place and time, rooted in different political realities in his two places of exile: Uganda and Canada. In Uganda, in 2002, Abdi was one of 217,302 refugees, many recently arrived, in a country of 25.7 million, with a GDP per capita of $923.77.[22] In Canada when he arrived in 2005, he was one of only 5,811 who arrived in the same year he did, in a country of 32.3 million, with a GDP per capita of $36,134.60.[23]

Abdi's countries of exile mirror the geography of sanctuary globally. The vast majority of refugees—73 percent—live in exile in countries that neighbor their conflict-affected countries of origin.[24] UNHCR reported that, at the end of 2019, 6.6 million primarily Syrian refugees lived in Turkey; more than 1.4 million primarily Afghan refugees lived in Pakistan; more than 1.4 million South Sudanese refugees in Uganda; and over 1.8 million Venezuelans in Colombia.[25] All of these countries share national borders. Canada was thousands of kilometers away from all of these conflict-affected countries and inaccessible on foot or by bus.

With prima facie refugee status, like Jacques, or the possibility of refugee status through RSD, like Abdi, refugees in Uganda lay some claim to their right of asylum. Yet their daily lives in exile are often an exercise in what a refugee in Dadaab, Kenya, called "don't die survival," focusing only on getting through each day alive.[26] I observed one family arrive in the Nakivale refugee settlement, in southwest Uganda, in the heat of equatorial midday: two women, one boy no older than fifteen, and seven small children, with one still carried on a back. With them, they had a laptop case, perched on one woman's head, and an L.A. Lakers backpack, stuffed almost to overflowing, balancing on the head of the other. A small girl carried a gunny sack filled with a few household items. It was 2004, and they had come from DRC, like Jacques, from Nord-Kivu province, where they had just witnessed the collapse of their hopes for political transition and peace. Fleeing indiscriminate violence, rape, and massacres, like Jacques, they made their way to Kampala only to be told by UNHCR, "*Allez au camp* [Go to the camp]."[27] So here they were. They had walked more than 200 kilometers from Kampala. And they had arrived to a place where these seven children, if they could be spared from the family tasks of fetching water and food rations, would be in classes with 150 children and where children like them, with some frequency, fell sick overnight and died of inexplicable fevers.[28]

In neighboring host countries, like Uganda, refugees' lives are generally characterized by these kinds of conditions: over-stretched social services systems and fragile political and economic institutions. Even in the presence of political will, these resource constraints make enforcement of refugees' rights both politically and materially challenging.[29] Further, in many neighboring host countries, refugees are not able to access the right to work, as Jacques and Abdi could not in Uganda at the time, given policies that made refugee status dependent on living in settlements.[30] And most refugees in neighboring host countries do not have an option of eventual citizenship—the naturalization of long-staying Burundian refugees in Tanzania in 2014 one recent exception—limiting their abilities to plan for a secure future.[31] The answer to the question of whether and how this kind of existence in neighboring host countries allows refugees like Jacques and Abdi to be safe from "pursuit, persecution, or other danger," whether and how it allows them to locate sanctuary, whether and how it might allow them to create opportunities, is core not only to their individual futures but also, as citizens of an increasingly connected world, to our collective future.

Outsourcing of Sanctuary

Collectively, we are all impacted by the inability for refugees to locate spaces where sanctuary is possible. Yet many of the world's would-be host countries focus instead on the greater perceived impact of having refugees inside their borders. Through distance, national laws, and walls, they—we—seek to enforce the absence of refugees by preventing them from crossing their—our—borders altogether. European and North American countries grant refugee status at a group level only in rare situations, as Canada did in the time-limited decision in 2015 recognizing all Syrians' right to claim asylum.[32] The norm instead is the lengthy, often expensive, and unpredictable processes of individual RSD, the criteria of which depend on the country and on the moment in time. Less than 1 percent of refugees globally are granted asylum through resettlement in these distant host countries, countries with high GDP per capita.[33] Compared to neighboring host countries such as Turkey and Uganda, the number of refugees who find sanctuary in these distant host countries is tiny: in 2018, Canada resettled the largest number of refugees, 28,100, up from 7,233 in 2014; in 2018, the United States resettled 22,900, down from 48,911 in 2014.[34]

Increased migration to Europe complicates discrete neighboring host country or distant host-country categories and the implications for refugee status. Like other distant host countries, countries in Europe do not neighbor the conflict-affected countries of origin of those seeking refuge, and they generally have much higher GDP per capita than do neighboring host countries. Like other distant host countries, the number of people in Europe who have refugee status remains small; in 2014, Germany and Greece resettled fewer than 6,000 refugees each. Yet the number of people arriving in Europe and seeking refugee status has grown dramatically. In 2015, the German government reported 467,649 formal asylum applications, with many more as yet unregistered asylum-seekers.[35] In this same year, almost one million asylum-seekers arrived in Greece, by sea routes alone.[36] By 2019, there were 1.1 million registered refugees in Germany, with an additional 309,262 seeking asylum.[37] While Germany now represents an exception in terms of successful asylum claims in a distant host country, across the rest of Europe and North America, few asylum-seekers are granted refugee status, either having been denied asylum or waiting years for RSD processes to take place. They are in similar limbo vis-à-vis permanent residence and possible citizenship to those living in neighboring host countries. In this way, the large numbers of and limited citizenship possibilities for individuals fleeing current conflicts and arriving in European countries are similar to those in neighboring host countries.

Yet these spaces of possible sanctuary are literally worlds apart in terms of the social and economic resources available in distant host countries. The GDP per capita in 2018, for example, in Uganda was US$642 and in Lebanon US$8,269, compared to US$47,603 in Germany.[38] In addition, different from neighboring host countries, distant host countries, even in Europe, to different extents, engage in "choosing" the refugees whom they accept. Admission of refugees to the United States fell by more than half between 2017 and 2018, with admission of Christian refugees falling 36 percent and admission of Muslim refugees falling 85 percent, despite the largest number of refugees in need of resettlement being Muslim.[39] In making decisions on asylum, distant host countries consider if and how they can justify—politically with their own national constituents and financially in terms of resource allocation—enabling refugees to cross their border and lay claims to their human rights.

While Abdi was peeking in as we sang "Blowin' in the Wind," Charity and her sister Simone were students in this class, some of my most engaged students. They would arrive to class early, they would stay late, and they would always speak in English, even though it was hard for them, because they wanted to learn. I could see sadness in their eyes. No words of any language were needed. Charity had become the caretaker for her family two years earlier when she and Simone had fled DRC. Their parents were killed, while they watched, and Simone was raped, repeatedly. When they too were told to "*allez au camp* [go to the camp]," Simone spent most of her days in the camp, curled up in bed or in a corner, wailing and unresponsive to anyone's approach. Charity brought her sister to Kampala, knowing that the necessary medical attention was not available in these camps. She sat outside the UNHCR office in Kampala every day, pleading for her sister to be allowed to see a doctor, coming back again and again, until it finally happened.

Charity soon learned that she herself was HIV positive. She came to me, passing me the piece of paper with the report from a doctor, saying she knew something was wrong but that she did not understand what, she could not understand the report written in English. The doctor had told her nothing, so as best I could I explained to her the virus, its causes, its consequences, and her treatment options, which at this time in Uganda were slim. She then pulled out another piece of paper and, crying for the first time with me, told me that her application for resettlement to Australia had been rejected. UNHCR had assured her that it would come through, and she did not understand how the letter could tell her otherwise. It, too, was written in English. Would I help her to understand it? From the Australian High Commission in Nairobi, it set out in six pages a cost-benefit analysis of admitting someone who was HIV positive to Australia. There was no mention of Charity by name, no mention of anything that in any way reflected who she was or what she had experienced. The Australian High Commission had simply determined that the cost per year of caring for someone who was HIV positive was a burden that Australian society could not take on. There was only one line that expressed any regret: "We are sorry to reject your application for resettlement," the letter concluded.[40]

While each refugee's experience is unique, the patterns of refugee experiences in distant host countries of North America, Europe, and Australia are markedly different from those in neighboring host counties. In distant host countries, the numbers of refugees are relatively small, they arrive over extended periods of time, and their populations are spread out geographically. Unlike in Lebanon in 2017, where one out of every four people was Syrian, less than one tenth of 1 percent of Americans were refugees in 2017.[41]

Asylum granted in a distant host country is also of a markedly different type than that granted in a neighboring host country. Most importantly, it comes with a pathway to permanent legal status and, in some cases, citizenship. Jacques had refugee status in Uganda for eleven years. Yet, like Abdi, this status came with an expiration date. And, crucially, he did not know what that date was. The 1951 Refugee Convention does envision an appropriate expiration to refugee status when the conditions of persecution have ceased in the country of nationality or when some other permanence of nationality is obtained. Yet the nature of contemporary conflict means that this resolution is elusive. So always in Jacques's mind was the fear that one day, this sanctuary in Uganda—limited as it was—might disappear. For Jacques, then, the granting of refugee status, with permanent residence and a pathway to citizenship, for him and his family in Canada, after eleven years of exile in Uganda, allowed sanctuary to take on new meaning.

On a Thursday in December 2011, Jacques received this news. He and his family—now four children—would begin a different kind of exile. That day, I received an email from him that read: *"J'ai finalement reçu le visa! Finalement à Ottawa!!!!!!!!*[I finally received the visa! Finally, to Ottawa!!!!!!!!] Marie, the children and myself have no words to say, we are filled with extreme joy!"[42] Seven days later, they were on an airplane for the first time, headed for a below-freezing day—also for the first time—in Ottawa, Canada. Jacques had spent most of that last week in Uganda working to see that his school in Kampala could continue. His now four children, he knew, would be assured of an education in Canada. He also needed to ensure his students in Kampala could continue building their present lives in Uganda and preparing for their as-yet-unknowable futures. In fact, Jacques almost did not get on that airplane, preoccupied with the tension between knowing that a future had opened to him but that the future he was trying to create for his students in Kampala would remain so uncertain.

Five and a half years later, Jacques and his family became Canadian citizens, achieving a permanence that had eluded him for eleven years in Uganda.[43] He wrote on the day he passed his citizenship test, "In a world where refugees and other people fleeing hardships are being shun[ned] away, this is something Marie and I, our children, their children will indefinitely be remembering every December 8, the day we landed at Toronto [on our way to Ottawa]. That is my family 'Canada Day.'"[44]

This sanctuary in Canada meant stability and the kinds of social supports and economic opportunities that permanence in a country could offer. Jacques's children have had access to free primary and secondary education, and the older two are now studying for their bachelors' degrees; Marie has graduated with her high school equivalency; and, after working for three years delivering furniture, Jacques himself has been able to pursue his long-time goal of postsecondary education. This permanence and feeling of security in Canada have also enabled Jacques to invest more deeply in expanding opportunities for children in Uganda and in DRC. Once a year since arriving in Canada, he returns to Uganda to work with the teachers at his school, to connect with the donors who support it, to visit each family, and to cultivate relationships with his students. In 2018, Canadian passport in hand, Jacques was able to return to DRC for the first time since he fled that prison fire in 2000. Now, as his own children near adulthood and build their futures in Canada, Jacques is shifting his attention back to children in the place that for him remains home, DRC. "I don't have a lot of money to contribute," he said, "but I have the rest of my life to dedicate."[45]

High-income countries allow sanctuary for a small number of refugees each year, like Jacques and his family, while stepping away from responsibility for the rights of refugees on a large scale. The geographic distribution of refugees is what Gonzalo Sánchez-Terán, a writer and humanitarian worker, calls a "global confinement crisis."[46] This distribution is not an accident of conflict and of migration patterns but rather a situation governed by policies and laws, most notably but not exclusively those of the European Union (EU) and the United States, that explicitly and forcibly contain refugees outside of countries.[47] The cost-benefit analysis of granting Charity resettlement may have seemed rational to an elected official or to an Australian citizen in Canberra, isolated from Charity and her reality in Kampala. The elected official or Ugandan citizen in Kampala may feel just as daunted by the possibility that conflict and strain will come from allocating resources to yet another person, moreover a noncitizen like Charity. But in Kampala, this kind of distancing from the needs of an individual is not possible. Charity is there, she is sick, and she needs sanctuary. A six-page letter can't make her need go away.

Yet through power and money, entrenched in colonization and its legacies, high-income distant countries are able not only to close their borders but also to outsource sanctuary, aiming to keep the "burden" or "threat" of refugees elsewhere. Elsewhere meaning neighboring countries, with less power and less money. It is a global refugee system that, as Bhupinder Chimni, a legal scholar at Jawaharlal Nehru University, described in 1998, "allows hegemonic states to turn to their advantage structural inequities constructed and sustained by them."[48] In Lebanon, for example, government officials noticed significant shifts in aid when Syrians began to reach European countries in large numbers. They saw more aid money from the EU become available to Syrians in Lebanon, which they interpreted as directly in line with European migration interests. Lebanese political scientist Carmen Geha and Joumana Talhouk of the American University of Beirut quote a government advisor in Lebanon commenting on these shifts between 2011 and 2016: "Now we are noticing a boost in funding for sectors related [to] livelihoods, which reflects donors' political interest to keep Syrians settled in Lebanon as opposed to resettling in Europe."[49] A precipitous rise in the number of higher education scholarships available to Syrians in Lebanon coincided with the 2015 peak of Syrians arriving in Europe, half of whom were young adult men between the ages of eighteen and thirty-four. Vidur Chopra, one of my former students and now collaborator, quotes a United

Nations staff member working in Lebanon who said, when asked to explain the rise in scholarship funds, that "the EU wants to keep refugees as far as possible from [their] own countries," and a foundation leader who described the scholarships as an "anti-immigration measure."[50] Better education in Lebanon, these international actors hope, means refugees can begin to see their futures—where they are.

Expanding Sanctuary

On September 2, 2015, three-year-old Alan Kurdi died, while attempting to cross the Aegean Sea with his family.[51] They had fled Kobane, Syria, where one reporter described what remained of his home as "a heap of dust," destroyed in an American airstrike.[52] Alan and his family boarded an inflatable boat to cross just five kilometers of sea, from Turkey to the Greek island of Kos. Like so many others, his boat filled with water and capsized. Alan, along with his mother and brother, drowned.

The photo of Alan's small body, lying face down on the beach in Bodrum, Turkey, was viewed on social media by more than twenty million people within twelve hours.[53] Like other horrific photos of children caught in the terrors of conflict, this one photo generated rage, disgust, and shame and transformed perspectives, even if fleetingly. Like nine-year-old Phan Thi Kim Phuc, screaming and naked, desperately fleeing a napalm attack in Vietnam in 1972. Like thirteen-year-old Hector Pietersen in 1976 in Soweto, South Africa, lying lifeless in an older boy's arms, a girl, in school uniform, running beside them, her right hand up, her palm outstretched, her mouth contorted with horror.

On a wharf in Boston, on a beautiful blue bright fall day, along with our two daughters, I stepped into an inflatable raft like the one that Alan Kurdi had boarded with his family in Turkey. It was a simulation, on dry land, not on water.[54] We were told that the boat was meant to hold eight people but that, at this same moment, in what was definitely not a simulation, sixty or more people would be getting into a similar raft in the

Mediterranean. Our then ten-year-old daughter looked to me with fear in her usually sparkling eyes. "But, Mama," she said, "if we were on the water, we would sink."

My own reality was so distant from that of Kurdi's parents and what brought them to their decision. As Kenyan-born Somali poet Warsan Shire writes, "no one leaves home unless / home is the mouth of a shark . . . you only leave home / when home won't let you stay."[55]

What are the possibilities of expanding access to sanctuary, so it is everywhere it needs to be? In their analysis of online searches and donation behavior, University of Oregon psychology professor Paul Slovic and colleagues argue that the effect of this "iconic photo of a single child [Alan Kurdi] was worth more than hundreds of thousands of statistical lives."[56] They find that donations to the Swedish Red Cross, to a fund set up to aid Syrian refugees, increased fifty-five-fold in the week after the image's publication.[57] In analysis of public opinion through Twitter data, a team at the Visual Social Media Lab at the University of Sheffield finds that there was also a swift and drastic shift in the terms that were used. Over the nine months prior to publication of the photo, the terms "refugee" and "migrant" were used with similar frequency (5.3 million vs. 5.2 million). Over the next two months the term "refugee" was used much more often (6.5 million vs. 2.9 million).[58]

This shift in Twitter rhetoric suggested, at least in part, a changed public view of Syrians, from those choosing to move ("migrants") to those in need of, or deserving of, sanctuary ("refugees"). Just two days after Alan Kurdi's death, German chancellor Angela Merkel decided to create an exception to the Dublin II Regulation that, like Abdi experienced in Uganda, required asylum claims to be made in the first point of entry to Europe, preventing asylum-seekers from crossing internal European borders.[59] Germany would admit Syrians who had previously been detained at the Hungarian border. The *Economist* reported on September 12, 2015, that 20,000 Syrians arrived in Germany over the first weekend of these suspended asylum rules.[60] After a summer spent negotiating how to preserve fortress Europe, *Der Spiegel* noted that "a link had now been established between affluent Germany and global suffering."[61]

Alan Kurdi's father, Abdullah, explained what he hoped might come from this link between a global public and his family's tragedy. "We want the world's attention on us, so that they can prevent the same from happening to others. Let this be the last," he said.[62] Because of that photo of his son, to Abdi's question, inspired by Bob Dylan's song over a decade earlier in Kampala—". . . how many deaths will it take till he knows / That too many people have died?"[63]—the answer, finally: one.

A year later, on September 20, 2016, then US president Barack Obama again invoked the image of Alan Kurdi, "lifeless, face down on a Turkish beach, in his red shirt and blue pants," as he convened the Leaders Summit on Refugees at the United Nations in New York.[64] He called for "collective action" to address "a crisis of epic proportions," further describing global approaches to displaced people as "a test of our common humanity—whether we give in to suspicion and fear and build walls, or whether we see ourselves in another."[65]

The New York Declaration, passed by the United Nations General Assembly the day prior, committed to "save lives, protect rights and share responsibility on a global scale," calling clearly on the need for high-income countries to step up their commitments to refugees.[66] Specifically, it commits "to a more equitable sharing of the burden and responsibility for hosting and supporting the world's refugees," recognizes the unequal contributions made by low- and middle-income countries that host the vast majority of refugees globally, and seeks to "expand the number and range of legal pathways available for refugees to be admitted to or resettled in third countries."[67] Unlike previous global commitments, the New York Declaration did not condone refugees' absence in high-income countries. But, at the same time, this declaration came on the heels of the "EU-Turkey Joint Action Plan," which had been agreed to on October 15, 2015, just over a month after Alan Kurdi's death, and which had come into force in March 2016. Rather than a commitment to collective action, as in the rhetoric of the New York Declaration, this plan put forth, again, a confinement approach.[68] All Syrians arriving to Greece would be sent back to Turkey, with the EU promising to Turkey €6 billion in refugee assistance funding by 2018, in addition to visa-free travel in Europe for Turkish citizens, and possible reengagement in negotiations on Turkey's EU membership. This commitment to "burden-sharing" between the EU and Turkey, like the allocation of scholarships to Syrians in Lebanon, was, in practice, a decision to outsource responsibility.

The Sanctuary of Belonging

Responsibility for sanctuary takes the form of national legal systems and global commitments, with no legal ramifications for noncompliance, that dictate who can cross which border and how long they can remain. What Abdi found in Uganda was generosity in allocating refugee status, despite Uganda not being his country of first possible asylum, but also an arbitrariness and a limit to that generosity in the form of an expiration date. Charity discovered the stark reality of exclusion in the letter she received from the Australian High Commission rejecting her claim for asylum based on what her asylum would cost Australian citizens. For the sultan's wise daughter in the Somali folktale, the sheep's gullet was the link between greed and generosity, and it was her answer to finding a way to bridge what divides us and what unites us. In seeking to locate sanctuary for refugees, we need this bridge.

The experiences of refugees globally teach us that relying solely on global institutions or on countries to create the conditions for sanctuary may be misplaced. Certainly, sanctuary for refugees in countries of exile is circumscribed by the permission to enter or permission to stay and by the geopolitical positions and financing power of global actors. Yet, at the same time, true sanctuary, not just the allowance of some physical space, is created through daily experiences of belonging and enough sense of stability to be able to see the future. These processes take place, by and large, at the intersection of individual relationships and institutional interactions, at the local level, in communities and particularly in schools. In the early 2000s, Uganda was implementing its Self-Reliance Strategy (SRS), which aimed "to integrate the services provided to the refugees into regular government structures and policies," including in education, and with the goal of benefiting both refugees and host communities.[69] This was not a new approach at the policy level; precursors included the "zonal development approach" of the 1960s, "refugee aid and development" strategies of the late 1970s and early 1980s, and UNHCR's Convention Plus framework, specifically "The Targeting of Development Assistance" (TDA).[70]

It was also not a new approach at the community level. The Kyaka area of Uganda was not formally included in Uganda's SRS, but teachers and school leaders in this area described how they had done the work of bringing refugees and nationals together for years both inside and outside of formal refugee settlements. Kyaka first hosted refugees in the late 1950s and early 1960s when thousands of Tutsi fled to Uganda from Rwanda in the aftermath of the Hutu Revolution and the installation of an all-Hutu government post-Independence.[71] The Kyaka II settlement was created in 1959, and many of the refugees who had come at the time stayed in protracted exile—which some argue was exacerbated by global political pressures—until 1994, when some refugees, but not all, returned to Rwanda.[72] After 1994, Kyaka II hosted primarily Congolese and ethnically Hutu Rwandan refugees. The schools in the Kyaka II refugee settlement, as the district inspector of schools for Kyaka Country explained, "are like any other schools because to us those schools are also government schools."[73] The district education officer for Kyenjojo District, in which Kyaka is located, echoed these sentiments: "I grew up and found that these people are studying together. . . . [T]here is no way you can say that refugees go there," he points to one side, "and those who are not refugees go there," he points in the other direction. "[T]he goal is to have the child educated. So we don't separate them."[74]

In her six-year study of refugees in Uganda, Lucy Hovil concludes from 1,115 interviews she conducted while research director at the Refugee Law Project in Kampala that refugees create these types of spaces for belonging within communities based on the shared needs of daily life, of local politics, and of the economics of survival in any given place.[75] In our collaborative work in Lebanon, Vidur Chopra and I find that Syrian refugees build relationships and engage in meaningful work, often related to education, that allow them to permeate, even if fleetingly, the physical and symbolic boundaries of their exclusion in Lebanon.[76] Peggy Levitt, sociology professor at Wellesley University, and her colleagues propose that people who move across borders create "resources environments" through relationships that span national boundaries to augment or replace state-centric social welfare institutions that are not set up to account for and respond to mobility.[77] In these spaces, refugees are locating elements of sanctuary, in particular a sense of belonging.

I teach a class at the Harvard Graduate School of Education on education in armed conflict. I assign students a semester-long project and ask them to interview one individual who has experienced education in a conflict setting. In the future, when they design education programs and make education policies, I want them to have actual people in their minds. I want them to consistently be asking themselves, how will this program, how will this policy affect the lives of people? Two hundred and twenty-five individuals have been interviewed for this project over the last four years, including a Nuer boy from Sudan living in Uganda, a Shi'a Hazara girl from Afghanistan in Pakistan, a Colombian girl in the United States, a Palestinian girl in Ramallah, three generations of a Sahrawi family in Algeria, a Chinese man who fled the Cultural Revolution to Hong Kong, a German girl living all over Europe in the early 1940s, and a father who fled Vietnam in the early 1970s for Indonesia.[78] In these interviews, students see that across all of these contexts, laws and policies almost never are the defining factors that individuals point to as enabling them to pursue their educational goals. What helped individuals to pursue these educational goals, including finding a sense of collectiveness that included rather than excluded them, were relationships. As it was for Jacques, these relationships are often with teachers. At the same time, laws and policies to support refugees' education are essential, albeit insufficient. Where refugees are excluded by laws and policies and not welcomed in communities, they find themselves, as Arendt observed, without protection. When Abdi was beaten with a stick in Kampala, he felt he had no recourse, given his lack of legal status. But Jacques, living in Kampala where refugees did not have the right to go to school, found a relationship that helped him mediate the liminal legal space: a local church leader who welcomed refugee students to use the space of his church as their school. Yet after a year using the church space for their school, and with mounting xenophobia from the surrounding residents who lived in such poverty that they themselves could not afford the school fees of local Ugandan schools, the church leader asked Jacques to leave. He and his students were no longer welcome.

It is hard for any of us to know, in advance, what the tipping point is, when the bounds of tenuous belonging will be stretched thin and finally break. Between February 2001 and May 2003, 1,200 Somalis arrived in Lewiston, Maine, a town of 35,690 people, 97.3 percent of whom were White at the time of the 2000 Census. A Somali community leader, arriving in Lewiston at this time, said, "Here was completely White, except for a few Somalis who were up here at that point. And everybody on both sides was in shock. The [Lewiston] people didn't know what this was all about. . . . And the Somalis were like, what did we get ourselves into? We came to a completely White state [and] a White city. An old mill town in the middle of nowhere. It was a far-away land."[79] Yet this small town in Maine, half a world away from Somalia, initially "felt more like home" to many Somalis who had previously lived in large American cities. The land around it seemed "big," just like Somalia. And people greeted each other on the street, just like in Somalia.[80] But as time passed, this small, safe town turned out not to be as hospitable as many Somalis first hoped.

A year and a half after Somalis first began to arrive, the Lewiston mayor wrote an open letter to the Somali community. He urged local Somali residents to communicate with Somalis in other states to discourage them from relocating to Lewiston:

> This large number of new arrivals cannot continue without negative results for all. The Somali community must exercise some discipline and reduce the stress on our limited finances and generosity. I am well aware of the legal rights of a US resident to move anywhere he / she pleases, but it is time for the Somali community to exercise this discipline in view of the effort that has been made on its behalf. We will continue to accommodate the present residents as best we can, but we need self-discipline and cooperation from everyone. Only with your help will we be successful in the future— please pass the word: We have been overwhelmed and have responded valiantly. Now we need breathing room. Our city is maxed-out financially, physically and emotionally.
>
> *Laurier T. Raymond, Jr.*
> *Mayor, City of Lewiston*[81]

The letter generated national and international attention. The World Church of the Creator group saw the opportunity to turn the events in Lewiston into a major victory for White supremacy and scheduled a public meeting in the city.

In response, between 4,000 and 5,000 people from Lewiston and neighboring communities came together, calling themselves the Many and One Coalition, and held a counter-rally to reject the hate group's position and celebrate Lewiston as a city that welcomed refugees.[82] This January 2003 rally marked a major shift in perception of Somali refugees in Lewiston by long-time residents. The city administrator described the complaints about Somalis he received before the rally: "I have a stack of communications, letters, emails. Without exaggeration, it's about this high," he said, his hand raised to about one and a half feet off his desk. But after the rally, "the telephone calls, the e-mails, the letters, and all of that literally stopped. . . . It isn't because there aren't people out there that aren't happy, or disagree with what's going on. But there comes a point where a community begins to understand that this is the way it's pretty much going to be."[83] His tone left open the question as to whether this is about acceptance or resignation.

On December 10, 2015, 163 Syrians arrived in Toronto, Canada, direct from Beirut. Prime Minister Justin Trudeau was at the airport to greet them. To the others gathered, he said, "Tonight they step off the plane as refugees. But they walk out of this terminal as permanent residents of Canada, with social insurance numbers, with health cards, and with an opportunity to become full Canadians."[84] Each of these refugees had been "sponsored" by a group of Canadians, who pooled their resources to raise the money required for their housing and sustenance during their first year in Canada. Most of these groups also had committed to helping these new Canadians build relationships and create community. One group I made a small donation to had a list of ways to support the sponsored family that included not only donations of new and lightly used household items but also teaching this newly arrived family to skate, taking them to get library cards, and having them over for dinner.[85]

The front page of the *Toronto Star*, Canada's largest daily newspaper, on that cold day in December read, in page-filling letters, "Welcome to Canada أهلاً بكم في كندا."[86] Yet two months later, residents of Calgary, Canada, would awaken to find the words "Syrians Go Home and Die" scrawled across the wall at Wilma Hansen School.[87]

These expressions of utter welcome and utter rejection may seem polar opposites, but they are not. They are often held together at the same time, in the same community, even within the same person. Imagining welcoming new people and being welcomed and doing the hard work of figuring out how to live together are entirely different endeavors. Being together in the same schools and in the same classrooms are new experiences for newcomer Syrian Canadians and for longtime resident Canadians. Mary Catherine Bateson describes how most teachers in the United States teach within 100 miles of where they were born. And yet, as she said to a group of educators, "Every one of you in this room today is an immigrant in the sense that you do not live in the country you were born in. It changed on you. You've got the same passport, you might even have the same address, but you live in a different world."[88] Liisa Malkki, professor of anthropology at Stanford University, argues that common rhetoric around refugees—"floodtides, waves, flows, streams . . ."—reflects a general bias toward geographic stability as we think about who we and others are, with these identities often called "roots," as if we live static lives, in one place, forever. She writes, "These liquid names for the uprooted reflect the sedentarist bias in dominant modes of imagining homes and homelands, identities and nationalities."[89]

As refugee and longtime resident teachers, parents, and students begin to feel this sense of a changed world *together,* they begin to ask of themselves and each other the hard questions on which the possibilities of true sanctuary depend. Who am I and what is my future? How does your right to be here and to be you threaten my right to be here and to be me? How might we be entwined?

On a warm November evening, I sat on the outdoor patio of a café in Beirut, across from a longtime activist, Gabrielle. Personally and professionally, she has dedicated herself to inclusion, participatory politics, and equity. In the midst of high-level analysis of policies in Lebanon and steps for transformation, she stopped talking. She put one arm down on the table and with the other lifted a cigarette to her lips. Then, in a quieter and more urgent voice, Gabrielle described seeing a car in the street that day, with a Syrian flag hanging out the window. She was afraid, she said. She remembered war, she told me. She remembered Syrian military in Lebanon, still so recent. She was afraid for her country, she was afraid for herself. She didn't want this fear to shift her commitments, but it was a constant battle.

The careful and deliberate cost-benefit analysis the government of Australia could do from a distance in evaluating Charity's case for resettlement happens in real time in Lebanon. Australia can set its policies preventatively, anticipating what might be the tipping point for welcome of refugees in Australia and then setting boundaries around sanctuary to reflect that. Lebanon, with its geographic proximity, cannot. Instead, sanctuary is negotiated, and created, in daily relationships that may or may not contribute to a sense of belonging for both refugees and nationals. Day to day, Lebanese and Syrians move about Beirut, each one with fear of what might, at any given moment, break the fragile bridge of what divides us and what unites us.

3

Power

Henri is twenty-four years old.[1] Not long before, he had come home from exile in Tanzania. In fact, exile had been his whole life. He was returning home, but he had never been there before. It was his first time in Burundi.

Henri was born a refugee. His mother had fled Burundi for DRC in 1972, a year of genocide, when more than 120,000 civilians were massacred by government forces.[2] The war in eastern DRC that eventually caused Jacques to flee to Uganda also led Henri and his mother to flee their first place of exile in DRC. They arrived in Tanzania in 1995, when Henri was six.

Through most of his young life, Henri lived in the Mtabila camp, in rural western Tanzania, not far from the Burundian border. "Life in camp is always difficult," he said. "You don't have any job . . . you are only there waiting for UNHCR to bring you what to eat. . . . Life there for sure was not a good life." Barred by the government of Tanzania from moving beyond the borders of the camp, Henri described the kind of fear and isolation he and his mother also felt. "Our mothers . . . they used to

leave the camp secretly in order to go [out] to fight for life." Since there
was not enough food, his mother worked small jobs for Tanzanian nationals outside the camp to make enough money to buy enough food. It
was a constant worry for Henri: "If the police catch you, you have to be
taken to prison." Already in a place that felt constantly insecure, he could
not imagine being without his mother.

In Tanzania, Henri found himself among a massively expanding
refugee population and, like Jacques in Uganda, among not only civilian
refugees but also combatants, seeking cover in the chaos of large numbers. In the late 1990s and early 2000s, there were nearly half a million
Burundian refugees in Tanzania.[3] By association, as a refugee, as a Burundian, as a boy, Henri knew he was perceived as a threat. And he was
treated like one. The Mtabila camp, during Henri's childhood, was part of
a new global approach designed to contain this "threat" of refugees: encampment. While the first refugee camps were built in the 1960s, UNHCR
and host governments—like Tanzania—found new favor with this model
as large numbers of refugees fled Rwanda during the genocide in 1994.[4]
The first refugee camp was built in Tanzania in 1990, but by the time
Henri arrived in 1995, there were nineteen camps, all, like Mtabila, in rural,
isolated areas designed for containment.[5]

If Henri's mother had fled directly to Tanzania in 1972, she would
have found a very different situation. There were no camps. She would
not have been waiting around for UNHCR to bring her food. She would not
have needed to sneak around, fearing arrest. At that time, Burundians
settled mostly in local villages with some initial support from UNHCR,
support that was then completely withdrawn by the mid-1980s. Refugees
were allowed to move freely, to grow crops, to be part of local economies. Refugees were allowed to create their own livelihoods in the rural
areas in which they lived, yet often eked them out amid volatility of rain
and entrenched poverty, as do subsistence farmers globally.[6]

Henri's education in Tanzania mirrored these shifts in global and regional refugee politics. Refugee students in the 1970s and 1980s lived and
went to school with Tanzanians in local villages. Even though Henri lived

in a camp from the time he arrived, the "old" policies were still in place when he was in primary school: he studied according to the Tanzanian curriculum in English and Kiswahili. As the director of pedagogy at a rural Burundian school described it, refugees "were integrated within the communities in Tanzania."[7] The Tanzanian curriculum and the national languages of Tanzania would be useful to refugees, as the abiding assumption was that Henri and other Burundians, even though now living in camps, might just well stay.

By the time Henri was in secondary school, though, refugees were increasingly unwelcome in Tanzania, accused of fomenting crime and contributing to land shortages.[8] Education policy shifted dramatically and swiftly and, all of a sudden, Henri could study the Burundian curriculum only, in French and Kirundi, languages that he knew were his birthright but that he did not know how to speak. Now UNHCR's and the government of Tanzania's assumptions, and intentions, were that Henri's future would be in Burundi. This intention was made all too clear to Henri in his last year of secondary school. Seared in his memory is the way he was forced out of the Mtabila camp. He watched the Tanzanian military burn down homes, ones he knew had been there for decades.[9] Rather than be shoved onto an overcrowded bus bound for a forcible return to Burundi, he fled with his mother to Nyarugusu, another camp in Tanzania. In this camp, the primarily Congolese refugees studied the Congolese curriculum in French. If he wanted to continue going to school, Henri had no choice but to join them. So he did, embracing a new language and a new curriculum.

When, at age twenty-four, Henri arrived in Burundi for the first time, he had spent his whole life so far in exile. With new peace in Burundi, he was hopeful he could join the university so that he could contribute to what he thought of as his country, and also support his mother, who remained in the camp in Tanzania. He was one of but a few secondary-school graduates in Burundi, where at the time fewer than 16 percent of young people were even enrolled in secondary school.[10] But without sufficient fluency in French or Kirundi, and having followed a different curriculum in Tanzania, he was denied entry to the university.

Henri's educational experiences are not unique among refugees. These experiences beg the questions that policymakers in Geneva and Nairobi, that teachers like Jacques in classrooms in Kampala and Beirut, and that families and students—like Henri—in Mtabila and in Bujumbura consistently ask themselves: Where will refugee children go to school? What should they learn there? What will they learn there? In what language? At the crux of all of these day-to-day questions are big, life-changing questions that face us all: What do I hope for my future? Can I belong here? And, as Henri reflected on, in retrospect, through the shifting landscape of his own education: Who has the power to make these decisions?

Locating Power in Education

These questions of where power resides shape education in all places and at all times. Education of refugees challenges dominant models of educational decision making about the ways education systems function and what young people learn, which generally focus on actors and politics inside countries, at various regional and local levels, and with concerns about the making of future citizens. Refugee education is embedded in global politics and power structures and concerned with the education of noncitizens, likely never-citizens. This makes refugee education somewhat of an extreme case, but also one that illuminates persistent tensions on the role of education in fostering unity and diversity within countries and particularly on the dilemma of who belongs. Global patterns and relevant nonrefugee examples illuminate the ways in which education navigates these tensions and provide context for the specificities of power in refugee education over the past sixty years, in four distinct historical eras: Liberation, Standardization, Localization, and Nationalization.

Prior to the emergence of modern states, local communities were at the center of education, and educators themselves had a great deal of autonomy over policies and practices in their schools.[11] Rarely do teachers have this autonomy now. Decisions to centralize control of education have a long history in some parts of the world, arguably with origins in the Prussian school system, which was established in 1808, and then later emulated by states in Eastern and Western Europe.[12]

Formal education systems are a key foundation of sovereignty for modern states and, historically and in the present, are strong nationalizing endeavors.[13] Textbooks reflect the knowledge considered legitimate by those with power at any given time and focus on the creation of national citizens.[14] Not at all surprising is that in schools in the United States, children learn the capitals of American states and American history and, at schools in Canada, they learn the capitals of Canadian provinces and Canadian history. Yet sometimes we don't realize until long into adulthood how connected to state narratives were the nuances of what we learned in school.

As we sit around our kitchen table at dinnertime, I listen to our daughter talk about what she is learning about the American Revolution in her fifth-grade classroom in Boston. She asks good questions about what life was like for an indentured servant at the time, what opportunities African Americans who joined the Minutemen might have had, how we might be overlooking leadership women provided. When she talks about the Loyalists, American colonists who were committed to the British, I can hear scorn in her voice. They supported the status quo, they wanted to prevent Americans from realizing their freedoms, they wanted colonization by the British to continue. I do a double-take, as I pivot into my own history. I had learned about these same people very differently. Sitting in a classroom in Toronto, Canada, I had learned of these individuals as "United Empire Loyalists," a grand-sounding title given to them by the then-governor of Québec. I had been taught that these people were refugees, fleeing persecution by Americans and seeking refuge in (similarly colonized) Canada.

What and how children learn is so important to countries that developing new school curricula is often high on the agenda in newly independent states. And, since an established curriculum can also be a prerequisite for education aid funding, there are many incentives at play. For example, South Sudan, the most recently independent country in the world, quickly shifted its language of school instruction from Arabic to English following independence in 2011. The interim Constitution stated that "English shall be the official working language in the Republic of South Sudan, as well as the language of instruction at all levels of education."[15] This interim Constitution, and the subsequent Education Act of 2012, also laid the legal groundwork for the formation of a new curriculum. In 2013, the government began a systematic curriculum review with the specific goals both to rid the country of curricula from Kenya, Sudan, and Ethiopia that had been in use and to develop a new national South Sudanese curriculum.[16] This new curriculum was launched in 2015. The then minister of education, science, and technology, Dr. John Gai Yoh, wrote in his introduction to the curriculum that it "sets out our ambition as a nation."[17]

Within these formal national education systems, a hallmark of recent global educational history is a vacillation between standardization across regions and schools, and autonomy at local levels, within cities and districts, both in the structures and content of schooling. These patterns are relevant, too, for the history of refugee education, in particular as they shed light on the implications of standardization and autonomy in education for experiences of marginalization both inside and outside of schools.

In Botswana, standardization in education has been pursued as a national strategy for conflict avoidance. While not a refugee context, Botswana provides a way to examine, over a protracted period of time, how ethnic and linguistic minorities experience school-based structures and narratives that position them outside of the national imaginary. Teachers are often teaching the same lesson on the same day with the same notes appearing on the board for students to copy, whether they are in the capital city, Gaborone, overlooking the shiny new tinted-glass windows of car dealerships or in a remote rural area where donkeys wander into the school grounds.[18] In Botswana, standardization in education has been a nationalizing project, an attempt to bring citizens closer together—both in terms of unity and equality—through sameness. Each primary school in Botswana receives the same amount of per-pupil funding, the same textbooks, and the same training for teachers, regardless of its geographic, economic, or social context.[19]

The abiding philosophy in education, dating to the time of Botswana's Independence in 1966, is that standardization is the pathway to equality, peace, and national development, a theory also often articulated in refugee contexts. The conception of equality as sameness often has its roots in experiences of conflict or, as in the case of Botswana, in explicit avoidance of conflict. Surrounded by Angola, Zimbabwe, and Mozambique that had recently been engulfed in violent conflict, Botswana's leaders at Independence sought to create conditions that would prevent that future.[20] As such, nationalized education was conceived as a way to redistribute resources with the aim of countering inequality and avoiding "a society which is polarised between rich and poor, urban and rural, well-educated and semi-literate, a privileged minority and an underprivileged majority."[21] With this kind of standardization, it was easier for a teacher to teach with little training. They could follow along specific and proscriptive textbooks and teachers' guides, which was important in a context where at the time of Independence in 1966 there were just one hundred secondary-school graduates.[22]

Postindependence education in the United States, in the late eighteenth century, followed this same intentional path of standardization in education, exposing another pattern relevant to refugee education: the "age-old problem of balancing order and liberty."[23] Vehement opposition to refugee-run schools in many contexts echoes this fear that freedom threatens order, framed in contemporary terms as fear of extremism.[24] In the development of American schooling, Stanford University historian of education David Tyack argues that leaders did not trust families and communities with the kind of socialization that would stabilize institutions and consolidate beliefs in the new country, and they turned to education as the space of deliberate instruction. In that endeavor, he argues, "Having fought a war to free the United States from one centralized authority, [the leaders] attempted to create a new unity, a common citizenship and culture, and an appeal to a common future. In this quest for a balance between order and liberty, for the proper transaction between the individual and society, Jefferson, Rush, and Webster encountered a conflict still inherent in the education of the citizen and expressed still in the injunction to teachers to train students to think critically but to be patriotic above all. Hence proceeded a paradox from their search for ordered liberty: the free American was to be, in political convictions, the uniform American."[25]

With the experience of conflict still fresh, unity (of White men) was paramount. As George Washington, the first US president, wrote at the time, decades before the advent of public education, "The more homogeneous our citizens can be made in these particulars, the greater will be our prospect of permanent union."[26] As in South Sudan and Botswana today, standardization in education resulted from belief in "conformity as the price of liberty."[27]

In certain times and in certain places, feelings of security and generalized trust translate, from the view of the state and those in power, into the notion that unity does not rest on conformity, allowing for autonomy in schools. At this other extreme, as a teacher in a public school in Massachusetts, I had the autonomy to decide more or less what I wanted to teach and when, as long as I loosely followed the state curriculum frameworks. During the 2001–2002 school year, I was teaching eighth-grade Humanities. I had long blocks of time with my students each day, which were intended to provide time for big projects and integrating social studies and literature. My teaching partner and I developed a mission for the course, which we excitedly shared with our principal: "This year, students will explore the origins and development of cultural interactions in a global context. Through studies of world religions and migration and trade patterns, students will examine the spread of ideas and resulting questions about power, diversity, and justice."[28] Prior to the start of the school year, we had designed this curriculum to take us from basic geographic principles into ideas of where and how development happens and is influenced by geographic features, into a study of Africa as the origins of civilization, and to the development of agriculture. It was to be a whirlwind year of global history and literature, greatly influenced, I see now looking back at my lesson plans, by the ideas I was grappling with at that time and the experiences I had recently had. I had spent time teaching environmental science to middle school students in rural Madagascar and decided to situate our study of human and environmental conflict in the rainforests and surrounding villages of central Madagascar. Since I had spent a year observing history classes in Cape Town that were focused on early African history, why not situate our study of ancient civilizations there, rather than in China as many other Massachusetts schools did?

Then, on a Tuesday in the second week of school in 2001, came September 11th. My brother worked at the time in the building across from the World Trade Center in New York. My cell phone, like everyone else's, didn't work. I sat by the pay phone in the teachers' lounge and loaded it up with all of the change I could find. I couldn't get through to my brother. A seventh-grade teacher whom I barely knew came in and sat down beside me and, without a word, held my hand while I tried, again, to reach someone who might know where he was. By mid-day, I knew that my brother was physically all right. I could now turn to the responsibility in front of me. I was in charge of explaining to my eighth-grade students— whom I had known for exactly one week—why the school had been on lockdown, what had happened in New York, what they might face when they set foot outside the cocoon we had created for them inside the school that day.

I remember asking my students to gather in a circle. I remember sitting with them in that circle. I remember feeling like what I said would be important but that I had no idea what to say. I remember Hadee coming to school early the next morning to talk to me. I wrote down what he said: "Islam would never allow this kind of terrorism to happen. . . . I know that people who are hating Muslims don't know any better. They are scared." Early African civilizations suddenly seemed less important. A village in rural Madagascar seemed no longer like the right way to examine human and environmental conflict.

We shifted our entire curriculum to center the year around "the lives, cultures, and religious beliefs of people during different periods of historical time."[29] We still were guided by the mission we had developed before the start of the year, but we shifted the frame, and we focused specifically on developing understanding of Islam as a religion and the experiences of Muslims in the United States both before and after 9 / 11. It was a study of world religions, as we noted in a letter to parents in January 2002, designed "as a way to understand global history and to build tolerance for differences."[30] As we noted in a reflection at the end of the year, we believed that we had given students the opportunity "to engage in authentic work that has real-world significance." But, at the same time, we also felt "like we were figuring [it] out as we went along," with little certainty that we were doing it right or well.[31] Eighteen years later, Hadee and I sat at a rough-hewn wood table in a local pizza joint, his favorite. I asked him what he thinks, in retrospect, about this decision by his teachers to spend the year studying world religions. "It filled a real hole," he said, not just an immediate one in the way we perceived the need at the time, post 9 / 11, but as part of "the education of all children in this country."[32]

In the year 2001–2002, in this school in Massachusetts, we had the autonomy for classroom-level decisions about what and how to teach. This autonomy evaporated in the second week of school, on September 11th, and took only months to turn into bipartisan-supported education reform for standardization. The No Child Left Behind Act (NCLB) passed in late 2001. It gave a stronger role for the federal government in school accountability, what Jal Mehta, a Harvard University sociologist of American education, describes as not the first but the most recent in a series of efforts in the United States to "'order' schools from above."[33] NCLB was about not only a drive toward conformity in order to prevent disunity, but also an attempt to use standardization to address rampant inequalities in schools—"closing achievement gaps"—and ensuring the economic competitiveness of the United States.[34] The frenzied search for unity in the United States post-9 / 11 helped to propel widespread support for this swing toward the kind of federal role so counter to recent Republican traditions.

Political and social context drive the pendulum toward standardization or autonomy. The swing to standardization can be magnified in countries where histories are contested and where governance is fragile, as is typical in refugee-hosting countries. In postgenocide Rwanda, for example, textbooks focused on conceptions of a united nation, with goals of overcoming past divisions and stemming possibilities for overt violence.[35] The new and united identities fostered in these history texts blur group differences.[36] In so doing, they leave "no room for any kind of ethnic identification," and they limit space for "productive conflict."[37]

Collaborative research that Bethany Mulimbi and I did in Botswana demonstrates the trade-offs between this approach to unity to avoid violent conflict, and opportunities for membership and belonging for those marginalized by the united narrative of a country, with relevance for experiences of refugee young people in schools.[38] In Botswana, eight Tswana ethnic groups constitute the majority in political and legal terms, while numerous politically unacknowledged but self-identifying non-Tswana ethnic groups make up the minority. As is customary in English, Tswana is used to describe the political-majority ethnic groups and the term Batswana—or, in singular form, Motswana—to mean all citizens of Botswana, regardless of their ethnicity. The education system in Botswana has been used to promote the assimilation of ethnic identities to a superordinate national identity, what Colgate University anthropologist Anne Ríos-Rojas describes as educational processes that "discipline difference in the interest of preserving the nation."[39] In Botswana, this national identity is constructed around the culture and language of the politically and economically dominant Tswana ethnic groups.[40]

A Tswana teacher at a school in the Tswana-dominant southeast region of the country explained the rationale, echoed in government documents, for this decision: "You know, we are a nation, yes, formed by different ethnic groups. But *kagisano* [social harmony, the national principle] is advocating for us to treat ourselves as Batswana, not identifying ourselves through our ethnic groups. . . . It does help a lot, because if there is unity there's usually less problem of ethnic conflicts, where ethnic groups will think they are better than others."[41]

In student surveys at three schools that were part of our research, students overwhelmingly agreed with the following statement: "At school I learn that it is important to treat all ethnic groups fairly" (the surveys showed agreement at 86 percent, 92 percent, and 93 percent at each of the three schools). In interviews and observations, students expressed their beliefs in the equality of all citizens and their faith in the government redistribution of resources for the good of all.[42] Even at a school in the northwest region of the country where only 9 percent of students identified as majority Tswana, 57 percent of the students reported that they "feel equally Motswana and my ethnic group," with Motswana being a way to describe a national identity. Yet, despite meeting many goals for unity through standardization, half of respondents at this school also described that their ethnic group was "treated unfairly at school" sometimes, often, or always, and 58 percent said that "students at this school get teased about their ethnic group."[43]

One Form 2 (Grade 9) student at this school, Thato, was a member of a small ethnic group, the Wayei. He described how "sometimes when you speak your own language they look down on you, thinking that maybe you're inferior or you don't understand some things. You're still not advanced."[44] Students like Thato expected that mastery of the standardized nationalized curriculum would create a path to paying jobs and inclusion in the modern state for all who buy into it.[45] But fewer than half of students (45 percent) in the largely ethnic minority district where this school is located make the transition to senior secondary school, compared to 65 percent of students nationally.[46]

In Botswana, this standardized, assimilationist approach to education has been extraordinarily successful at mitigating conflict, a similarly expressed goal in many refugee-hosting countries. At its Independence in

1966, Botswana was among the poorest and with the least formal education of all countries in the world, surrounded by countries engulfed in civil war, with an economy based on natural resources, and with high ethnic diversity and one dominant ethnic group.[47] Conflict seemed inevitable. Yet in 2016, on the Global Peace Index, Botswana ranked 27 out of 163 countries.[48] This index measures the absence of personal or direct violence, what Johan Galtung, social theorist and builder of the field of peace studies, calls "negative peace," echoing Dr. Martin Luther King's earlier characterization of peace in this way in his 1963 "Letter from a Birmingham Jail."[49] As young people like Thato describe it, the absence of violence in Botswana is a huge achievement. But Botswana has done much less in creating conditions for "positive peace," which is not only the absence of violence but the presence of conditions that allow individuals, like Thato, and groups, like his Wayei ethnic group, to access equal opportunities.[50]

Access to equal opportunities, or possibilities for what Nancy Fraser, a New School for Social Research professor of social and political theory, calls "parity of participation," requires redistribution of resources, like wealth and land, to counter resource-based inequalities and also recognition of individuals and groups to counter identity-based inequalities.[51] In education, in refugee and nonrefugee contexts, redistribution to address resource-based inequalities can be done through standardization and centralized control, providing access to schools, teachers, and materials for every community, no matter its size or amount of wealth. Yet recognition to address identity-based inequalities requires at least some autonomy for teachers and their students to create the kind of teaching and learning that enables opportunities within unequal power structures. What are the trade-offs between the autonomy needed for recognition to enable full participation by all, particularly marginalized groups, and the potential costs of this autonomy vis-à-vis "weakening citizens' ability to communicate, trust, and feel solidarity across group differences"?[52]

This tension, so challenging to resolve within national education systems, is heightened for refugees. Refugees are living, and being educated, outside of their countries of citizenship. Modern states are premised on

assumptions that the provision of services, including education, is a responsibility of that state to its citizens. For noncitizens like Henri, living
as a refugee in Tanzania, who is responsible for their education? Under
a standardization approach, what entity is the standardizing power: the
country of origin, the host country, a global actor? Under an approach
of autonomy, autonomy from what, toward what end, and with what consequences for recognition and opportunity?

Power in Refugee Education

It was a breezy November night in Beirut, Lebanon.[53] In a high-ceilinged
yet warmly lit and cozy restaurant, I listened to stories. Some about childhood magic: the feeling of lying in bed and waking to the pop-pop-pop
sound of the pistachios ripening on the trees, their shells splitting open,
knowing that, come morning, the trees would become a snack-filled playground. Other stories about childhood terror. The knowledge that to
get to school, during the Lebanon Civil War (1975–1990), you needed
to cross "the line." The Green Line or Demarcation Line that divided
West (Muslim) and East (Christian) Beirut. A line through the city, green
with foliage, where nature had re-taken the places people could not tread.
But crossing that line anyway because the university was on the other
side and the university represented the only possible future. Then crossing
one day to the explosion of a car bomb. Being separated from your sister,
who later comes home to explain how she had been left for dead on a pile
of bodies.

The woman I am with, Dina, with her stories of magic and terror, is
a Lebanese teacher. She exudes energy, warmth, patience, curiosity:
everything you would want your child to be enveloped with in their
school. Her students are Syrian, living in exile in Lebanon. In this restaurant, we are on the Damascus Highway, an extension of the central
Beirut street that was once the Green Line, the same road that would lead
us, about a hundred kilometers away, to Damascus, Syria, a city no longer
green but filled with concrete rubble and rebar. Dina knows that for her

students, now is their one shot at education. And there is no teacher in Lebanon who does not know the importance of education for the Syrian refugee children in their classrooms. They know this because they, too, have experienced conflict.

Gordon Brown, former prime minister of the United Kingdom and, since 2012, United Nations Special Envoy for Global Education, calls the students Dina teaches "the lost generation." Yet Dina, and most other Lebanese adults today, remember feeling that they too were, or could have been, a lost generation.

Global policy and practice in refugee education rarely recognize the cyclical nature of conflict and displacement and how we might learn from the history of refugee education. It is a history that has mirrored global trends that reflect where power is located, has vacillated between standardization and autonomy, and that, like in other contexts, is largely ignorant of the lessons of previous eras. This historical amnesia has consequences for students like Henri who ride the seesaw of shifting policies and practices derived from single moments in time. A focus on this history—through the eras of Liberation, Standardization, Localization, and now Nationalization—makes clear the timeless nature of the question Henri needs answered: How can my education prepare me not only for this moment in time but for long-term future opportunities?

Liberation

Refugee education as a coherent field has its origins in World War II and its aftermath. The needs of refugees were at the forefront of the work of the nascent United Nations in postwar Europe and then in emerging Cold War conflicts and Independence movements.[54] The nature of conflict changed at this time: not bounded by battlefields, conflicts had become more dangerous for civilians and led to burgeoning refugee populations, including large numbers of children. UNHCR was established by the United Nations General Assembly in 1950 with the mandate to assist Europeans who were displaced during World War II. The

UN General Assembly initially mandated UNHCR to operate for three years, from January 1, 1951, to December 31, 1953. The idea was that this would give UNHCR sufficient time to complete its task of finding "permanent solutions" for displaced Europeans and, in so doing, would work itself out of the need to exist. Instead, UNHCR now works in 134 countries.[55] UNHCR has its headquarters in Geneva, in a fortresslike building that occupies a full city block. Its entrance is on a corner, a small opening into the expansive seven-story building, with a tall, glass, light-filled atrium occupying its middle. While the building is understated, UNHCR's mandate is not. It is nothing less than the physical, political, and social protection of refugees both through the delivery of humanitarian assistance such as food, shelter, water, and education and through negotiations with host governments about these services and other rights. UNHCR is an intergovernmental and constituent body, which means that it must coordinate with donor and host governments and work within the parameters defined by each country, or else risk expulsion. So UNHCR can advocate for Abdi to be granted asylum in Uganda or for Charity to be resettled to Australia, but only the potential host country (in Abdi's case, Uganda, and in Charity's case, Australia) can make those decisions. Expulsions do happen, and the risk of it circumscribes the actions UNHCR can—or is willing to—take in a given situation. While I was living in Uganda in 2003, the head of UNHCR in Uganda was expelled from the country over a disagreement about where refugees who had been attacked in one camp would be moved.[56]

UNESCO, established in 1945, was initially the global institution to hold the mandate for refugee education. However, UNHCR quickly assumed this responsibility as its decentralized structure was well suited to the local provision of education for refugees, who remained outside the purview of national education systems.[57] UNHCR took on the mandate for refugee education in an ad hoc manner immediately upon its formation in 1951 and then in a more formal way with the signing of a Memorandum of Understanding with UNESCO in 1967.[58]

Article 22 of the 1951 Refugee Convention defined global norms and obligations of the state vis-à-vis refugees' education. It specified that signatory states "shall accord to refugees the same treatment as is accorded to nationals with respect to elementary education . . . [and] treatment as favourable as possible . . . with respect to education other than elementary education."[59] While 145 countries are party to the 1951 Convention and 146 to the 1967 Protocol, there are notable exceptions, including states where large numbers of people seek asylum: India, Lebanon, and Malaysia, for example. In these states, the rights of refugees are not bound by international conventions. In addition, some states have ratified only portions of them. Egypt, for example, does not endorse Article 22 on education, noting "reservations because these articles consider the refugee as equal to the national." Zambia, Zimbabwe, Mozambique, Malawi, Monaco, and Timor-Leste have also registered their reservations about Article 22, noting that they consider access to education for refugees within the country a recommendation but not a legally binding obligation.

Despite the creation, at global levels, of institutions like UNHCR and conventions such as the 1951 Refugee Convention, obligations to refugees from the 1950s and into the 1980s played out not primarily with global actors or at national levels, but at local levels. This was a time when global illiteracy stood at 49 percent and the mean years of schooling was four.[60] The role of global institutions in refugee education was limited in scope, focused on postprimary education through scholarships for an elite few. In 1966, a postsecondary scholarship program launched with 1,000 scholarships; the number increased to 1,200 in 1982 and to 3,950 in 1987.[61] The decision to focus financial resources and staff in this way was intentional, targeted to what could not be provided locally within communities. Refugee communities organized themselves to create primary education opportunities, and sometimes secondary, where none existed, mirroring the situation for nonrefugee communities throughout Africa and Asia at this time.[62] In these countries, the schooling that was available was not largely provided by the state but instead by local communities and religious organizations.

Refugee education at this time, too, was organized by communities. These educational initiatives were local endeavors to an extent, but they were also transnational, connected to refugees' aspirations that spanned countries. In particular, refugee education was often linked to refugees' struggles for self-determination, as in the anti-apartheid and anticolonial movements, which connected individuals and organizations across borders. This education joined an exiled present to visions of future rebuilding of countries of origin. For example, Palestinian refugee teachers in Gaza started schools in 1949, Eritreans and Tigrayans started schools in the 1970s in Sudan, Nicaraguans in Honduras in the 1980s, and South Africans in Tanzania in the 1980s.[63] Anti-apartheid leader Oliver Tambo explained that these schools for refugees "consciously prepared our people to play a meaningful role in a liberated South Africa," a clear vision for the connection of refugee education to future participation in countries of origin.[64]

Forms of refugee education in exile often lay the foundation for education upon return. About 210,000 Zimbabweans lived in exile in Botswana, Zambia, and Mozambique during Zimbabwe's liberation war (1964–1979). Largely they were people who fled for political reasons, having been threatened with, or experiencing, detention for engaging in struggle against the White Rhodesian state.[65] Others fled seeking opportunities for education outside of a country where the minister of education had said to Parliament that "for the great majority of Africans there is no purpose in education other than literacy," and where White education was funded at a level thirty-six times that of Black education.[66] The schools that Zimbabweans created in exile offered a new form of education for Black Zimbabweans, designed to prepare students to contribute to the ongoing struggle from their place of exile and for their eventual return. Stella Makanya, professor in social work at the University of Zimbabwe, writes that the "focus of the teachings was to show how the people had been dispossessed of their birth-right and had been denied basic human rights by the system of government in Rhodesia [later Zimbabwe]."[67] Over time, the content of this education also came to focus on such pragmatic considerations as self-sufficiency in the camps, including manual skills needed for food and clothing production. This education in exile would later become the basis for the socialist education system that was developed in an independent Zimbabwe, after refugees' return to a country where 2,000 of the 2,500 primary schools had been destroyed during the war.[68]

The *nakba*, meaning "disaster" or "catastrophe," describes the displacement of Palestinians from their homes and to neighboring countries, including 110,000 to Lebanon in 1947–1949.[69] The United Nations Relief and Works Agency for Palestinians in the Near East (UNRWA) was created by the United Nations in 1950, and it inherited 33,000 students and 62 schools that had been set up under what was initially intended as a temporary program, the United Nations Relief for Palestinian Refugees (UNRPR).[70] Unlike in other situations of exile at the time, Palestinian refugees had widespread access to education. Middle-class Palestinians in Lebanon, for example, freely attended Lebanese schools at all levels (until 1975). Poor Palestinians aged six to sixteen, who settled in both rural and urban camp spaces, accessed free schooling up through the level of the Brevet or Grade 9 through UNRWA.[71] Unlike UNHCR, UNRWA has a population-specific mandate, Palestinians, and education has been a priority since its inception. In 2008, for example, UNHCR spent 4 percent of its budget on education while UNRWA spent 59 percent.[72] The result was that there was near-universal enrollment of Palestinian refugees in basic education as early as the 1960s.[73]

UNRWA schools follow the curriculum of the country in which they operate, so refugees in Lebanon received instruction in the Lebanese curriculum, in Jordan in the Jordanian curriculum, and in Syria in the Syrian curriculum. Although the government authority differed between sites of displacement and occupation, across countries and over time, Palestinians have been subject to "alien curriculum, in which Palestinian culture and history have been ignored or actively suppressed."[74] Yet de-

spite the layers of standardization that result under a global body like
UNWRA and national education systems in the countries where refugees live, Palestinian leaders asserted some autonomy over the content
of what children learned. The Palestine Liberation Organization (PLO)
created a national curriculum in exile in Lebanon in the 1970s, and educational guidelines, which focused on history, geography, and culture.[75]
Similar to the way Oliver Tambo later described education for South Africans in exile, the PLO curriculum, developed and implemented unof-
ficially in Lebanon in the 1970s, had goals of creating anew the nation in
exile, including disrupting the colonial education of the British mandate
(1917–1948) and articulating new identities.[76]

During this first phase of refugee education, both the content and the
structures of education were centered in communities and shaped by local
power and decision making. The focus of instruction was largely on liberation, connected to the political struggles from which people fled and
that were waged through the creation of nations in exile, and with the
purposes of preparing leaders for decolonizing states, such as South
Africa, Zimbabwe, and Palestine. In contrast, the 1951 Refugee Convention was clear that "the work of the High Commissioners [for Refugees]
shall be of an entirely non-political character; it shall be humanitarian and
social."[77] In education, though, UNHCR and UNRWA were largely
hands-off at this time, allowing for the development of refugee education that, decentralized and with local autonomy, was not apolitical but
instead highly, and overtly, political. Standardization of refugee education, and concurrent attempts at depoliticization, would follow global
trends in institutionalism in education and the proliferation of refugee
camps.

Standardization

Cold War politics led to the rise of influences in education outside of communities and national systems. Many donor countries targeted their

bilateral aid to education in ways that directly conformed to their own interests.[78] The rise of the Education for All (EFA) movement, leading up to the first World Conference on EFA in 1990, was a departure from a "fractious epistemic community" with little coordination among global and national actors, as we saw play out in early refugee education.[79] Post-1990 multilateralism, or cooperation among countries, on the other hand, represented growing consensus—shaped by varying power dynamics—among countries about educational priorities and targets and an "unprecedented" commitment to coordination among actors to achieve these goals.[80] The implications for countries, especially those that were aid recipients, were immense. Through his studies of globalization, Roger Dale, professor in education at the University of Bristol, described the increasingly "globally structured agenda for education," as involving the "ceding of some of individual states' powers to supranational bodies," bodies that became critical determinants of national education policy, including for refugee education.[81]

Multiple theoretical perspectives seek to explain how globalization influences national education systems, including world culture, world systems, postcolonial, and culturalist, with considerable debate over both the normative implications and empirical viability of each position.[82] Dale provides a productive framework for identifying the mechanisms and institutions by which global influences come to bear on national education systems, including through borrowing, learning, harmonization, dissemination, standardization, installing interdependence, and imposition.[83] Important to this conceptualization is where the "locus of viability" of the mechanism is, essentially asking the age-old question: where does power lie?[84] Is it external to a country, internal to a country, or somewhere in between?

On one end of the spectrum, the "imposition" of policy in countries occurs through explicit and compulsory relationships with organizations that hold power, such as World Bank education loans tied to structural adjustment or education aid tied to security interests.[85] It is dictated by the donor. The receiving country has little choice. In the middle are a wide range of voluntary relationships for countries that come with less explicit external influences, such as membership in supranational organizations to which cohere certain principles, norms, and rules. The United Nations, for example, has facilitated a growing convergence in education approaches and thinking across countries, despite diversity in its members' resources and histories.[86] On the other end of the spectrum are voluntary relationships with centers of power and decision making within the country, itself exemplified by policy borrowing or the movement of educational policies and practices across national borders.[87]

In these ways, policy reforms currently take on "international reference frames," rather than bilateral ones, and education policy more generally has been broadly deterritorialized.[88] From the 1980s, refugee education exhibited these same trends in globalization, with governance by global institutions. As a result, refugee education became increasingly standardized by policies made at global levels.

The year 1985 marked a major shift toward a central role for UNHCR in articulating the purposes and mechanisms of provision of refugee education across all countries in which refugees resided. A review of refugee education programs concluded that UNHCR's approach of providing individual scholarships to students "requires a disproportionate share of resources for a small amount of refugees both in terms of staff time and project funds."[89] As a result, in response, UNHCR shifted funding away from individual scholarships to support populations of refugee children, such that by 1986, 95 percent of UNHCR beneficiaries in education were primary-school children.[90] No longer was the focus on developing an elite cadre of leaders through postprimary scholarships but instead on providing access to education for all refugee children, mirroring national trends in countries of exile that emphasized mass expansion of primary education. This shift was driven by two main global developments. First was the wide consensus on the right to education for all, institutionalized in the 1989 Convention on the Rights of the Child (CRC).[91] Second, the related commitment to global action to achieve universal access to education, formalized in the 1990 EFA Declaration and incorporated centrally in the MDGs. The declaration recognized "war, occupation, [and] civil strife" as some of the "daunting problems" that "constrain efforts to meet basic learning needs."[92]

These normative shifts and formalization of commitments through conventions and declarations, as well as the economic globalization that accompanied the post–Cold War era, marked the development of new forms of global authority in education. Refugee education, under the mandate of a UN agency, was outside of the structures of any national system. As such, it was not beholden to macroeconomic stabilization policies, yet it did follow the emerging pattern of global influences on the local provision of education. At the same time, sovereign states were not without power.

Unique to refugee education was a duality: it was dictated by the political and economic interests of the host country while at the same time it was outside of the host-country structures of service provision. This here-but-not-here situation was made possible through the advent of the refugee camp. Camps isolated refugees from nationals and ceded power over their education from the country in which they lived to a global actor, UNHCR. This era included large refugee camps such as those for Vietnamese and Cambodians on the Thai border, Rwandans in eastern DRC, and Afghans in Pakistan, such that refugees lived distant from national populations and in circumscribed areas.

Afghans did not initially live in camps in Pakistan, instead settling in rural areas amid local populations. While Pakistan is not a signatory to the 1951 Convention, its government granted temporary asylum to Afghans fleeing the 1978 Saur Revolution, or communist coup, and subsequent arrival of Soviet forces.[93] The government declared that "the asylum has been granted on humanitarian grounds . . . as well as for reasons of cultural, ethnical and religious affinity between the peoples of the two countries."[94] For the first year of mass displacement, the government of Pakistan took responsibility for assisting the more than 100,000 refugees who arrived. A year later, in 1979, as tens of thousands more refugees arrived, UNHCR took on a more active role.[95] By 1982, there were more than two million Afghan refugees in Pakistan, and UNHCR and the government of Pakistan began to set up camps to "avoid their numbers [of refugees] exceeding those of locals and to be better able to control them."[96]

Practices of encampment developed out of complex sets of interests. They became favored by UNHCR for reasons of efficiency of delivering services to large refugee populations and by many host governments for reasons of security and of allocation of financial responsibility for refugees to the global, not national, community.[97] Alex de Waal, research professor at the Fletcher School of Law and Diplomacy, argues that in most cases "the mandate for humanitarian imperium," of which refugee camps are part, "has been acquired by default, driven not by grand designs in the metropolis but more by the incremental logic of trying to address these complex emergencies themselves without appreciating the endpoint of escalating the relief, security and diplomatic engagement."[98] Yet, despite operational rationalizations and lack of intentionality, most refugee camps globally resemble open-air detention centers. This "warehousing" of those fleeing persecution across national borders has a many-decades-old history around the world.[99]

Large numbers of refugees and their locations in isolated refugee camps led to the structural necessity of refugee children attending schools separate from nationals. UNHCR policies aligned refugee education as closely as possible to the country of origin, specifically in terms of curriculum and language, with the purpose of facilitating a swift return and enabling future participation in the country of origin.[100] This orientation toward the home country echoed the earlier era of refugee education that was focused on liberation, but the nature of this orientation was radically different. As camps began to develop, approaches to refugee education shifted from Liberation to Standardization.

For example, in the 1980s, more than 500,000 school-aged children lived in camps in Pakistan, and primary schooling was financed by UNHCR with some oversight by the Commissionerate for Afghan Refugees, a Pakistani government agency charged with overseeing Afghan refugees in Pakistan.[101] Research done at the time suggests the tension between standardization and autonomy played out in local decision making, as many families elected not to send their children to these schools. They instead chose religious schools that did not use the "politically neutral [schoolbooks], centered on a Pakistani context" that were used in UNHCR-run schools.[102] Others associated these refugee schools "with a communist regime that played down the importance of the Qur'an and encouraged atheism."[103]

The institutionalization of global influences on refugee education took the form of policies created in and implemented from UNHCR headquarters in Geneva. In many ways, UN agencies at this time acted as a "pseudo-state" for refugees.[104] Between 1988 and 1995, there were four sets of global guidelines on education that provided detailed instructions for UNHCR staff members working in host countries.[105] These guidelines explicitly focused on the value of education for refugee children and included checklists of important elements of education. Yet they provided very little substance on how to create these educational opportunities. The 1993 UNHCR document "Refugee Children: Guidelines on Protection and Care" notes: "This book is not a practice manual. Unlike the manual you may get when you buy a car, this book will not tell you how to fix something when it is broken or how to keep it from getting broken; it will not tell you, 'In situation X, you must do Y.' By contrast, guidelines help you solve problems by pointing out things that are important for you to keep in mind. In using guidelines you must always rely on your knowledge of the local situation, your skills, and your common sense to get the job done."[106]

At the same time, UNHCR abolished field-based education posts. Education typically became part of the work of staff members working in the areas of Community Services or Protection, often who had little in the way of education-specific "knowledge of the local situation," "skills," or "common sense." One former senior education officer with UNHCR, who had worked both in field offices and at the headquarters in Geneva, noted, "My impression is that we have lots of guidelines, lots of international meetings. There is a lot of superstructural knowledge and guidelines and standards that serve as a point of encounter."[107] So guided was UNHCR by global-level policies at this time that even in Côte d'Ivoire, where the government opposed camps and allowed refugees to settle amid local populations, UNHCR created parallel social services for refugees, including in education.[108]

By the mid-1990s, refugee education entered a phase where it was led by policy checklists and not by people. Between 1998 and 2011, UNHCR did not have a single education officer working in a refugee-hosting country. In 2004, only 0.1 percent of UNHCR's total budget was allocated to education staff.[109] There was what one former senior education officer described as a "total lack of expertise" in education within UNHCR.[110] During the era of Standardization, refugee education became more and more distant from local education expertise in host countries and also lost any education-specific expertise within UNHCR.

A 1997 evaluation conducted by UNHCR internally concluded that these education guidelines gave "limited guidance to managers, and allow[ed] for differences in interpretation of policies, determination of methods, and implementation."[111] UNHCR staff working in different offices and over time have suggested the guidelines were drafted this way on purpose, with the goal of creating enough latitude to allow for the continued existence of education programs in an environment of limited technical capacity.[112] Yet with so few education specialists working on education, policy was not enough, and refugee education programs were "plagued by inconsistencies."[113] In 2000, 98 percent of refugee children in Uganda had access to primary education, while in Sudan it was only 25 percent.[114]

Segregated education for refugees was premised on efficiency in service delivery but it could only be efficient over the short term. It rested on the assumption of a speedy return to a country of origin, both for sustainability of financing and also in terms of the ways in which it prepared refugees for their futures. Education guidelines during this Standardization era reflected this vision of refugees' futures. UNHCR's "Revised

Guidelines for Educational Assistance to Refugees" (1995) explained the revisions in this way: "The text has been rewritten to take account of the circumstances of the mid-1990s, and in particular the emphasis on the durable solution of voluntary repatriation. This has major implications for refugee education policy."[115]

While refugee education policy shifted to reflect a vision of short-term exile and swift return to the country of origin, the realities of conflict reflected different futures. In the aftermath of the Cold War, conflicts were increasingly protracted. In 2016, the average length of exile without a permanent place of sanctuary (such as return to the country of origin or citizenship in a new place) was estimated at between ten and twenty years, up to three times as long as it was in the early 1990s.[116]

Despite shifting rhetoric and realities, approaches to how refugees lived in exile were quite stagnant. The Dadaab and Kakuma refugee camps in Kenya were established in the early 1990s with the idea that they would be temporary, that the Somali and Sudanese refugees fleeing civil war in Somalia and Sudan at the time would stay in the camps for a few years at most and then return home. Dadaab was built in 1991 by international agencies to accommodate 90,000 refugees. Aerial photos taken at the time show neat rows of tents, ready to accommodate the arriving refugees. The camp quickly grew past its capacity; as political theorist Jonny Steinberg writes in his ethnography *A Man of Good Hope*, "when one goes back to the reports written about it in the early 1990s, it feels as if one is reading in dry officialese a description of hell."[117] This hell was not short-lived. By November 2011, the population of Dadaab was 463,500, making it by population the third largest city in Kenya, after Nairobi and Mombasa.[118]

Kakuma, too, was built to be temporary, established in 1992, in response to an influx of Sudanese refugees fleeing the civil war in Sudan. In our research, we have met children who are third-generation Kakuma residents. Raphael, an NGO staff member in Kakuma, pointing to the generations of young people who have been born in Kakuma, explained how their experiences are misaligned with the practices of refugee assistance. "We can't keep talking about emergency," he said. "It is no longer an emergency in some of these cases, because if people have been here for twenty years . . . when does it stop being an emergency and then we design programs that now become developmental? Because if I was born here and this is how I wake up and this is what I see around me, then you keep telling me I'm in an emergency. First of all, I've not come because I'm running away from anything—I am here. So when you design things that are emergency in approach and in context, then you are not addressing my needs as I grow up."[119]

Localization

Just as in Pakistan, and among Palestinians in exile, refugees and teachers in Kenya responded to the misalignment between the situation of exile and the available education by creating new forms of education. In camps in Kenya, teachers and students began to use the Kenyan national curriculum, rather than the curricula of refugees' home countries. By 1997, conflict conditions in Somalia were such that return for Somali refugees living in Kenya was not likely in any foreseeable future. Reflecting this longer-term view of exile, first there arose possibilities of postprimary education for refugees.[120] The orientation of responsibility for education of refugees in Kenya also began to shift at this time toward the hosting country. Until 1997, students followed the Somali curriculum with Somali refugees as their teachers. After that, refugees began to follow the Kenyan curriculum, they had more Kenyan teachers, the language of instruction changed from Somali to English, and they sat for Kenyan national exams.[121] Not until 2012 was there official policy to include refugees in the national education system in Kenya, but decisions about curriculum and language were made by teachers and students, and with local autonomy, long before then.[122]

Also in the late 1990s in Uganda, conflict conditions in what was then Sudan and in DRC began to force similar reconceptualization of refugee education. When Annette arrived in Uganda, she thought that her exile in the Kyaka II refugee settlement would be short-lived and that she would soon return to her home in eastern DRC. Yet in 2002, as she looked through the faded cloth that created a door to her family's home in the camp, she noticed that her father had planted bananas. Bananas can take up to a year to produce fruit, and she knew he would never have planted them if he expected the family to soon return home.

District and national officials in Uganda were at this same time also taking a longer-term view, like Annette's father. Integration of refugees into national schools became part of Uganda's new Self-Reliance Strategy (SRS) in 1999, designed jointly by the Uganda Office of the Prime Minister and UNHCR. The goal of the SRS was "to integrate the services provided to refugees into regular government structures and policies."[123] An education advisor to UNHCR at the time, noted that "the SRS is not a theory. It is a practical solution" to shifting educational opportunities for Annette and the more than 100,000 other refugee children in Uganda.[124] At a consultation meeting in 2001, a technical advisor from the Ugandan government endorsed this "farsighted approach," but also indicated that this kind of policy should be understood as temporary "until repatriation [return] becomes possible."[125]

By responding to the local conditions, education policy for refugees began to shift away from the global norms of isolation in parallel systems. It was a time of massive change in education for nationals in Uganda as well. In January 1997, the government introduced Universal Primary Education (UPE), exempting four children per family from paying primary-school fees. The number of children enrolled in primary school that year more than doubled, from 2.6 million to 5.5 million. By 1999, the numbers had further increased, and 6.5 million children were enrolled in primary school in Uganda, equivalent to a net enrollment rate of 85 percent.[126]

While administration of refugee affairs in Uganda was sequestered in the Office of the Prime Minister, support for including refugees in national schools was growing out of the larger national education movement, connected to the global EFA movement. The SRS aimed to develop "mechanisms for the inclusion of the refugees into the Universal Primary Education (UPE) being implemented in Uganda" and to ensure that "the conditional grants provided to the districts for UPE . . . be increased to include refugees."[127] Under this approach, schools would receive an allocation of UPE funds from the Ugandan government for all students, regardless of whether they were refugees or nationals, in addition to funds provided by UNHCR designed to specifically target the needs of refugees in schools.[128]

Some of the very same questions that Henri's experiences in Tanzania raised shaped initial discussions on how to integrate refugees into national schools under the SRS in Uganda. In a consultative workshop, participants who included staff from government, United Nations agencies, and NGOs raised "fears" of the experiences that Henri had: Would refugees be neglected in the national system? How would language differences be addressed? Would refugees lose their identities or become "assimilated"? Permanent residency or citizenship were not on the table for refugees, so would the education received in Uganda fit into the education in the home country when return happened?[129]

Yet these questions became invisible as the policy was implemented. The staff member working on education at UNHCR described the tension this way: "The districts host the refugees, but the central government has the mandate to protect them."[130] She explained that the implementation of programs was the responsibility of the central government, in terms of guidance and monitoring. But that meant that decisions were made in Kampala, on questions like how many students, how many new classrooms, how much money to transfer. These decisions were isolated from the complexities of teaching and learning at local levels. Discussions of the purposes of integrating refugees centered on improving the quality of education for both refugees and nationals and of "better social cooperation and understanding between refugees and nationals."[131] Yet as the SRS was implemented in the districts and schools, none of these issues emerged as priorities. Instead, the programs were focused on what could be counted easily, such as the number of refugee students in classrooms, but not on processes of teaching and learning. Integration tended toward standardization and not autonomy. It was structural and not relational. Like in other periods in history and in other contexts globally, putting power over educational decisions at the center did not resolve the day-to-day challenges in schools and classrooms.

Annette's home in the Kyaka II refugee settlement was more established than some: her house was made of sticks and mud without any tarps. The long-to-mature banana plants were all around the compound. As we talked, Annette's father moved quickly to his main point: he wanted me to know that language was the central barrier to his daughter's success in school. He explained that Annette had been in *première secondaire*, the first year of secondary school, in DRC and then was forced to go back four years to Primary 3 when they arrived in Kyaka II so that she could learn English with the Ugandan students.[132] She had persevered, and was now in Primary 6, but he felt that she was just continuing "like that" with no real learning. While she once had dreams of being a nurse, certain that "my studies will lead me there," she now had a different conception of herself. "I am a refugee, I am poor," she said.[133]

At school, Annette sat at the back of a class of forty-nine children. She was never called on to speak in class, her teachers rarely had the chance to look at her exercise books, and she never interacted with her teachers outside of the classroom. Annette and her father were not the only ones preoccupied with these challenges. Another student in her class, Kito, was the same age as Annette, having also been held back when he arrived from DRC. He, too, was struggling. His mother said, "I see every day that my son's teacher has written 'good, very good, excellent' in his exercise book. But I ask my child to read me what is in his book and he cannot do it. Alas, where does this work come from and why are there such remarks in the book when the pupil does not even know what he is doing?"[134]

Wilson, a Ugandan, who was the head teacher at the school and also Annette's English teacher, had taken this teaching job in a refugee camp as a hardship post, agreeing to live far from his family and to work under "such conditions." Yet he was a dedicated teacher, spending his evenings reading about refugees in Uganda and about ideas for pedagogy to teach new languages to children, a topic never touched on in his teacher training. "I know my children struggle in English," he told me in a three-page letter. "What shall I do is my question."[135]

Sonal, a usually reserved Indian woman who worked in Kampala for UNHCR as an education advisor, also felt at a loss for how to address the issue of pedagogy and language for refugees. She had just returned from a site visit to Kyaka II and called to ask me to come into the office, "immediately," deeply troubled by the rows and rows of children like Annette and Kito—"almost men and women"—whom she saw populating the schools of Kyaka II. "What can I do?" she exclaimed.

Sonal felt her hands tied at all levels.[136] At that time, refugees did not have the right to live in Kampala but were instead told, like Jacques, to "*allez au camp* [go to the camp]." As a UNHCR staff member, Sonal was thus prohibited from working with refugees in urban areas. As a private citizen, though, she gathered some chalk and other teaching supplies and asked me to deliver them to Jacques's school. This workaround to provide what Jacques explained that his school needed was far simpler than any solution she could think of regarding the lack of learning among refugees, which we both observed in Kyaka II.

One day, Sonal called me. "I have it!" she yelled into the phone.

I had no idea what she was talking about. "The curriculum," she said, almost breathless. "My contact brought it over the border two nights ago, and it arrived in my office today."

In her office a few days later, Sonal still looked triumphant. She carefully opened her locked filing-cabinet drawer. Under her purse was the *Guide Pédagogique*, the primary-school curriculum from DRC. She held up the tattered book in front of me as if it were the Nobel Prize.

"Please take it to Kyaka II for me," Sonal asked, knowing that I was going the next day to continue my research. "Caroline is waiting for it."

I knew Caroline well. With warm creases around her eyes and always dressed in a long skirt with a frilly white blouse, Caroline was not the White savior, motorcycle-riding aid worker of the movies. She was

Ugandan, grew up in the Kyaka area, and, over her lifetime, had seen refugee children from Congo and Rwanda come, stay, leave, and come again as the conflicts in their countries cyclically continued. Where she was once a student, she now was working for a Ugandan NGO, in charge of the schools in the settlement as well as all other education and social services.

Caroline knew everyone in the settlement. A good listener, and constructive gossip, she knew everybody's business and their needs. She had sat with Annette's father, too, in the shadow of their newly planted bananas, listening about the problems of language. But she spent most of her work days making lists: the number of children present in each class, ration-card numbers, missing uniforms, bars of soap distributed. Knowing that this was the nature of her work, I could not imagine what Caroline would do with the curriculum from Congo. But I had agreed to take it with me to Kyaka II, and Sonal watched as I secured it in my backpack.

"You won't carry that bag on your back, will you?" she asked, alarmed.

"No, Sonal, I won't," I promised. Abdi had learned in Toronto that he could carry his backpack on his back and not fear being robbed; I had learned in Kampala that a backpack did not belong on my back.

I delivered the *Guide Pédagogique* to Caroline, and we talked over how it could be used in Kyaka II schools as her grandchildren played on the floor by our feet.[137] "*Une bonne idée,*" she said about hiring teachers from Congo to teach the complete primary-school curriculum in French. "A good idea . . . ," she trailed off, sipping her ginger tea. But she kept the *Guide Pédagogique* safely stacked on her bookshelf at home. It was a good idea that never left the bookshelf. When I pointed to the book one evening as we talked again at her home, she said, "Yes, we are responsible for these refugee children, but they are pupils in *Ugandan* schools. I think you understand that there is little we can do."[138]

The challenges of being a refugee in a Ugandan school were not limited to language. Refugee students in Annette and Kito's class described how the national students in their class refused to sit with them. Nationals sat two to a bench, refugees sat four to a bench, and they knew they could not move to even out the numbers.[139] Yet despite what the children experienced, Caroline explained the rationale for not collecting data on ethnicity. "When they come here," she said, "we ask them not to be their nationalities anymore."[140]

Instead, each day, Annette, Kito, and their peers stood in front of the Ugandan flag in their school's compound singing the national anthem: "Oh, Uganda! the land of freedom . . . Oh, Uganda! the land that feeds us." Annette sang loudly when she arrived at this line: "We lay our future in thy hand."[141] Yet as she laid her future in the hands of the state, she soon came to realize that her future could not be *of* the state. For the next five years, Annette continued to go to school every day. When she stopped at age eighteen, she was not allowed to vote, she was not allowed to own property, and, since she did not have the right to work, she would not be able to practice as a nurse, as she had dreamed about. Five years later, Annette was still living in the same refugee camp. She was a subsistence farmer who tended, among other crops, her family's bananas.

In 2012, the shifts in practice toward the education of refugees in national schools that had taken place in Kenya and Uganda were codified into global policy, in a new era of Nationalization, the focus of Chapter 4. Refugee education now sits between a reawakening of the potential of local autonomy to meet the needs of marginalized students, and the expansion of one-size-fits-all national and global policies and structures that aim for quality at scale. Students like Henri and Annette were, and continue to be, often caught in the middle between these principles and approaches, between these local, national, and global goals. What does my right to education mean? Can I use what I learn in school? Where? Like with refugees' claims to sanctuary, in their education they are caught in the cracks of possible belonging that place them, and the futures they dare to imagine, outside of any country. As for Dina in the 1970s in Beirut, and Hadee post–September 11th in the United States, Henri and Annette ask themselves each day, what are the purposes of education, in creating our own individual futures and those of our families and communities?

4

Purpose

When Aliyah fled Syria with her four children, she imagined returning home within a few months.[1] Like most refugees, she left with clothes that would keep her warm only one season, never expecting that her exile would be protracted. Yet now, in 2014, she had already been in Egypt for three years. Nevertheless, the drawings of her daughter, Manar, always rendered the nostalgia of her once-upon-a-time life in Syria. She might envision herself in a different place, her mother explained, if she could go to a "good school." The government schools in the area of Cairo where the family could now afford rent were of poor quality, and her mother felt as if Manar was learning little. The only other school options were problematic also: at the costly private school she initially attended, her teachers were "warm and caring," but other Egyptian children bullied her incessantly, making her feel unsafe; and the nonformal Syrian school, which was free and followed the Syrian curriculum, kept her connected to a Syrian community but isolated from Egyptian society and the credentials necessary to move forward her education in exile.

Manar's life as a refugee in Egypt was filled with the uncertainty of her future, which affected her mother's criteria for a "good school," a school that would allow her to bridge her present reality with an imagined, yet uncertain, future. Would she return to Syria? If so, the nonformal Syrian school would provide a safe temporary environment and perhaps ease her transition back to school in Syria. Would she remain in exile, as Annette and Henri had for so long? If so, following the Egyptian curriculum and obtaining Egyptian certification would be critical for her livelihood prospects, and creating strong relationships in Egyptian schools would be worth the challenging, long-term investment. Would she seek to move onward, toward Europe, or would she be formally resettled to a distant country of exile, such as Canada as Jacques had been? If so, strong basic skills that could be transferred to another national context would be key, as would credentials to certify her learning. Yet Manar and her family could not predict which of these pathways might be open to her.

Slogans on schools serving refugees all over the world shout out the connection between education and futures, often hand-painted in lively colors by students. "Help me build my future!" radiates off the front of a primary-school building in the Kigeme camp in Rwanda. "Education is our only route out of poverty" is painted in bright bubble letters alongside drawings of students and teachers reading and carrying books on the wall of a secondary school in the Dadaab camps in Kenya. Yet as for Annette, on whose school wall in Uganda was painted "Education Is Light," Manar and her family faced a future in which these routes and the light were undetermined and hard to locate, circumscribed as it was by sanctuary and its expiration and by the power of states over where and how they can live. In the face of this unknowable future, they struggled to determine what kind of education might best meet Manar's needs now and in the future.

The Canadian Arctic is very distant from Manar's life in Egypt, yet the snowshoe hare that lives there offers a helpful metaphor in understanding the type of uncertainty that refugee young people like Manar face in thinking about the purposes of education. These large hares are so adapted to their environment, with big feet that allow them to move gracefully across the snow. Most remarkable is their capacity to change the color of their coat—brown in spring, summer, and fall when the Arctic land is scrubby and earthen; and white in the winter when the Arctic is covered in snow. Snowshoe hares' coats change in response to the number of hours of daylight, not to when snow falls. As the earth heats up, the snow and the light are no longer in sync. There is no longer snow on the ground when the light begins to fade in autumn, yet snowshoe hares still turn white. Their adaptation works on a clear theory—follow the light to be successful and make it. A warming planet, altered by climate change, has changed the color of the ground under their feet.[2] And a bright white bunny on an open brown earth, who has indeed followed the light, cannot make it.

Snowshoe hares have long been the poster-child example of adaptability. But in order to be adaptable, the signals they have access to need to be accurate. Annette could believe for quite some time that "Education Is Light," but the restrictions placed on her using that education for her future did not add up to making education the light that was promised to her. As the ground shifted under their feet, and once in Egypt, Manar and her family began to question the purposes of education. What kind of education could align with her possible futures, could support her in adapting and making it?

Refugee families, along with policymakers and practitioners, struggle daily with the uncertainty of unknowable futures as they must make and abide by decisions in the present. Often these decisions are made in urgent situations, with reverberating consequences. A protection officer from UNHCR in Egypt at the time Manar lived there described the kinds of calls that came to the hotline that UNHCR had set up to respond to refugees' questions. Calls that came right from the cusp of stepping onto a boat, like the ones from which Alan Kurdi and thousands of others have drowned, asking, "should I go?"[3]

Decisions about education can be just as consequential for the futures of young people such as Manar. Like Jacques at his school and Sonal at UNHCR in Uganda, decision makers at all levels struggle over what curriculum refugees should follow and what the implications are not only for their certification, but also for their feelings of belonging and for their possible futures. Like Henri experienced in Tanzania, what languages refugees learn have consequences regarding whom they can communicate with, where they can live, and what jobs they might have access to. Vulnerable and exposed in situations of newly confusing signals, refugee young people, families, teachers, and policymakers must make decisions about the types of schools that might best prepare them for work and life, both in the present and the future, without knowing what futures might be possible. Just like snowshoe hares signal a warning for the future of our planet, the experiences of refugee young people like Manar may signal a warning both for the future of education and our collective futures.

Reimagining the Purposes of Refugee Education

Out of the history of refugee education, with its varied approaches based on Liberation, Standardization, and Localization a radical new movement in refugee education has developed that seeks to address these very questions of uncertainty: Nationalization. Through previous eras, the purposes of refugee education have always been to prepare refugee students for the future. Yet the nature of this future has not been fixed. It cannot be fixed. Until recently, refugee education policy and practice assumed an eventual return to the country of origin. Reflecting that purpose, refugee students were isolated, largely in camps, and attended refugee-only schools, usually with lessons conducted in the languages of their country of origin.

The UNHCR Global Education Strategy released in 2012 assumed a different future. For the first time, global policy articulated an approach of including refugee students in educational structures of host countries, rather than isolating them in parallel systems, following the early local approaches in Uganda and Kenya. The 2018 Global Compact on Refugees, the Comprehensive Refugee Response Framework, and the 2019–2030 UNHCR Education Strategy have further codified this approach of inclusion.[4]

The processes of shifting to this approach were not straightforward or universally agreed upon. In 2009, Jeff Crisp, who was then director of policy and evaluation at UNHCR, approached me to undertake a "state of the field" study of refugee education. This review—described by a senior UNHCR staff member as "a hard-hitting and independent evaluation of the state of refugee education"—jump-started conversations on education within UNHCR in a new way.[5] Education, this staff member characterized in an email, "is the one issue which refugees prioritize above all others but in which we fail to deliver."[6] The plan had been to distribute the review I authored at the Executive Committee (ExCom) meetings of UNHCR in October 2011.[7] But with "UNHCR . . . not shown in a positive light," there was some "panic," and a last-minute decision was made to allow me to present the review, even though the text of the review itself was embargoed until after these meetings.[8]

Yet, in his closing speech to the Executive Committee that same year, António Guterres, then the high commissioner for refugees, and now the secretary-general of the United Nations, emphasized the importance of renewed focus on education: "Another area that was discussed by different delegations concerns gaps in education. Education and vocational training are key to finding solutions for refugees. We had a side event on Monday presenting the evaluation that was done on education, and a new strategy is now being prepared. We have made an important step forward in health, nutrition and water / sanitation in recent years, although much remains to be done. We now also need to make education a center piece of our strategy for solutions, namely in protracted refugee situations."[9]

In 2012, I worked with the Education Unit of UNHCR to draft this new education strategy, which focused on "access to quality education," in particular learning that enables refugee young people to build "relevant skills and knowledge . . . to live healthy, productive lives and . . .

[build] skills for self-reliance." As an overall approach to meeting these goals, the strategy focused on "integration of refugee learners within national systems where possible and appropriate and as guided by on-going consultation with refugees."[10]

The language of "where possible and appropriate" was often forgotten in conversations on this new approach, an approach that struck many with long-term experience in the field of refugee education as too radical and impractical. What happens when national teachers do not want to work in areas of Pakistan where Afghan refugees live? What happens when "half a million or more refugees with a different language of instruction cross the border"?[11] What happens, such as "in the case of Mozambique"—and reminiscent of Henri's situation—when refugees who studied in Portuguese (while in Malawi and Zimbabwe) were able to reintegrate after repatriation whereas those who had studied in English in Tanzania and elsewhere were unable to access education on return?[12]

Despite the apprehension and opposition in global-level conversations about the overall approach of integration and how it applied in each context, there was a glimmer of new possibilities for education to be more of the "light" Annette sought, which emerged from new policy recognition of the long-term exile that had been, for decades, embraced by teachers and students in their local and school contexts. Once introduced, there was rapid uptake of this new approach. In 2010, only five of fourteen countries identified by UNHCR as "priority countries," those hosting large numbers of refugees, integrated refugees in the national curriculum and language but, by 2014, eleven of these fourteen countries did. By 2016, UNHCR had formal relationships on the provision of refugee education with national authorities, such as national ministries of education or departments of refugee affairs, in twenty of its twenty-five expanded priority countries, having negotiated access to national schools for refugees and established means of coordination. This was up from zero formal relationships in 2011.

The 2012 strategy was not intended as a global blueprint—"integration of refugee learners within national systems *where possible and appropriate*"—but instead as a set of strategic objectives to be contextualized within each country. An education manager with an NGO in Ethiopia described the global document as the "mother document."[13] Training her colleagues on the new strategy, a UNHCR staff member based at its headquarters encouraged them to "think of the Strategy as a verb, not a noun," as something active, not inert.[14] Documents created by UNHCR at the global level emphasized the need to analyze situations in each country to inform decision making about whether and how to take up the approach of integration. UNHCR staff in each context engaged in activities designed to answer questions such as "What does UNHCR hope that children and youth will be educated for in your country context?"[15] Global policy was clear that local priorities should drive national approaches to refugee education.

And they did: the new global approach to refugee education was interpreted in different ways in different places. These differences reflected priorities in each country but also different ways in which the present situations of refugees were connected—or could be connected—to their futures. Globally with UNHCR and within countries, there was a quick shift in rhetoric from the word "integration" to the word "inclusion," signifying a focus on the structural processes of making national education available to refugee young people, rather than on relational or long-term social processes.[16] In some countries, like Malaysia and Bangladesh, governments have rejected even the structural elements of this approach, such that refugees and nationals attend separate schools, generally with refugee education being informal, ad hoc, and with few certification options.[17] While UNHCR staff in these countries express hope that including refugees in national education systems might become possible, they see limited political space for it. A government official from Iran, speaking at a coordination meeting on the implementation of the UNHCR strategy, described including refugees as "our duty and our job to do [even if] the result is somewhere else," meaning that, despite the country's investment, the refugees might well in the future take the benefits of their education outside of Iran.[18] On hearing this, a UNHCR staff member working in Malaysia said, "When we heard the presentation from Iran it took time for us to pick up our jaws from the floor. We hope perhaps one day we can say the same about our country."[19]

In other countries, especially where refugees live in camp settings such as in Kenya, inclusion involves using the Kenyan curriculum and English and Kiswahili as languages of instruction, even though refugee and national children are geographically isolated from each other and do not attend school together. In some places, like Lebanon, inclusion involves refugee children attending the same schools as Lebanese children, with most of the same teachers, using the same curriculum and examination systems, but at a different time of day, Lebanese students in the mornings and refugees in the afternoons. In a few situations, particularly in urban areas of refugee-hosting countries, refugees and nationals attend school together at the same time in the same classrooms.

The dynamics of this inclusion vary widely, depending on various factors. It can depend on whether there are few refugee students among many nationals as for Hadee in my classroom in the United States and Jacques's children in Canada, or many refugee students with few nationals as for Annette in rural Uganda or Henri in Tanzania. For Manar, in Egypt, access to national schools depended not on her refugee status but on her country of origin. While the policy in Egypt shifted in 2017 to include all refugees, Manar had access to Egyptian schools because she was Syrian, but her peers from Sudan, Somalia, Iraq, DRC, Eritrea, and Ethiopia did not. If Abdi or Jacques had fled to Egypt rather than Uganda, they and their children would not have had access to national schools.

These different structures of refugee education both reflect and circumscribe the possible futures Manar and her family were trying to create. UNHCR has long outlined three possible "durable solutions," or futures, for refugees: "resettlement" to a distant country; "return" to the country of origin; or long-term "integration" in the host country.[20] Since 2016, UNHCR has additionally focused on futures that are flexible geographically and less unidirectional, recognizing ongoing "human mobility" and the "precarious" nature of any possible future.[21] Leveraging the global scope of the studies I draw on, across countries patterns emerge in the futures imagined for refugees at global and national levels, by refugees, by teachers, and by policymakers. They fall into four general categories: a future of resettlement, a future of return, a future of integration, and futures that are less-bounded. The future imagined and the structures and content of education are tightly connected, both shaped by and shaping each other. Their synthesis is central to how the purposes of education are defined and experienced in each context.

A Future of Resettlement

Resettlement is a process by which refugees receive legal status in a distant country, usually a high-income country, before departure from the previous country of exile rather than applying for asylum when they arrive. Most refugees in the United States arrive in this way. Jacques and his family were granted this resettlement to Canada after eleven years of living in exile in Uganda. Yet a future of resettlement, where one's legal status is secure before setting foot in the new country, is unavailable to the vast majority of refugees globally. Jacques and his family were among the 1 percent of refugees who had access to this future.[22]

Resettlement comes with a high degree of permanence, including a pathway to citizenship that is typically unavailable in neighboring host countries. For this reason, refugees, who increasingly find themselves in protracted displacement, often perceive resettlement as the ultimate future, especially in terms of the educational possibilities offered in distant countries that usually provide free and mandatory schooling, including for high school and, in some cases in Europe, for university. Many refugees also make decisions about the kinds of certification they seek and the languages they learn in light of a possible future of resettlement. A young Syrian may ask herself if it is worth it to learn Turkish if she imagines her future to soon be in Germany.

Malaysia is one country with high numbers of refugees who leave for resettlement. In 2014, 15 percent of all resettled refugees globally departed from Malaysia in response to the extremely limited possibility of long-term residence in Malaysia, which is not signatory to the Refugee Convention and which has no legal system for asylum.[23] Without legal status, individuals fleeing to Malaysia are at risk for arrest, detention, and deportation, in other words for ongoing persecution that makes them candidates for resettlement. Under these conditions, refugee families and NGOs providing education perceive instruction in the Bahasa Malay language as counterproductive to possible futures for refugees. Thus, in Malaysia, refugee education takes place in separate schools run by NGOs, typically in English, and is aimed to foster opportunities upon resettlement. As a teacher in a refugee school said, "This is the preparation time to have a better education in the third county. This is our main purpose."[24]

Despite the elusiveness of resettlement for most refugees, the stakes of these decisions about curriculum and language that look toward resettlement can be unknowingly high. Ramazani's family was well-off compared to other refugees in Kampala, Uganda. They lived in a house with concrete walls and floors and a high, tin roof. Their sofa and chairs had new, soft cushions. In the main room, one of only two in the house, there was a small black wheeling cart that held four videotapes and a paraffin lamp, indicating lives that included at least some leisure and nights filled not only with sleeping.[25]

Ramazani, age fifteen, and his family were registered refugees in the Kyangwali refugee settlement, in western Uganda, but they decided to make their life in exile in Kampala. Ramazani's father was an artist, and an urban area was the only place he could practice his profession and support his family. While their present lives were in Kampala, the family planned for a future of resettlement in Canada or Australia. The problem, however, was that in order to be eligible for resettlement, the family was required to live in a refugee settlement as almost no refugees were resettled from the city. But Ramazani's parents were not willing to give up their present livelihood and what they perceived to be better education for their children in Kampala for the long-shot opportunity of resettlement. So they played their odds, living in both the city and the refugee settlement. When they got word that UNHCR was conducting a census in Kyangwali—because staying on UNHCR's list for possible resettlement depended on them being counted in this census—they quickly traveled back to the settlement and took up residence there. As soon as the family had been counted, they moved back to Kampala. When I met them, this pattern had continued for three years. The timing of the census in the previous year, however, had meant that Ramazani was forced to miss his final exams in Kampala and spend the next year repeating his Senior 2 (Grade 8) year.

The consequences of this kind of setback in education can be huge for a young refugee like Ramazani, including in the case of his eventual resettlement. On a nippy spring day in Oslo, Norway, a young Somali graduate student told me of the consequences of educational roads taken and not taken.[26] He and his cousin were about the same age. They both grew up and attended schools in the Dadaab camps in Kenya. He obtained his Kenyan Certificate of Secondary Education (KCSE) not long before being resettled to Sweden, enrolled almost immediately in university, earned his bachelor's and master's degrees, and then was funded for his doctorate. His cousin, just as capable and hardworking, was resettled a few months prior to sitting for his KCSE exam, so he arrived in Sweden having done all of the same coursework but without a diploma. This cousin was too old to complete high school in Sweden, the high school equivalency courses were hard to access, and he was denied entry to higher education. He decided to return to Kenya to sit for his exam. Only then, with Kenyan certificate in hand, was he was able to enroll in a university in Sweden.

A Future of Return

Fourteen-year-old Bakari arrived at the Kyaka II refugee settlement in Uganda as an unaccompanied minor. His father was killed in eastern DRC, not far from where Jacques had fled. Bakari explained to me, in short phrases, and almost out of breath, that "during the war, enemies burned the houses, and when people made to flee, the enemies cut them up with machetes."[27] That the war had come to his village had been a surprise for Bakari, as it is for most refugees.

As a child, Bakari had been content in DRC. "I used to study," he said. "I used to play, and life was good."[28] In Uganda, on his own, he had to take on so much more responsibility, figuring out ways to care for himself in a new and unfamiliar place. But he still looked so young, ears sticking out slightly from his school-required shortly cropped hair.

A year after he arrived, Bakari's mother also came to Kyaka II. She had a thin face and high cheekbones. She smiled readily, to reveal a mouth with few teeth. As we talked, she sat on a small stool beside a pile of beans awaiting threshing, and she told us that they had begun to plant crops, certain that their exile would take them into the next season.[29] A year earlier, Bakari had said, "I would choose [to go home] to Congo, if there would be no war."[30] What he would choose and what he was safely able to choose continued to be misaligned as one year stretched into the next.

Bakari's desired future, a return to DRC, echoed Jacques's preferred future as well: return to the place where one truly feels at home. Refugee testimonies and memoirs and decades of research are filled with this same clear choice most refugees would make, if that choice were available: to return home. As a Congolese refugee teacher working in the Kigeme camp in Rwanda described, "every human being loves being home."[31] In an interview with Elizabeth Adelman, one of my former students and now collaborator, Lina, a Syrian teacher teaching at a nonformal school in Lebanon, expressed her conundrum: balancing her personal uncertainties about the future with a responsibility to provide for her students more stability than she felt. "I feel that is my duty to make kids understand this situation is temporary and things will become better." She laughed self-consciously. "Even though I am not true [honest], at least this gives them hope that we are going back."[32]

While home is not a possible present for most refugees, the desire to plan for a future that includes home never goes away and is reflected in aspirations around education. Until 2014, Sudanese refugees in Chad followed the Sudanese curriculum, in Arabic, sat for Sudanese government exams, and received official school-leaving certificates from the Sudanese government. Facing an increasingly protracted situation, refugee education policy in Chad shifted, such that refugees would follow the Chadian curriculum and be eligible for Chadian certification. The country's National Education Sector plan, the policy document that provides long-term vision and strategy for reaching national education goals, also included the provision of education to refugees, making Chad one of only a few countries globally to take this inclusive, long-term step with national policy. This access to national education opened the possibility of creating a future for refugee young people that did not depend on a return to Sudan. Yet the future that Sudanese refugee young people imagined for themselves did not always align with this approach. Several NGO staff members described how some Sudanese refugee young people decided against sitting for Chadian final exams, and instead elected to re-enter Sudan temporarily in order to sit for Sudanese examinations. They took this action even at great physical risk, so strong was their desire for an education that could prepare them for a future of return, improbable though it might be.

The Dadaab camps in Kenya, established in 1991 in the Standardization era of refugee education, are the only home that hundreds of thousands of Somali refugees have ever known. Salim arrived in Dadaab when he was a small child, and he doesn't remember Somalia. He says he feels that he is "not Somali, not Kenyan. I identify myself as Dadaabian. . . . In my heart I am a Somali. I know that is who I really am. But even though I am a Somali . . . I have never been [in] Somalia. I don't have a lot of experience with Somalia."[33] Becoming Dadaabian, a word now widely used by young people who have grown up in Dadaab, did not seem to Salim like a process, but more like a realization. "When I was in primary [school]," he said, "I didn't even think that I would finish high school in the camps. . . . I felt people would be taken back to Somalia somehow, or someday a solution would be reached. But it never happened."[34]

Despite the realization that return is improbable, like Annette's when her father planted bananas, Somali young people in Dadaab think about their education in terms of how it connects them, or could connect them, to Somalia. Salim's peers are a small cadre of students who have graduated from secondary school in Dadaab, a place where only 2.3 percent of young people have access to this level of education.[35] The current poverty, inequality, and conflict in Somalia, and what they might contribute to its reconstruction, is consistently on the minds of these refugee students as they pursue education. One explained, "One of my educational goals is to become someone, then take part in the reconstruction of Somalia."[36] Another stated that his "burning issue is to go back to Somali country and construct that collapsed country."[37] A third, who completed his secondary schooling in Dadaab and was sponsored for a bachelor's degree in Nairobi, said, "Why not . . . come back to Somalia and add a value on this tree that's growing called Somalia. It's very small and very delicate now."[38]

The education that was accessible in Dadaab—free, certified, and in English—was one way for refugee young people to build a future of return, while continuing to live outside of Somalia. One noted that as a teacher he is "making a good contribution to society . . . because I am building [my students'] brains and their future. . . . If you run away with only your shirt and you have the brain, you can work somewhere else and earn a living."[39] Another saw a direct link between his teaching and the future of Somalia: "the work I am doing now is related to Somalia because if these people [my students], I teach them well, they will be going back, and they will teach there."[40] More than five thousand miles away, in Lebanon, Lina, the Syrian refugee teacher who was torn about how honest to be about a future of return, gave this same message to her students: "If we do not like our current situation, we can think of how we want it to be in the future. I constantly tell them, 'Try not to go back to Syria the same way you came out of it.' I mean to go back in a better position than we left."[41]

What the best educational investment is for a future of return is an open question. One NGO staff member articulated what is "common knowledge" in South Sudan: "those who can speak English and do something are the people who return from Kakuma [refugee camp in Kenya]" to South Sudan.[42] Not in all cases, however, does an education acquired by a refugee outside their country of origin hold currency if and when refugees return. Henri, arriving in Burundi with a secondary-school diploma from Tanzania but lacking consistency in his education vis-à-vis languages and curricula, was denied entry to universities that required a Burundian education for admission. An education leader from UNICEF, two years after she had participated in a class discussion about Henri's educational trajectory, wrote, "Good morning from steamy Dakar. I will be thinking about Henri and others like him today as I meet colleagues from the region, along with MOE [Ministry of Education] and partners, working on different refugees responses."[43] Yet as these colleagues think about Henri and his trajectory through education as a refugee in Tanzania and what it means for the kinds of policies and programs they develop, the question remains: aside from recognizing the immense uncertainty refugee young people face, what kind of education can prepare them for their futures?

A Future of Integration

Given the slim prospects of resettlement or return, long-term exile is an increasingly likely reality for most refugees. Salim and the majority of his peers arrived in Dadaab as small children or were born there. Decades later, they find themselves still in this same place of exile, now finished secondary school and determining what the possible options are for this next stage of their futures. The approach of including refugees within national education systems was created with this common reality of Salim's in mind: more than three-quarters of refugees at the end of 2018 were living in protracted displacement, meaning more than five years, and one-third of these refugees—5.8 million—had been displaced for more than twenty years.[44] At the same time this approach also reflected a pragmatism related to the "confinement crisis," whereby the politics of migration limit the spaces globally where refugees can locate even temporary sanctuary. The motivations of global actors to push for opening national schools to refugees in the neighboring countries in which 73 percent of refugees live globally are certainly tied to their own political pressures to keep refugees out of Europe, North America, and Australia.

While Aliyah and Manar left Syria with one season's worth of clothes, they quickly realized that they would need to think of their exile—and their futures—in much different terms. As UNHCR High Commissioner Guterres noted at the 2011 Executive Committee meetings, education was a key part of "solutions" in protracted situations, but the protractedness of situations also meant a rethinking of the purposes of refugee education and how to achieve them. The UNHCR education strategy, "Refugee Education 2030: A Strategy for Inclusion," articulates this "new understanding that short term approaches to refugee education are insufficient and inappropriate to displacement realities, which require medium- to longer-term development perspectives and opportunities for knowledge and skills acquisition that lead to economic inclusion well beyond the margins of informal economies."[45]

Promises of Integration

Does this global policy of inclusion open a crack in the limited sanctuary that now exists for refugees, and to a renegotiation of opportunities for refugees through education? On the surface, it does. In Rwanda, including refugees in national education was presented as a commitment of the state to refugees, with broad-based support across the country, from top-level government officials to teachers. "I haven't seen anyone who's against it," said a UN agency staff member.[46] When Rwanda's government expanded fee-free education through secondary school, refugees were included in the mandate. A government official described this situation as win-win: "the local population benefitting from the expansion of existing infrastructure [paid for by international donors] and the refugees benefitting from teachers being hired by the government, being paid by the government."[47] For a district government official, the issue was equity: "We allow this [inclusion] because this issue of global education is universal. It's not a country-based policy. It's even in the MDGs [now SDGs]. So we can't say that Rwandans should complete 12 [years of schooling] but others who are in Rwanda shouldn't study."[48]

An explicit purpose of access to quality education for refugees in Rwanda was to enable multiple futures, renegotiating the limited ways in which education within a state means imagining futures within that same state. A government leader explained that the goal is to "gain . . . the skills that could help them in their future anywhere."[49] A refugee teacher in a camp-based school, with students primarily from DRC, emphasized ongoing pursuit of a future that could be "anywhere." He referred to both Rwanda and DRC as "our country," signifying the possible dual nature of his and his students' futures.[50] A government leader in Kenya echoed how access to quality education "would enable them to settle . . . to help them fit into society and be a useful member of society . . . to help the refugee to integrate." These are the "same skills that any other Kenyan would need," she explained, such as critical thinking, communication skills, and technical skills that match workplace demands they will face in their futures.[51]

Another NGO staff member envisioned the need to plan refugee education with these multiple possible futures at the forefront of the mind: "I would like [refugees] to go away with something. . . . And for me education would be key. Because even if they relocated to a different country today, they would go with the knowledge, they would go with a paper [certificate], something that would help them in their life and the years to come."[52] To prepare for these multiple futures, a government leader in Kenya underscored the need for children to learn not only to read and write but also to "contribute to nation-building."[53] What "nation-building" entailed, though, was nebulous, and visions for where

refugees' futures would be had implications for which "nation" education should prepare them to contribute to. One teacher described wanting
his students to be in a "position to influence the governance in any country
you want to go to. . . . You need knowledge to change government." He
wanted education in exile in Kenya to "make them a better citizen [so]
they can transform their society into a better society," wherever that society may be.[54]

Yet for a young person like Annette, the process of schooling in Uganda
was, in her mind, preparation for life in Uganda. She learned the Ugandan
curriculum, in Ugandan languages of instruction, sat for Ugandan certification exams, and each day as she stood before the Ugandan flag she
sang "We lay our future in thy hand." Annette felt this as a kind of social
contract and acted to uphold what she saw as her part, by going to school
each day, adapting to the new curriculum and language through challenges and senses of loss, and preparing herself for a future that was not
how she imagined it would be, when, as a young girl, home was DRC.
Yet what she felt as a promise to her by the Ugandan state, enacted through
her education, was not in fact the promise that the state was making.
While opening schools, policies enacted by the state and UNHCR simultaneously maintained structural bars, to freedom of movement, pursuit
of higher education, and the right to work, which limited how she could
"be a useful member of society," "influence the governance," or have an
education that could "help . . . in . . . life and the years to come."[55] Rather
than using her education to fulfill her dreams of becoming a nurse, she
tended her family's bananas.

There is a dilemma at the heart of education policymaking: what entity is responsible for the education of a child, and to what entity do the
collective benefits of investment in education accrue? Modern states take
on the responsibility of education and the provision of other social services,
with belief in the benefits of economic, political, civil, and social future
returns. But will the future returns of education of refugees accrue
to the hosting country? Rights for noncitizens within countries have
been precarious, resulting in a historical cornerstone of humanitarian

governance being that it operates largely outside the state, through global institutions.[56] In situations of internal conflict, this status quo stemmed from the understanding that states are complicit in the suffering that humanitarian governance seeks to assuage; and in refugee situations, from the often limited capacity of host countries to uphold fundamental rights that require resources, including the responsibility of service provision to noncitizens.[57] In the Standardization phase, UNHCR acted as the "pseudo-state," and it was an era of the "rule of the NGOs."[58] Financed by bilateral and multilateral funding, these global actors took on responsibility for the education of refugees.[59] In the current Nationalization phase, the question of responsibility for education is being renegotiated.

Michael Barnett, political scientist at George Washington University, argues that humanitarianism, as ideally constructed historically, is a "cosmopolitan option to a system of states," "creating a world defined by the values of humanity."[60] Yet he is critical of how these values not only can operate for good but also can "make possible new forms of violence."[61] In refugee education, financing power—answering the question of who is responsible for education—makes possible new violence within geopolitics. In theory, the Global Compact on Refugees advocates that refugees are included in national education systems but that global actors take responsibility to provide the financing power needed to meet the educational needs of refugees in these already over-stretched education systems.[62] At the same time, over the past decade, an average of less than 2 percent of all humanitarian funding was allocated to education, making the kinds of sustained investments needed to expand education systems elusive.[63]

An NGO staff member in a camp in Rwanda discussed how the scale at which national education systems operated could absorb some of the volatility of funding: "If we had to initiate our own [refugee] schools, we would have to pay teachers. . . . But now because children are integrated in the national schools, the government is taking responsibility. The big responsibility is on the government. The government has to pay teachers;

it has to provide the capitation grant for all children—refugees and nationals. It is a good system."[64] An NGO staff member in Egypt said of inclusion of Syrians into Egyptian schools, "it is easy and it is cheap."[65] Yet government officials across refugee-hosting countries, sitting not in schools but with balance sheets in capital cities, do not agree. Including refugees in national schools is expensive. Even in a double-shift system such as in Lebanon, infrastructure needs to be maintained for the larger number of students, more supplies have to be provided, and more teachers and other school staff need to be paid. The Lebanon Ministry of Education and Higher Education (MEHE) reported that 12,251 staff members worked in the second shift, the shift for refugee children, in the 2017–2018 school year, which meant 12,251 more salaries to fund in a national system already struggling to cover the basic costs of public education.[66]

A mapping exercise of out-of-school children by UNHCR and UNICEF in Lebanon, shared with education partners in September 2018, stated that, "in light of the funding gap still remaining for school year 2017 / 2018, and for the upcoming school year 2018 / 2019, MEHE has expressed that they are not prepared to accommodate any exercise leading to an increased demand for enrollment."[67] MEHE reported the funding gap for enrollment fees at US$30,055,613.[68] Marwan Hamadeh, then the minister of education and higher education, circulated a memo to all schools noting the freeze on enrollment of non-Lebanese students unless funding was made available: "Priority shall be given to the registration of returning students, then to children who successfully completed the Accelerate Learning Program (ALP) and are able to enroll to formal education based on an official certificate in this regard, as long as the number of enrolled students in each school does not exceed the number of enrolled students last year. Lists including the names of new children wishing to enroll to formal education shall be prepared, regardless of the school's capacity, pending the availability of required funds to take the appropriate decision regarding their final registration. The school's principal shall be responsible for any surplus exceeding the number of last year's numbers."[69] Understood in the memo was a message to donors: without additional funding to fulfill the commitments these donors had made to supporting the inclusion of refugees in the Lebanese education system—at the London Conference (2016), and Brussels I Conference (2017) and Brussels II Conference (2018)—the Lebanese state would not take responsibility for the education of refugee students.

MEHE forced an answer to the question of "whose responsibility" the education of refugees is by refusing to allow new enrollments by Syrian students pending donor funding. National governments may recognize the possibilities for efficiencies of scale, but in the absence of substantial and predictable global funding, inclusion only shifts the "big responsibility" for refugee education from a global collective commitment to being borne by national actors. The approach of including refugees in national education systems is described in global instruments as "responsibility-sharing," but it can only be such if it includes financial support to the primarily low- and middle-income countries that host refugees.[70] Without that, the approach places the "big responsibility" of education on refugee-hosting countries, especially those that are least resourced to support it.[71] As for individual refugees, for countries too, there is a disconnect between present investment and possibilities for future returns. This period of Nationalization of refugee education forces a rethinking of the collective benefits of education, nationally and globally.

Possibilities of Integration

While long-term residence in a country of exile is a reality for the majority of refugees today, permanence in that state is most often politically untenable and not what refugees desire over the long term.[72] Why then should a state invest—financially, politically, morally—in the education of refugees?

Mass schooling developed alongside shifts in economies, from agrarian to industrial forms of work and to professions. The rationale for national investment in education is framed in most foundational documents for national education systems globally as a catalyst for economic growth, even if access to education is necessary but not sufficient for future labor-market participation. In most refugee-hosting countries, though, refugees are unable to access the formal labor market due to restrictions on their right to work, to access capital, and to own property.[73] Given these constraints, a country's investment in refugees' education cannot translate into economic growth in that country, limiting the perceived collective benefit. Annette could not become a nurse as she once dreamed, given the restrictions that existed at the time on her freedom of movement in Uganda and her possibilities for higher education.

Instead of education focused on ways to create futures, then, teachers within these systems often feel the responsibility to focus on helping their students to cope in the present. In an interview with Elizabeth Adelman, one teacher explained the negotiation he needed to do with himself about how to teach students to live productively in Lebanon: "The Lebanese people rejected the Syrians, so this makes it difficult for me to tell the student that he should fuse or adapt in the Lebanese society. . . . I cannot teach a student how to adapt in a society that is rejecting them."[74] Five years later, in a collaborative study with Vidur Chopra, Joumana Talhouk, and Carmen Geha, another teacher in Lebanon explained to us how he rationalized teaching a history he did not agree with to his Syrian students. "All history books are biased," he explained. "But we have to learn the history the way it is, in order to get the grades. We are merchants in grades."[75]

Syrian Grade 9 students in Lebanese public schools in Beirut, studying for their Grade 9 exam—on which grades would open a path to more education or would shut them out of any further education—still could not be sure what passing grades at this level would do for them in the future, if they were unable, without the right to work, to put their education to use in Lebanon. Khawla, a sixteen-year-old Syrian girl, arrived in Lebanon when she was nine. Departure from Syria came as a surprise to her and, as she remembers it, one of the hardest moments was needing to leave behind her favorite teddy bear. In retrospect, she laughs at being worried about her toy, but her life in Syria at that time did not force other preoccupations.

Khawla's early years of school in Syria were formative, both in terms of how they made her feel about school and about relationships with teachers. Khawla described her school, smiling as she remembered the painting of SpongeBob visible as soon as she entered, the blue windows, and a garden with olive trees and flowers. The walls were covered with the children's drawings, "so that we would be more encouraged and motivated," she said.[76] At home, she watched a medical television show, which inspired in her a goal to become a doctor. Her kindergarten teacher encouraged this idea, and Khawla remembers how "she used to always make me feel optimistic and say, 'You're going to become a doctor. You'll achieve your dreams.'"[77]

This dream remained with Khawla and, as a sixteen-year-old, it had become a specific goal of being a surgeon who helps people in need for free.[78] After Googling the requirements for this training in Lebanon, she wrote out a detailed series of steps covering the next twelve years of her life by which she could accomplish this goal. But each step was accompanied by a set of factors over which she had no control. Would refugees be allowed to continue to go to school in Lebanon? Would she be allowed to work in Lebanon if she did become a surgeon? She had top grades, the kind that, according to the logics of exam systems, would facilitate her further study and enable her to reach medical school. But what Khawla heard from her teachers when she began primary school in Lebanon shook her trust in whether these opportunities would be open to her. She explained that she began to think, "Maybe they're right, maybe we are coming to Lebanon, it's not our country, we can't study here, we can't work here, we can't stay here. Maybe they're right. We are occupying their country."[79]

When Khawla's family arrived in Lebanon, her mother found the very same stuffed bear that Khawla had needed to leave behind in Syria. She bought it for Khawla, and Khawla still has it, one of her most special possessions. The bear was a kind of continuity, a connection to her life in

Syria, and the childhood dreams that seemed so possible. But the bear stayed at home, away from the encounters Khawla had each day that made that future instead seem elusive. "In the end," Khawla said of Lebanon, "this is their country and maybe we are intruders in their country but the situation in our country doesn't allow us to return."[80] Khawla and other refugee young people knew they were at the mercy of cyclical and conflicting logic: educational policies that allowed them to study but social and economic policies and politics that did not allow them to participate. How can they not be burdens on the Lebanese state without opportunities to put their education to use?

On top of legal restrictions, in Lebanon and in most other refugee-hosting countries, the kind of learning that would enable young people to complete school ready to be economically productive is limited. For example, in Kenya, the classrooms for refugees were so overcrowded—with upward of 200 children at times—that even children sitting next to their teacher could not hear. In a collaborative study with Michelle J. Bellino, Nasra, a Somali refugee who had attended primary school outside the Kakuma camp but returned to Kakuma when her family could no longer afford the school fees, described how she felt the stark difference between the national schools outside the camps and the ostensibly national schools inside the camps. "No one wants to attend school in a refugee camp," she said. "The syllabus is the same, but the education it is not the same."[81] While feeling like inclusion in a national school promised a pathway to broader inclusion in Kenya and opportunities for upward mobility, Nasra instead found herself ensconced in the downward mobility of ethnic, class, and regional inequalities in Kenya.[82] The district where the Kakuma camp is located, Turkana, has some of the highest levels of poverty and the lowest levels of access to education in Kenya.[83] In a recent study of early grade literacy, we found that young children in Kakuma have some of the lowest documented scores anywhere in the world.[84]

How possible is a future of integration for refugees if they access low-quality education within contexts of few postschooling opportunities, even for nationals? A teacher in Kakuma, who arrived from South Sudan as an upper-primary student and completed his secondary schooling in Kenya, also questioned the value of pursuing a future in a situation where there are so many "challenges": "There is no future. . . . [I]t gives me a divided mind whether . . . I want to be integrated. . . . If I am integrated as a citizen of this country, what will be my life? Will it be better or worse than the way I am [now]?"[85] A refugee teacher in Rwanda noted that his own desire for a future of integration in Rwanda was not high, especially when he looked at the lives of Rwandan nationals. "Their lives are not even better," he said bluntly.[86] Similarly, in Egypt, an NGO staff member noted "there is no benefit" to including Syrian refugees—for either Syrians or for Egyptians—in a system already struggling to implement quality education.[87] In Pakistan, an NGO staff member said, "it is hard to take on [the] additional task of Afghan refugees."[88] As the newest country, challenges of inclusion in South Sudan were similar. South Sudan "is a country in the making," and the Ministry of Education is also "in the making," said a UNHCR staff member. For these reasons, UNHCR staff explained that schools are "barely functional" and act in "haphazard" ways while trying to include refugees.[89] In Lebanon, where Khawla is in school, under one-third of Lebanese children enroll in government schools, the ones to which refugees have access, as families with options doubt their quality and choose private schools instead.[90]

In addition to economic benefits, collective benefits of education to the state include social and civic development. Education systems—in both their structures and content—historically and in the present orient this social and civic development toward the state, with goals of generating unity and social cohesion, as Thato understood but struggled with in Botswana.[91] In 576 textbooks from 78 countries, a recent study found that, despite globalization, these textbooks continue to center on nationalist narratives and are oriented toward the creation of national citizens.[92] The authors do find that diminished nationalism is more present in globally dominant countries, in the form of cosmopolitanism and global citizenship.[93] Yet concerns over cosmopolitanism echo Barnett's critique of western hegemony, with the benefits of this cosmopolitanism still accruing to these globally dominant countries.[94] Other research has shown that access to the experiences that global citizenship education promises may be possible for young people with multiple citizenships and access to money, but not for the majority of the world's children who face one form of geopolitical restriction or another, and in particular not for refugees like Khawla who are noncitizens in their sites of education.[95]

In the case of refugee education, then, under new policies that include refugees in national education systems, incentives on the economic, political, civil, and social collective benefits of education are misaligned: we have a case of education by the state but not for the state. Refugee young people find themselves within the systems of marginalization that already exist within the hosting countries and perceived as a potential threat to limited economic opportunities. Because of refugees' unpredictable future geography and inability to legally work or grow the economy, host countries are unconvinced of any politically viable economic or civic benefits for meeting their educational needs.

The Futures School, in central Beirut, is right off a main road.[96] Tall buildings and bumper-to-bumper traffic give way to a small entryway that quickly opens into an expansive courtyard. The three stories of classrooms around it have windows onto the courtyard, and its top opens to the sky. The exterior wall of the school is bright and lively, painted with mottos and pictures, including a graffiti-style tag saying "I Love School." Inside the courtyard, there is again art on the walls, including students' colorful drawings. There are Lebanese army flags on the courtyard windows and a Lebanese flag flying outside the school.

There are symbols of an education connected to global as well as national influences, as well.[97] The graph-paper notebooks that Grade 9 students take out in Physics class are imprinted with the logo of the United Nations, and each student sports a large green and yellow backpack boldly embossed with two crossed swords and a palm tree, the emblem of Saudi Arabia, and with the words "The National Saudi Campaign to Support

Our Brothers in Syria." A Grade 9 student at another second-shift school in Beirut described being confused as to whether he should accept the backpack. He recalled when two people came to the school from Saudi Arabia to pass out bags. Some students said they thought Saudis were involved in the war in Syria so they did not want their bags. Others, he recalled, said that the Saudis are giving us all of these things, and it's generous of them as they are helping us to study, so we should take them.[98]

At Futures, there are twenty-seven students in the late afternoon Arabic class, each of them in school uniform. There is one empty desk; one student is absent. Boys are seated beside boys, and girls beside girls. The desks have little shelves under them with space for supplies. There are cut-out birds on the bulletin boards around the room, and there is a drawing of a Christmas tree on the back wall. At the front of the room, there is an audio-visual cabinet with a USAID sticker on it. Inside is the equipment that would be used to control the projector, which is tightly fixed to the ceiling. The projector is not used in this lesson, though. One student explained, almost nonchalantly, that the projector is only for the first-shift students and stays locked when Syrians are at school.[99] He was so habituated to these messages of exclusion, to the second-class status of the second shift, that he did not question it.

In addition to these structural messages of exclusion, Syrian young people find themselves excluded from what they are taught in the curriculum. All Grade 9 students in Lebanon learn about "The Right to File Administrative Complaints" in Civics class. In two public Lebanese schools, this lesson was straightforward. The teacher drew a chart on the board illustrating the government institution that was responsible for receiving each kind of grievance, by geographical region. "For example," she said, "if someone wants to raise a complaint to the Ministry of Education and Higher Education, and they live in Beirut, they go to the 'Educational District' in Beirut and file a complaint there."[100] At a private school with all Syrian students and Syrian teachers, the teacher subtly called out the contradictions for Syrian students learning about these methods of filing complaints, when as Syrians they did not have the right to do so. The teacher said, "Let's say Leila Ali takes her relative to the hospital for an emergency. The hospital was late to admit her relative. Let's say Leila Ali is Lebanese. What does she do? She filed a complaint."[101] Just like a "merchant in grades," as the one teacher called himself, Syrian and Lebanese teachers reflected a stance that they would teach within the nationalized system of education, even if it did not apply to refugees: if Leila Ali was Syrian, she would not, she could not, file a complaint.

But Munir, age sixteen and in Grade 9 at Futures School, lodged complaints against his teachers' way of teaching each day through his battery of spot-on questions. In a Civics lesson on education, the teacher explained that "education challenges poverty and is a pathway for a better life." He went on to explain how "if a person is not educated, they cannot contribute to the benefit of society." Munir asked, "Who chose presidents and prime ministers . . . ?" The teacher, clearly uncomfortable, responded, "They are special people, that's why they were chosen." After the teacher turned his attention away from the class and responded to a text and listened to a WhatsApp voice note on his phone, Munir asked, with a sarcastic tone, "You find these people special?" The teacher smiled, seeing his student understood more than his lesson intended. "The problem," he said, "is that sometimes they have money and influence, and that's how they reach these positions."[102]

At break time at Futures School, all of the students played in the interior courtyard. It was chaotic, children running around in all directions. Some of the boys were fighting—pulling each other down, wrenching each other's arms and twisting. There were teachers walking around as if on autopilot, ringing the bells they held in their hands loudly in no particular direction as they walked, then suddenly walking up to particular students whom they deemed too unruly and ringing the bell loudly right beside their ears, with no words. I watched as the children didn't change their behavior and simply ran away. The teachers didn't change their behavior either, continuing to ring the bell alternately in no direction and toward specific children, with no effect, caught between their senses of responsibility and powerlessness.

There were soccer nets at either end of the courtyard, but there were far too many kids to play a proper game. There was a basketball net in the far corner, and a few children played there, creating a world of their own outside of the melee. As the break came to a close, most of the children lined up by class, but some continued to run around in circles. One male teacher forcefully grabbed the male students who were still running around, each by one arm, and pulled them into their places in line. Another teacher did the same by grabbing one boy by the ear. From the reactions of the teachers and the reactions of the students, this all seemed routine.[103]

The exclusion from relationships that Munir and his peers faced while being included in Lebanese public schools often felt like a punch in the face, even though the violence was not as often physical as it was for the younger children. Munir didn't have any close Lebanese friends of his age, but he did have Syrian friends. For their Chemistry project, his friends made a chart of the periodic table, a beautiful chart with lots of bright colors, in big and clear handwriting. It was clearly the product of time and thought. Their Chemistry teacher was impressed and, to show her pride, she put it up on the wall so the entire class could see it. She told the class that she thought even the Lebanese students who came in the morning shift could use this chart, and so she left it hanging on the wall. When Munir and his friends came to school the next afternoon, they found that the chart was torn to pieces and lying on the floor. Munir's friends were upset that someone would do that to their chart. When the Chemistry teacher came, Munir showed her the torn chart and explained how upset his friends were. By way of explanation, the teacher said that the students in the morning shift felt like Munir and his friends were "intruders on the school." This idea made Munir even more upset, and he wanted to "rip all of theirs [work]." He said, "They should respect us the same way we respect them," using an Arabic proverb to emphasize his point: "When I look at you with one eye, look at me with both your eyes."[104] It seemed only to make it worse when the principal told the class that maybe the Lebanese students did this to the chart because, after all, it was their school first. Munir, upset as he was, was also resigned in some ways to this second-class status. He said, "It's like they're giving [the school] to us so we can learn, not to be established."[105]

The policy of inclusion of refugees in national education systems exposes divergence between promises and possibilities in the future of integration. In particular, the position of refugees within host countries creates gaps in the ways in which education can connect past, present, and future for refugee young people, their teachers, and the state, which I explore in Chapter 5. As Munir described, his commitment to education involves trade-offs: learning now but with the impossibility of ever being "established," with no guarantee of where that education can lead. Munir's teachers feel a responsibility to teach refugee young people like Munir in the present, yet with ever-encompassing concern for the stability of their country and the accompanying need to assert that the school is, after all, for Lebanese children first. At the same time, countries like Uganda, Kenya, and Lebanon invest in refugee education in the present—supported by funds from external donors, unpredictable and limited through they may be—with uncertain future collective benefits, in terms of the economic and social returns by which national investment in education is generally politically justified. Amid these trade-offs at all levels, the future of integration also turns out to be elusive for refugee young people.

Imagining Less Bounded Futures

The elusiveness of an education that can prepare refugee young people for the future stems from the reality that futures of resettlement, return, and integration are often close to impossible for the vast majority of refugees. Educational decision making is entangled in politics and power and in the ever-shifting landscape of what kind of sanctuary is possible for those who migrate. The future of integration exposes a stark disconnect between the present education a refugee young person like Manar in Egypt or Munir in Lebanon has access to and the futures they imagine and would like to plan for. It is tied up simultaneously in the politics of curriculum (of what they learn) and the politics of migration (of where and how they can use what they learn).

As Thato experienced in Botswana, centralized control of education more easily tilts toward a politically convenient and short-term focus on unity and cohesion in ways that overlook inequalities that prevent students, particularly marginalized students, from experiencing unity and cohesion both inside and outside of school in long-term, sustainable ways. This standardization is predicated on an unrealistic assumption that students will encounter equal opportunity structures as they pursue their futures. The centralization of refugee education within national education systems means that decisions around refugee education are often disconnected from the politics of what young people learn and the futures they will confront.

Initial integration of refugees in national schools in Uganda in the early 2000s, for example, focused on how many children could attend Ugandan schools and how global actors would pay the Ugandan government the needed school fees for refugee children. Aside from what Sonal could hide in her locked filing-cabinet drawer at UNHCR, global and national policymakers paid little attention to the curricular aspects of this integration: the lack of possibility for Congolese children to learn the history of their country, the challenges of transitioning from a French-language school system to an English one, or the dead-end that Annette would face in continuing her education. Nor was there attention at the policy level to the social aspects of integration. How would refugee and national children build relationships with each other? How would Ugandan national teachers interact with refugee children? What would it mean to Congolese refugee children to stand around the Ugandan flag every morning and sing "We lay our future in your hands"?

In the face of mountains of logistics and technical challenges, we see a similar lack of attention from global and national policymakers to what refugee children learn and don't learn through their school experiences around the world today. Syrian students in Lebanon learning a Lebanese curriculum with Lebanese teachers have few opportunities to discuss how their learning applies—or does not apply—to their daily lives as Syrians in Lebanon and to their possible futures. Munir and his friends, their hard work ripped into pieces on the floor, remained without opportunities to process that experience or to think collectively about how to address the tensions they experienced as Syrian and Lebanese students sharing the same physical building but not sharing any time together. Possibilities for different kinds of learning and belonging are the focus of Chapters 5 and 6.

These daily experiences of exclusion in school play out against a backdrop of the global and national politics of migration, of locating sanctuary and spaces in which one might use one's education. As Jenny Erpenbeck writes in her novel *Go, Went, Gone,* "Must living in peace—so fervently wished for throughout human history and yet enjoyed in only a few parts of the world—inevitably result in refusing to share it with those seeking refuge, defending it instead so aggressively that it almost looks like war?"[106] While Erpenbeck writes about Germany, Munir's and his friends' experiences in Lebanon take on this character. They fled one war for their own physical safety and find themselves in another war for social, economic, and psychological safety in their daily lives in Lebanon and for a future of unknown opportunities without the right to work and ongoing xenophobia. Yet their education goes on, and they continue to learn about what Lebanese citizens would do if they needed to file a complaint, their teachers ignoring the politics of migration that at that very moment prevented any new Syrians from even registering for legal status in Lebanon.

During the recent period of Standardization, responsibility for the education of refugees was globally held, by a constellation of United Nations and NGO actors, funded by external, usually western, donors. The prevailing assumption by these same global actors was that countries within which refugees lived were not capable, or were unwilling, to take the responsibility for educating these noncitizens, despite evidence that, historically, in the periods of Liberation and Localization, responsibility for refugee education was generally local and community driven. In the current period of Nationalization, this responsibility has been centralized with the host country, through the introduction of a new global policy in 2012 that was rapidly taken up by global actors and refugee-hosting countries. However, this policy has come with no indication that a refugee-hosting country is able or willing—or should—shoulder this responsibility, financially or politically, systemically and over the long-term. It has also come with no definition of the collective benefits that might drive host countries' engagement with the politics of curriculum—what children learn—and the politics of migration—where and how they can use what they learn—especially in the presence of continued policies of containment by which high-income countries shirk their own responsibilities. At its core, this dilemma forces a reckoning with if and how education can be a collective and transnational good and if and how its opportunities can be realized for students, for teachers, and for countries in both the present and the future.

5

Learning

"A people without a history is like a vehicle without an engine."[1] Siyabulela, age eighteen, wanted to tell his granny about this idea and ask her
what she thought.[2] He was always so interested in what his grandmother
thought. But he also knew that she had stopped listening for the night.
Her arms, so used to hard housework, were already deep in the soapsuds
of dishes from dinner.

"Thandiwe! *Hamba!* Go! Bring me some more water," Granny said,
calling out to Siyabulela's younger brother, Thandiwe, in her firm but pa-
tient way. Thandiwe scampered out of the dimly lit room, grabbing the
red plastic bucket on his way out the door. Siyabulela knew the door
would not shut properly with Thandiwe's little hands and he was already
pushing himself up from his sagging chair to close it behind his brother
before Thandiwe made it to the doorknob. Last time, Granny had asked
him to get the water. This time he was left free to think. He glanced about
the room, mulling over the best work spot for tonight, somewhere he
could just be and not need to move about the room to make space for
others.

It was September, in Khayelitsha, outside Cape Town, South Africa, with the promise of a southern hemisphere summer hinted at each sunny afternoon, but with the air still nipping at night, especially with the new gap in their corrugated aluminum roof. That hole had appeared the last time the Cape Doctor came to town, the name of the wind that blew so strongly that women had to hold on to their skirts. Not to mention the sandstorms that followed, bringing fine sediment through the slash in the roof. All of Khayelitsha, where Siyabulela's family had lived since moving from the rural Transkei just after he was born, was sand. "The Black man's soil," Siyabulela had heard his teacher say once.

Siyabulela longed to broach his questions again, and he often asked them in quiet tones, knowing Granny did not want to hear him. His questions became whispered, like "Can you tell me about the history of the Xhosas in Transkei?" "Why did our family move here?" Granny's eyes would leave her dishes for a moment but just as quickly return to the blue enamel plate she was cleaning, all traces of food already erased by hungry Thandiwe.

At that moment, Thandiwe rushed in, water sloshing back and forth in his bucket. He had been out to (what was then called) Lansdowne Road already, to the spigot shared by as many as 5,000 people. He knew not to spend much time in the street, especially not at this time of day when this area of Cape Town was among the least safe places on earth. Siyabulela recognized the relief on Thandiwe's small face as he entered the house. He got up to close the door once more.

"*uThandiwe usebenza kakuhle*," Granny patted Thandiwe on the head. "Thandiwe works well." Siyabulela longed for Granny to say something like this to him. But his work these days was head work and he wasn't good for much around the house. Five hours a night he was spending studying.

Siyabulela tried to formulate a question that Granny would want to answer. He knew when she wanted to talk, there was no stopping her. There were so few moments when they were alone, just the three of them in the house. Finally, he remembers muttering, "How am I supposed to understand the present if I don't understand the past?" The minute his words escaped his teenage lips, he felt a wave of uncertainty and slumped in his seat, almost touching his bum to the floor through the sag of his favorite chair.

"What did I do to bring Steve Biko into my house?!" Granny's outburst punctuated the room, and Siyabulela recalls sitting up very straight. Granny knows about Steve Biko, early leader of the Black Consciousness Movement? Siyabulela marveled. When he opened his own mouth to respond, to really talk to Granny as he had been yearning to do, she was already back to the dishes, her eyes glued to *Isidingo*, the then new show on TV that was playing across the room.

Siyabulela opened his notebook and placed it gently on the coffee table in front of the TV, the only table in the house. He was eager to deal with something he understood.

Siyabulela began to read over his notes from class that day: "Aware that they were the moral and intellectual equals of White students, but that they were the pawns in the racial and economic policies of the White government," he had written, "African students began uniting under a new and highly significant banner: Black consciousness (see box)." He knew his teacher had copied these words straight from the *Reader's Digest Illustrated History of South Africa*, the book that he was using as a resource since he did not have a new textbook.[3] Then, of course, Siyabulela had dutifully copied these same words into his own notes. Even "see box." Yet there were no boxes in his notes. Still, Siyabulela knew that his teacher wanted to make a point, as always.

"Beware the box," his teacher had warned them, he remembered. "When you are asked to see the box, you must ask yourself why." He could hear the teacher still in his head. He knew his teacher didn't really want him to ask himself why. He knew the teacher wanted him, the student, to ask him, the teacher, why. Twelve years of schooling had taught Siyabulela that teachers liked to hear themselves talk.

Siyabulela told me how he imagined his teacher there in front of him and began to play a game with himself. "So, teacher, why? Why am I being asked to 'see box'?"

In his mind, Siyabulela saw the teacher waving his long arms out to each side, sweeping dramatically to say, "*Abafundi,* Students, do you know what this history is about? No, you cannot know. You are the post-apartheid generation. I, on the other hand, *Abafundi,* have lived in the time of 'Black consciousness.'"

"My teachers can go on and on but all they ever tell me is that I cannot know what this history is about!" Siyabulela explained how he grew tired of his own game. At his old school, he had once flipped to the index of the history textbook he did have, down to the Bs, thinking, "I will educate myself, if I need to." B-l-a-c-k . . . Black consciousness was not there. He had another idea. "What is the last chapter of this textbook?" he had wondered. "1948," its title read, "Victory for the National Party."

"History doesn't even want to know that I was born," Siyabulela said, as he had told me more than once, usually followed by a shrugging of his shoulders. "Maybe I am not supposed to understand." But right there in his notebook, he read, "A study of recent History is essential for an understanding of the present."[4] Siyabulela wondered if maybe he was not meant to understand the present.

Linking Past, Present, and Future

Like Munir, Siyabulela was looking to his school to help him un-do exclusions of history. While Siyabulela was not a refugee, his recent past and schooling within the country of his citizenship were circumscribed by many similar factors. His family was barred from free movement, limited to certain kinds of work, and forbidden from using their own languages in schools. He and his family migrated to Cape Town from Transkei, in what is now within the province of the Eastern Cape. Transkei was one of ten areas of South Africa designated "homelands" under apartheid. Not too dissimilar from the refugee camps where Jacques was told to relocate in Uganda, homelands were areas of land—rural, isolated, and often less fertile—assigned to Black South Africans by the White government. Black South Africans, like Siyabulela's family, were exiled within the country of their own citizenship, echoing the contemporary global refugee confinement crisis and with resonance for understanding of learning and belonging in contexts of exclusion.

In 1948, fifty years before Siyabulela began secondary school, apartheid became state policy in South Africa under the leadership of the National Party. Laws this government enacted and enforced entrenched already-existing racial disparities and discrimination, denying rights to vote, movement, and employment to the country's Black majority. Apartheid also consolidated a system of unequal schooling, with education for Whites, Indians, Coloureds, and Blacks—the four racial groups defined by apartheid laws—governed by separate departments of education. Students could attend only schools that accorded with the racial group listed on their state-issued documents, and funding and quality among these schools was widely divergent. In 1969–1970, for example, for every one rand (R1.00) spent on a Black child, R4.29 was spent on a Coloured child, R4.76 on an Indian child, and R16.59 on a White child.[5] In broad strokes, the curriculum in White schools prepared students for professional employment and the curriculum in Black schools for agriculture, low-wage mine and factory work, and servitude.[6] It was in protest against this curriculum, and specifically the dictate that all students in South Africa learn in the Afrikaans language, that thousands of young people gathered in Soweto in 1976, the day Hector Pietersen was killed by South African police and the photo of him shifted global anti-apartheid public opinion, just as the photo of Alan Kurdi shifted global public opinion toward welcome for Syrian refugees four decades later, as discussed in Chapter 2.[7]

Siyabulela's Granny had lived through decades of nonviolent struggle like that intended in Soweto that day in 1976 and armed struggle that included bombings of government buildings and arson that engulfed whole townships. In 1992, the African National Congress (ANC) and the National Party reached a power-sharing agreement followed by democratic elections in 1994 that brought ANC leader Nelson Mandela to the presidency. A top priority of the new government was to build a racially integrated education system. The 1994 ANC Policy Framework for Education and Training proposed a new curriculum that would promote "unity and the common citizenship and destiny of all South Africans irrespective of race, class, gender or ethnic background."[8]

Siyabulela had one teacher who brought new resources into his teaching and began to teach about recent South African history. But the curriculum used in the two schools Siyabulela attended over secondary school, up to eight years after the introduction of the new curriculum framework, remained largely unchanged. The school where Siyabulela began secondary school opened to make space for a large number of new students arriving from the Eastern Cape. Siyabulela's family, like so many others, had come to Cape Town from the Transkei area of the Eastern Cape, intent on building new opportunities they thought they would find in the city. They settled in Khayelitsha, then the fastest-growing city in South Africa. Siyabulela's school was founded in 1990 and then renamed for an anti-apartheid leader after the 1994 elections to reflect hope for a different future. This hope that hung in the air seemed to act like helium on even the most skeptical, buoying them up to face ahead and confront the present with optimism. Despite this air of hope, the air around the school choked with smoke. This smoke, which obscured even the not-so-distant mass of Table Mountain, was not only from cooking fires. One of the Grade 9 history teachers at Siyabulela's school explained that it was also the houses burning, burning so easily because they were shacks made of corrugated tin and pieces of wood. "We have to reissue books all the time," she said. "They burn with the houses."[9]

Students and teachers were ambivalent about whether they wanted these books. This teacher explained that "even if we are now in the new South Africa, still our history books haven't changed. We're still using those old books. Those old ideas where there's no truth. . . . You're still teaching apartheid."[10] She pulled a textbook from under the pile of papers on her desk, and it fell open to a page she clearly had looked at many times, with the spine of the book broken in this place. "Look at this," she said. The topic was South African society at the turn of this century.

She had penciled a star beside the first two items in a list of groups considered "social problems" in South Africa: "1. Poor-Whites, 2. Black People."[11]

Siyabulela was in this teacher's class, where she used this textbook, before he went to a different school for his last two years of high school, where the teacher was confident enough, and resourced enough, to scrap the textbook and bring Steve Biko into his teaching of South African history. Sitting in this classroom, with houses burning around him, Siyabulela felt an immense weight of the past on his present. In 1998, I spent two months in Siyabulela's school. One day, as we both exited his history class, he stopped me in the crowded open-air corridor. He said, "I think history is a wrong subject, just because I've told myself that we must make peace in our land."[12] He could not see how the past could be a conduit toward the future, especially as what he was learning about as the past seemed all too consistent with the poverty and exclusion of his present. Just like Munir in Lebanon two decades later, Siyabulela was looking for his education to help him figure out how to make sense of the present so he could envision for himself—and for his Granny and Thandiwe—a future in which he did not constantly feel himself to be treated just as the textbook described, a "social problem." What kind of learning can build these connections between past, present, and future for young people?

Education might build these connections by disrupting two main types of inequalities: resource-based inequalities and identity-based inequalities. Under apartheid, the kind of education available to Siyabulela's Granny was unequal to that available to Whites, both in terms of how much funding the government allocated to it and its different content that prepared Blacks and Whites for vastly different futures. What Siyabulela had thought was promised to him after Nelson Mandela became president in 1994 was a different kind of education on both dimensions: one that was funded equally for all students (which would disrupt resource-based inequalities) and one that would enable him to see himself and his future in the opportunity structure in South Africa (which would disrupt

identity-based inequalities). Examining the difficulty of creating these possibilities for citizens within national education systems like South Africa
underscores how hard it is to meet these challenges in refugee education,
as refugee young people and their futures are typically outside the bounds
even of educational policies and practices that attempt to break with the
status quo on resource- and identity-based inequalities.

Resource distribution and identity recognition have important implications for learning that might enable futures for all students.[13] Resources
must be distributed so as to mitigate disparities that prevent full participation. In most cases, this requires the *re*distribution of resources in order
to rectify existing inequalities. Structural changes in the education system
in postapartheid South Africa, aimed at consolidating government
spending on schools that served poorer and Black, Coloured, and Indian
students, represented a redistribution aimed at redressing such past inequalities, even if it was largely unsuccessful. Access to social services,
including education, could allow for full participation in society. Yet that
notion is based on an "assumption of equality" that does not consider
identity-based inequalities.[14]

In order to counter identity-based inequalities, redistribution of resources must be accompanied both by recognition, all people having equal
respect, and by participation, including access to power that enables status
and the ability to participate fully in society. The fires that raged through
Siyabulela's neighborhood, the dated and racist histories in the books in
use in his school, the fact that Thandiwe needed to brave threats of
twilight streets to fetch water to wash dinner dishes, all represented messages of nonrecognition and limited opportunities for participation for
Siyabulela. Nonrecognition and exclusion from opportunities created
disconnects between the present he lived daily and the future he felt was
promised to his generation by the new postapartheid government.

One way education can foster recognition is through history and
civics curriculum. To do so, it must ensure that the contributions of diverse groups in the past and present are integrated, and that it embodies
"respect for individuals and their equal rights as citizens."[15] In South

Africa, textbooks in the postapartheid era focused heavily on ideas of a united nation to overcome past divisions and to promote the basic conditions—such as a lack of overt physical violence—in which equitable opportunities might be created.[16] Yet South Africa has taken a guarded approach to individual and group identity recognition. Other research demonstrates that curriculum and classroom discussions can become "race-neutral discourses," with a commitment to include "both sides of the story" in ways that may help to prevent acute violence but which often de-racialize and de-historicize the experiences of individuals and groups.[17]

Like in Botswana, these conditions can enable negative peace, the absence of acute violence, but they do not enable positive peace, the absence of structural violence, which "shows up as unequal power and consequently as unequal life chances."[18] Positive peace includes the presence of conditions that allow individuals and groups to access equal opportunities. In education, positive peace therefore rests not only on the intent of a curriculum's recognition but on its outcomes: recognition is only realized when diverse children have an equal chance at school success.

Often assumed is that refugees find "negative peace," or the absence of direct violence, when they arrive in a host country. Yet the kind of sanctuary that would provide freedom from direct violence is often incomplete, as Jacques and Abdi experienced in Uganda when they were involuntarily questioned and beaten, and as Munir and his peers experienced in Lebanon as their work was torn up and left in pieces on the floor. Addressing this acute violence in refugee settings is essential, just as addressing direct violence related to racism and colonialism is key to systemic approaches to inequities in settler settings like the United States and Canada. In these ways, work toward negative peace is critical but insufficient.

As in postapartheid South Africa, in refugee settings, through eras of Standardization, Localization, and early Nationalization, so urgent have been needs to focus on violence prevention in daily life that dimensions of positive peace, and connections between present experiences and future outcomes, have been all but ignored. In many ways, what refugee young people learn through their educations reflects the hard-learned pragmatism of a Congolese man who had recently arrived in the Kyaka II refugee settlement where Annette lived: "We don't know if we will die here or if we have fled death," he said. "This is semi-death."[19] Could education—in enabling learning and futures—be a pathway out of this "semi-death" liminality, so widely experienced in exile, and a pathway toward positive peace?

Unlike the 2012 UNHCR education strategy, its newer strategy, published in 2019, clearly sees education in the present as connected to refugee young people's aspirational goals for the future. Also unlike previous global policies, during the eras of Standardization, Localization, and early Nationalization, this new strategy recognizes ways in which educational experiences in exile and sociopolitical conditions in exile work together to limit future opportunities. In 2018, I worked with the UNHCR Education Unit to help develop this new strategy, grounding the overall approach of the strategy in research, research on the kinds of education that could enable the global consensus goal of "learning for all students"—as articulated in Sustainable Development Goal 4 (SDG 4)—and a more ambitious goal outlined in the strategy, to "enable learners to use their education toward sustainable futures."[20]

In this work, I listened to staff from ministries of education in refugee-hosting countries, bilateral donor agencies, UN agencies, and NGOs debate how to articulate this approach to refugee education through a model of including refugees in national education systems. It was a process for me of trying to consider the perspectives of differently positioned states, and of the humanitarian and development actors beholden to the politics of those states, while keeping at the forefront the experiences of individuals like Jacques, Henri, Manar, Annette, Khawla, and Munir. There were clear tensions both across and within these different positions and experiences. In countries where "refugees are barred from legal work and face very serious consequences if caught working," education then can be a "frustrating exercise when refugee children and young adults know and later experience first-hand that they cannot put these skills into practice."[21] At the same time, even in these same countries, policymakers, teachers, and students espoused aspirational beliefs that "education is not an end in itself, it is a way to achieve something else [such that] once finished studies, [refugees] ideally would have access to labor markets and further studies."[22]

The question of responsibility for education pervaded these conversations, not just in terms of financial and political feasibility but also in terms of the content of learning. Many working for international NGOs and UN agencies insisted that a global strategy advocating learning for all and opportunities for sustainable futures for refugees was in reality a "wish list" since "all of the ideas here are very good but many require significant funding. In most operations, we don't have the money."[23] Beyond funding, UNHCR staff members also asked themselves the obvious next question—"What to do when quality is not there?"—to which they had no concrete answers.[24] The distribution of access to quality education is massively unequal across the world, and yet "UNHCR does not have a standard for education, the standard is what it is in the country we work in."[25]

The question of how to address unequal distribution of access to quality education was accompanied by a question about recognition within the schooling experiences available to refugees. "Curriculum is a national role and refugees are included in national systems," an education specialist with longtime experience in Jordan explained, very familiar with the alienating educational experiences of young people like Munir in Lebanon.[26] Given the tight connection between national sovereignty and what is taught in schools, was it even reasonable to think that Munir might be taught anything other than the way administrative complaints were filed in Lebanon? Students themselves recognized these seemingly irreconcilable disconnects between prioritizing citizens and the inequity of the exclusions they faced. Munir's friend explained the logic: "They're Lebanese and their school is Lebanese," she said. "For sure, for sure, for sure, there's no country that favors others over their own citizens, right? In Syria, we also have our school and it's not theirs."[27]

On the question of language of instruction, a senior staff member with UNHCR summed up the overarching dilemma of the sovereignty of states and the educational content that refugee young people experience. There are great benefits to young people of having instruction in their home languages both for learning and identity development.[28] Yet even Thato, a citizen of Botswana, found his minority ethnic language unwelcome in his own school in Botswana. Was it reasonable to expect recognition of refugees' home languages in their schools in exile? This UNHCR staff member wrote, "From a learning perspective, I'm 100% behind you. From a reality perspective, my heart sinks."[29] What possibilities are there for positive peace when refugees are caught within national spaces in which they are marginalized from the redistribution of resources, the recognition of identities, and the power for participation that would enable learning and equal opportunities for life outcomes?

In addressing these power and opportunity imbalances in schools, conflict can be productive, as individuals and groups negotiate their inclusion, opportunities, and access to equitable outcomes.[30] Yet in volatile regions—like the ones in which Munir finds himself in Lebanon and Annette in Uganda—there is already tenuous national unity on which to base any kind of productive conflictual dialogue. Ongoing fears of direct violence lead to conflict avoidance and a repression of dialogue in reaction to the fear of provoking or reinvigorating conflict and in the name of stability. Such was the case in Rwanda, where education following the 1994 genocide focused on the creation of new and superordinate identities of being Rwandan, intended to erase individual and group differences.[31] This approach limited space for any divergent perspectives.[32] The teaching of history, banned for a decade after the 1994 genocide, was reintroduced in a nonnegotiable and centrally standardized way, based on one official historical narrative that prioritized unity of the collective and ignored individual and group histories and identities.[33]

While not the same as refugee contexts, situations of postconflict and protracted marginalization, as in Rwanda and South Africa, are instructive in looking at the possibilities for redistribution, recognition, and participation that could support refugee young people in threading together their pasts, presents, and futures. Thirteen miles away from Siyabulela's high school, right under Cape Town's Table Mountain, which he can't see through the smoky air, students of his same age at Central High had a very different kind of school experience. Unlike Siyabulela's Granny in the 1970s, who by law could attend school only with other Black students and unlike Siyabulela could not afford the school fees or transport costs to a school that had other than all Black students, Central High was one of the first multiracial schools in South Africa. In 1998, its students—about one-third Black, one-third Coloured and Indian, and one-third White—came from still racially segregated townships, all over the greater Cape Town area, traveling many miles each morning and evening to and from the school located in the center city at the hub of all the transport lines.

Keisha, a history teacher, was one of the first teachers of color at this formerly all-White school. Young, with long hair and a welcoming smile, she managed her classroom with the easy air of someone students wanted desperately to like them. "Our kids are having the chance to experience the diversity of South Africa," Keisha said. But "they have difficulties dealing with each other on an individual level and knowing who they are . . . I don't think people seriously think that it's an issue to be considered. . . . I think they think that it's just going to happen by natural osmosis or something. That it's something you'll grow into, because that is what the government is telling us, 'Give it time, it [diversity] will just grow on you,' you know. And it doesn't just grow on you. You can grow averse to the thing as well; you could dislike it precisely because you don't understand it and it's just forced on you. So, it's not something that is just going to happen like that. You must want it to happen and you need to understand it to happen. . . . [The students] are always clashing in terms of beliefs and understanding and values. As a teacher, you have to negotiate those differences. . . . History can help them to have the discussions they need to have, to understand each other.

They must learn to live in the kind of South Africa that is made up of diverse people, who are equal."[34]

"It starts with simple things," Keisha said, in explaining her own approach to teaching and building relationships with her students. "Like how you pronounce words." Keisha did not speak any African languages, but she was committed to learning. "Some people will say 'Causa' because it sounds better to them, but it's '!Xhosa.' And I will make sure that I pronounce it right. . . . I'm not always right or doing it well, but I'll ask 'Now how do I pronounce it?' And it starts with something as small as that." Keisha knew that this was a small act, necessary but insufficient. She continued, "And I can tell you this, not everybody really tries to reach out and actually show students that they are of value."[35]

Keisha carefully considered how she could make each of her students feel visible in the space of school. But she was adamant that recognition could not happen through individual teachers' practices or by simply adding small elements to existing curricula to make it more "sensitive" to the diverse experiences of people. "Children know when something is an aside," she said. "And we don't want to make them to feel that they, as people, are an aside."[36] The history curriculum needed to be redone completely, she asserted, to reflect goals of recognition.

South Africa provides a context to see what happens over the longer term, in redressing resource- and identity-based inequalities connected to long-term conflict, mass migration, and social and economic marginalization, adjacent to refugee experiences in neighboring host countries. In 2019, twenty years after Keisha was one of the first teachers of color at Central High, the school continued to be a commuter school, drawing students from the still-racially segregated townships that surrounded the city. The almost 700 students of Central High now were almost entirely Black and Coloured, with some immigrants and refugees from other parts of Africa, and three were White. The history curriculum at Central High, and in all of South Africa, had been completely redone. The textbooks in which Siyabulela found himself described as a "social problem" were found now only in the archives, and core to the Grade 9 curriculum, the last year in which history was required of all students, was recent South African history, the formation of individual and group identities, negotiations of power including along lines of race, and it included Steve Biko.[37] Yet twenty years later at this same school, students understood this history as a distant past, disconnected from current inequities and future outcomes as they relate to opportunities for economic, social, and political participation in society, which remain vastly unequal.[38] Teachers and students alike shared the deep-rooted understanding that students' life chances still could go either way. Grade 11 students led one of the first assemblies of the year in 2019, which focused on "commitment" and "integrity" and gave younger students advice about such big-picture ideas as holding themselves accountable and always telling the truth, and also practical suggestions of writing down their goals. Following these Grade 11 students, one of Central High's teachers sought to provide life advice as well, but his tone was almost threatening. He explained that he had watched students who sat in this very auditorium follow one of two paths: grow up to be someone who has their house cleaned, or be someone who cleans others' houses.[39]

Education has not moved these students closer to the equal life chances that Siyabulela so strongly believed in when he was these students' age. Even in places like South Africa, with school-based momentum to transform what and how young people learn, where students are citizens, and where their futures are presumed to be long-term within the country, redressing resource- and identity-based inequalities remains a persistent challenge, magnified in refugee contexts.

Building a New Politics of Curriculum

At school in Beirut, Munir learned many things. He learned how to factor numbers.[40] He learned how covalent bonds form to share electron pairs between atoms by watching his teacher grasp hands with two other students.[41] He learned when the tank was first used as a weapon, by whom, and in which battle.[42] He learned that he could ask certain teachers questions and they would give "me good and accurate answers . . . and [keep] explaining things to the extent where we almost fall asleep."[43] He also learned that teachers he thought cared about him and his friends would not stand up for them when Lebanese young people treated them unfairly.[44] He learned that he did not have the same rights as his Lebanese peers and, at the same time, he learned how to productively navigate life in Lebanon without these rights. But, like Siyabulela, Munir did not learn in school how to thread strands of the past with his present and his hoped-for future.

As a teacher, I search for how to create opportunities for students to weave together their pasts, presents, and futures, and I have felt the immense challenge of this undertaking. When I met Hadee again, eighteen years after I was his teacher, I told him that I've often wondered how he felt as the only Muslim, child or adult, in our school in Massachusetts, on September 11th, 2001, and through his Grade 8 year. "I've been isolated by geography," he explained, in the northeast of the United States and in this Massachusetts city in particular. He said he personally had been sheltered from most overt Islamophobia by how others perceived him. "Often people just think I'm Dominican," he laughed. He also noted that his name doesn't identify him as Muslim and about how assumptions about Muslim Ethiopians are not the same as the "ugly" assumptions about Muslim Arabs. But, more important, he reflected, his ethnic identity has protected him. "Ethiopia was never colonized," he said, "not like the rest of Africa . . . not just [unlike] *some* other parts of Africa, [unlike] *any* other part of Africa." He told me about the Battle of Adwa, where the Ethiopians defeated the Italians and resisted and defeated colonialism. "Adwa is in Tigray," Hadee said, and his father is from Tigray. "It is his home."[45] Hadee found belonging in stories of his family and in an ethnic history that centered him, enabling him to weave together his past, present, and future. He did not, however, find this at school.

Rhetoric on refugee education among global actors continues to focus on avoiding a "lost generation." These campaigns emphasize that no refugee child should be denied their right to education while in exile, and they focus on access to school. Yet for teachers like Jacques and for students like Munir, "lost generation" has a different meaning. They have not lost access to school, even if they must create it themselves. For them, a "lost generation" is one that misses out on an education that provides the resources and recognition, the skills and the knowledge, for each child to create a future where they have equal opportunities and life chances.

Alex Hutchinson, a sports scientist and writer, uses the term "limit breakers" to describe the people and approaches that expand "the apparent boundaries" of what any of us thought previously would be possible, in his case in terms of endurance running.[46] A limit breaker and Kenyan runner, Eliud Kipchoge, for example, set out to and then succeeded in running a sub-two-hour marathon. I use the phrase "limit breakers" in relation to shaping a new politics of curriculum. What people and approaches expand the apparent boundaries of what and how young people learn in view of equal opportunities and life chances?

Many refugees are limit breakers as they live, maintain relationships and communication, engage politically, and work in ways that transcend national borders. Those who are in places and situations where they, and their children, have access to opportunities often hold particularly strong commitments to and shared identity with those who remain in precarious situations.[47] These lasting connections and commitments make them more likely to espouse Harvard University economist and philosopher Amartya Sen's view of development as beyond "having more," in terms of material resources, to also include "being more," in terms of recognition, participation, and collective social well-being.[48] They are thus particularly well positioned to understand how refugee young people might learn in schools in ways that allow them to weave together a past that can seem distant and exclusionary, a present that often maintains inequalities of resources and recognition, and futures that are unknowable, given protracted conflicts, limited access to postschooling opportunities, and a global politics of migration that limits sanctuary.

Like Jacques, teachers who have lived amid conflict or fled conflict often orient their work on education toward transformation of conflict dynamics. In particular, through educational programs and policies that focus on addressing historical inequalities and persistent drivers of conflict, they seek to shift opportunity structures within and outside of schools. In other words, they design education that connects past, present, and future in ways that allow young people to better understand the origins of the inequalities they are experiencing and to learn how to address them in the present and for the future.

Mohammad Khan Kharoti was born to what he called "a nomadic family" in Afghanistan. As an eleven-year-old, he enrolled himself in primary school and "found this great treasure of education from my childhood that I can never forget."[49] He explained that his own educational experiences and his experiences of conflict and flight, including to Pakistan and the United States, have motivated him to work in the field of education in Afghanistan. Of the future of children in Afghanistan, he said, "peace is the best, the most gracious gift they can ever get, education is the tool, the way for that."[50] He started a school in 2001 in an area of Helmand Province that had no schools and where he said he could "not find one woman who can read or write." The school, which is free and follows the government curriculum, had over 1,200 students at the time of our interview in 2013. Although literacy has been a focus of his work, and a set of desired skills that his students are seeking, Mohammad has a broader view of what quality education in Afghanistan entails. "A quality education is [when] somebody can use it positively for a particular job, *and* environment they're living in," he said in a pensive tone. "I cannot teach somebody in Afghanistan how to swim in the ocean. The ocean does not matter in Afghanistan . . . , a landlocked country." He has experienced the imposition from outside of a curriculum that holds no relevance for the students to whom it is taught.[51] "For Afghanistan, an education is how to be able to read and write, for Afghanistan [it is also learning] how can we bring our resources, how can we connect to the country." He stopped and added, with emphasis, "How can we bring peace to the country?"[52]

Like Salim and his peers in Dadaab, Mohammad knew from his own experience that for someone who grows up with and lives amid conflict, getting an education is tightly bound up with hopes of—and belief in—working for and / or living in conditions of peace. Despite unlikely prospects of peace, refugee young people the world over strive for a future of peace, whether it is probable or not. They commit themselves to their education as if peace were possible. We learn from them that a new politics of curriculum could support these commitments through recognition of identity and history and a critical understanding of the drivers of conflict and resultant inequalities.

Leonie Hermantin, who helped run an NGO that built and ran schools in Haiti, explained how she—who moved from Haiti to the United States when she was twelve—thought about the ways in which education can support young people for this future of working for peace. "How do you provide [young people] with a very positive sense of who they are? That's not just talking lightly in Haiti. When you are talking about children who are poor, who are Black, and who are growing in a culture that despises itself to some extent, because it's Black, because it's poor, or because you're a girl . . . our children really need to be equipped with the tools that will make them productive citizens, but also teaches them to love themselves."[53] Like my student Hadee in Massachusetts, Leonie emphasized the importance of history in working toward these goals. "I'm just one of those nuts who actually take[s] our history very seriously and very personally." She seeks in her education work to "really show that my country of birth has given something to the world." She described her education work in Haiti as a "chance to celebrate not destroying, but building."[54]

Nedgine Paul Deroly runs a movement that recruits and equips a network of Haitian teacher-leaders to become civic leaders throughout rural Haiti. In college, she chose to study Haitian history. She learned, among much else, about the ways in which the Haitian education system "perpetuated inequity," particularly under the US occupation of 1915–1934. From her own understanding of the past, Nedgine began to imagine what could be possible if education in Haiti were equitable. In the educational programs prevalent across Haiti, she also became aware of the damage an ahistorical understanding of Haiti could cause. Nedgine described how Haiti's Constitution, passed in 1806, "said every kid deserves to have public education."[55] She paused for effect. "That's pretty revolutionary."[56] It runs so counter to the media portrayal of Haiti that Nedgine experienced as a child growing up in Connecticut, which focused on "the poverty," and also to the state of education in Haiti today, where less than 15 percent of schools are government-run.[57]

Suraya Sadeed, founder of an NGO that works with a network of schools in Afghanistan, described the present-oriented focus on building schools: "The sign for success [for the Ministry of Education] is building more schools. . . . [T]hey're visible; people can see it; people can take pictures. But what they're [the students] being taught is not something that people are interested in." This lack of interest in learning was what Suraya wanted to turn on its head through her work: "after 9 / 11, and after the intervention of the U.S. and NATO forces in Afghanistan, I refocused my efforts into what I believe can rescue that nation, and that is providing education and innovative programs to new generations of Afghans." Suraya explained that Afghans have become suspicious of hidden agendas in educational materials developed outside the country. Yet "the Ministry of Education, unfortunately, is a donor-driven ministry" and makes decisions "that donors want," including taking textbooks and teacher-training materials used in Sri Lanka and Minneapolis and translating them for use in Kabul. This kind of education development, she said, will not contribute to the peace she envisions: "Democracy is not one size fits all. . . . [I]t has to be homegrown. If every time that you want to import or export democracy in another country, it's bound to fail . . . so what we did, we tried to make this [curriculum] as Afghan as possible."[58] By doing this, Suraya encouraged her students to critically engage with a past that was relevant to them—unlike Munir and Khawla in Lebanon—in order to imagine the possibility of answering Mohammad's question, "How can we bring peace to the country?"[59]

Education that addresses historical complexity and engages teachers with origins in the community contrasts with refugee education in the current Nationalization era. Within national schools in host countries, the alienation that refugee young people experience by way of curricula not recognizing them limits the ways education might disrupt cycles of conflict and alter structures of opportunity. Assata Shakur, in her autobiography, states as related to the Black Liberation Movement, "No one is going to give you the education you need to overthrow them. Nobody is going to teach you your true history, teach you your true heroes, if they know that that knowledge will help set you free."[60] Power imbalances endemic to refugee education mean that education is often similarly a tool of domination and control, where aid is tied to market and antiterrorism interests.[61] In these settings, "expert" authority often dominates as well, as Suraya experienced in Afghanistan.[62] These "experts" are frequently outsiders, who are often culturally distant from students and schools and can have transient rather than long-term interests in transforming conflict dynamics.[63]

We have seen the ways in which refugee education is limited in terms of learning, experiences of discrimination, and mismatch between current education and imagined futures. We also see examples of generativity in the practices of refugee teachers. They engage their students in learning about historical inequalities and contemporary unequal opportunities with the intention of transforming underlying and persistent drivers of conflict. These teachers disrupt the status quo and reimagine links between an imperfect yet longed-for past, a present exile of frequent exclusion, and an as-yet-unknowable but aspirational future of opportunities. Many of them have experienced the same disconnects between their pasts, presents, and futures and live the daily dissonance between the aspirations they hope to cultivate in their students and the realities of exclusion that they fear will limit realization of those aspirations. They, like their students, must navigate between the probable and the possible. Together, they share the inability to live with the bleakness of the probable, and so they take the risks of embracing the possible.

These steps toward positive peace are generally isolated in private spaces or small-scale endeavors that preclude equal chances for all that positive peace is premised on. Yet they hold fragments of the puzzle on which our collective future depends. The gap between accepting the probable and embracing the possible is the collective challenge. What if, like refugee teachers, Munir's nonrefugee teachers also could not live with the prospects of the probable, for both their students and for themselves? What if I, at this moment 5,400 miles away from Munir, cannot, or should not? What if we saw the opportunities of our futures as entwined, one with the other? Would a shared belief that the probability of what the future held for Munir—if there were no disruptions to the cycles of conflict he has faced—was not acceptable for Munir, for the teacher, for me, or for a global collective enable Munir's teacher to react differently when faced with the torn pieces of the periodic table on the floor?

Henry Shue, a normative philosopher, argues that each of us has both negative and positive duties to one another. We all, no matter where we live, and no matter what actual contact we have with each other, have these obligations to each other, no matter, as Shue writes, if they are "strangers." A negative duty means "not depriving other people of what they have rights to . . . simply not interfering with others."[64] He argues that this duty is universal and applies to all people, no matter their relationships to each other. Positive duties, on the other hand, Shue says, require "the expenditure of some resource I control, like time, money, energy, or emotional involvement."[65] Since everyone's—and every state's—resources are limited, the "positive duties need to be divided up and assigned among bearers in some reasonable way."[66] Shue asks us to think about the ways in which we allocate this sense of positive duty, to whom we give priority. He questions how most people think about the ways in which this priority of duty declines with each degree of separation, such that our duty to "strangers" reduces to nil. This is an outgrowth of a very distant time, he argues, in which our interactions with these strangers—our abilities to have any effects on them—were in fact nonexistent. That reality, with colonialism, political and economic globalization, with transportation and communication, no longer holds for almost anyone on the planet; we have become "interdependent," or entwined. Yet we continue to see this way of understanding play out in the confinement of refugees to neighboring host countries, through the outsourcing of sanctuary. Shue puts his finger on the dilemma that plays out each day in the educational experiences of refugees: refugees and their national hosts are "entangled with each other to some degree but . . . have no agreed-upon reciprocal rights and duties toward each other."[67]

Munir and his teacher, though they share the space of a school for a certain number of hours a day, are connected to each other in ways that are structural, not relational. They lack a public space, as philosopher of education and teacher Maxine Greene describes it, "for the sake of coming in touch with the common, of making something audible and visible in between."[68] Without space in the curriculum to talk about their own histories, understandings of the present, and experiences of life in Lebanon at this moment, their pasts and presents run parallel to each other. They therefore do not see ways in which their futures might be woven together. They are without a collective understanding and rationale of why rejecting the probable and embracing the possible could re-create the future.

What refugees learn in and through their education is a policy challenge, a problem that needs to be solved. It is also an opportunity, as another philosopher of education and teacher, John Dewey, believed, to create the world anew. Refugee education opens possibilities for "a community in the making."[69] A new politics of curriculum, already led by refugee teachers, engages relationally with the past, the present, and the future, with orientations not only toward the probable but toward the possible. In this way, it can allow refugee young people not only to see the dissonances between their present situations and their imagined futures, but also to understand how inequalities, rooted in the past, create these dissonances. With that, they are set free to disrupt them.

6

Belonging

Abshir was born in 1991 in central Somalia, just as the regime of Major General Mohamed Siad Barre fell and the country was engulfed in a conflict that would last his entire childhood and beyond. Through this childhood, he had "no parent to guide" him, he said, as his parents were killed in the war. As the conflict in Somalia intensified, his older sister fled with him—he was just a baby at the time—to the Dagahaly camp in northern Kenya.[1] Dagahaly was one of three camps in the Dadaab complex, set up just a year before Abshir's arrival. Abshir experienced the camps grow from their capacity of 90,000 refugees to more than 463,000 in 2012.[2]

"The agencies have supported us very well," Abshir said, looking back to the era of Standardization that brought with it the "rule of the NGOs" in refugee education. He described how, as he got older, classrooms were constructed, replacing the patch of open ground under some trees where he used to learn. Like those of Annette and Henri, these classrooms were crowded. Abshir recalled that his classes often had seventy children or more and, even still, there was not enough space in the schools for all children to attend, especially girls. His sister never had the chance to go to school, put to the margins by what Abshir labeled as a "community belief" that "there is no need [for girls] to go to school. Even if she learns, her knowledge will be wasted," he said, ". . . [as] she will just stay home, she will care for the children."

For children like Abshir who did have the chance to go to school, education was of limited quality, a pattern that persists two decades later. Abshir did not believe that his teachers could "teach you properly." He said, "We used to have only our teachers who are just like us. . . . They were not trained. . . . My [social studies] teacher, he was a Standard 8 failure." Abshir was the only one in his class to pass the primary-school leaving exam. By age twenty, in 2011, he was a Form 4 graduate, with a Kenyan Certificate of Secondary Education (KSCE), having benefited from the national certification that accompanied earlier Nationalization efforts in refugee education in Dadaab. He was also a primary-school teacher employed by the international NGO CARE and about to begin studying for a bachelor's degree. How did Abshir navigate his way through education in a place where only 2.3 percent of young people even attended secondary school?[3]

"There was a teacher," Abshir explained. "He used to encourage me. He used to push me all the time." This teacher had lost his parents, like Abshir, and "he used to tell me, 'Your parents have passed away. . . . So you study so . . . you have a good future. Tomorrow, you may become even a president.'" Abshir recounted that his teacher would take a loan to buy books for him, and he would not have been able to continue studying without them. With these words and actions, this teacher helped Abshir to link the threads of past, present, and future, by recognizing and engaging with his difficult past, by providing resources to address the challenges of the present, and by understanding Abshir's imagined future of contributing to peace and a rebuilding of Somalia.

Abshir's teacher now lives in Canada, granted resettlement through a scholarship he received to pursue higher education.[4] He remained connected to Abshir on Facebook. On the day that the Kenyan minister of education announced the results of the KCSE, the teacher picked up the phone in Toronto and called Abshir in Dadaab to find out his score. Despite geographic distance, this teacher remained a role model for Abshir in the face of obstacles to school success. When Abshir got news of his acceptance into a bachelor's degree program, it was this teacher and his sister whom he shared the news with first.

Not all of Abshir's friends had these kinds of relationships. When the costs of his education became prohibitive, one friend decided to return to Somalia. He told Abshir in a series of text messages, "[I do not] do anything. I just stay here . . . [while other classmates have] passed to the next degree of letters." Even friends who were able to continue their education were often sitting around doing nothing, Abshir observed. Some who finished secondary school chewed *miraa*, plant leaves with an amphetamine-like effect; others sat all day in small film and television screening rooms in the marketplace. They had been able to continue in school, they had graduated from school, and they believed they were creating a more certain future for themselves through education.

Then, they came smack up against the limited opportunity for sanctuary. "We cannot proceed our education further," he said. Despite the freedom he thought the KCSE he held in his hand had promised to him, Abshir remained confined in the isolated area of Kenya where he had been relegated for the past two decades. We "cannot go to other parts of the country," he explained, "because [we] don't have any kind of ID." Refugee camps, like Dadaab, embody a logic of dependency, with policies and rules that limit and stymie the opportunities that Abshir felt ready to take up and create.[5]

These experiences left Abshir questioning the purposes of persisting through all of the challenges to complete his education. He felt as Abdi had expressed in his poetry, from his tiny shack of a home in Kampala in the midnight hours when he could not sleep: "I have no place to go, I'm just like /The air blowing around, no stay. . . ."[6] Abshir had sought and had succeeded in completing an education so that he could pursue a future that was not confined to the anemic geography of the barren ground of sanctuary in Dadaab that was all he could claim. Yet stuck in one place, the wrong place, with no ability to move, he had no tangible opportunities.

Abshir and his peers faced daily the limited sanctuary that refugee status in Kenya provided and the unshakable power that the nature of global policies of confinement have over the ways in which they can use their education, or not. As a result, they questioned the purposes of their education and if and how their learning could disrupt the barriers to their opportunities.

How might we redraw these maps of sanctuary through a focus on belonging? While maps of countries remain unyielding in terms of controlling borders and movement, refugee young people are redrawing their own maps of belonging through their relationships. In particular, through intentionally forging relationships that link local and global and self and other, they are creating new forms of belonging by figuring out and practicing how to be not dependent but interdependent. Even in situations of such limited sanctuary, they are creating belonging that enables new ways to address persistent resource-based inequalities, allowing them to get by, and new ways of belonging that reshape identity-based inequalities, allowing them also to create opportunities and their futures.

Linking Local and Global

Abshir's trajectory through school was marked by his relationships—with NGO staff, with teachers, with peers, and with family—and the resources those relationships enabled. While refugees often find their relationships fractured through conflict and displacement, students like Abshir demonstrate the ways in which refugees also intentionally re-build and re-create relationships, sometimes in new forms.[7] Refugees may have little or no contact with nationals, given policies that isolate them in camps like in Kenya or different school shifts like in Lebanon, but given migration patterns and transnational interactions, they frequently have virtual connections that can jump isolationist policies and span geographies.

One way to think about these relationships and the ways they func-
tioned for Abshir, as with his teacher, is as "social capital."[8] "Bonding"
social capital describes the social ties within communities that are
bounded, for example, by geography or class, such as the relationships
Abshir had with his peers and his family that helped him to get by in his
daily life. "Bridging" social capital, on the other hand, enables people
to extend their opportunities through social ties built across communities, which often span differences of geography or class, such as the relationships that Abshir built with NGO staff. These two types of social
capital can form the building blocks of belonging, expanding access to
material and relational resources and shifting the kinds of opportunities
refugee young people have to prepare for the futures they imagine for
themselves.

Young people like Abshir demonstrate ways in which their unique position as refugees enables them to create new forms of social capital as
they transform their bonding relationships into transnational bridging
relationships, as with his teacher. Transnational ties—economic, social,
political—among migrants and their countries, cities, and towns of
origin are well documented.[9] Despite being often constrained in their
physical mobility due to ongoing conflict and camp restrictions, refugee
young people too have interactions and connections that are not only local
or only global but that "travel" between the refugee camp and other
places. Anna Tsing, anthropologist at the University of California at
Santa Cruz, documents in her study of capitalism and environmentalism
in the rainforests of Indonesia in the 1980s and 1990s that these traveling
relationships run counter to conventional views of how resources flow.[10]
They do not, she writes, begin—or end—in "imagined world centers
such as New York, Tokyo, or Geneva" but instead circulate through
informal networks with origins and destinations in all geographies.[11]
Tsing further describes how interactions and connections are often made
in "fragments," as individuals collect and piece together the ideas and resources from a wide array of sources. By linking local and global relationships, refugee young people like Abshir show how they work against

the dependencies created by global and national refugee policies to create new opportunities of interdependence.

Urie Bronfenbrenner, who was born in Moscow on the eve of the 1917 Russian Revolution and whose ideas would become the origins of the US Head Start Program, famously described ecological systems in which children's development occurs. It is a useful model for envisioning this interdependence, seeing the connections among Abshir's individual relationships (the micro-processes) and his encounters with and interactions within institutions (the macro-processes). In Bronfenbrenner's model, individuals operate within nested systems: the microsystem, which is the family, peer group, and school; the mesosystem, comprising interrelationships between microsystems, such as between parents and schools; the exosystem, such as institutions and practices that affect the individual; the macrosystem, such as social and cultural norms; and the chronosystem, including historical and environmental transitions over time.[12]

In Dadaab, interactions across these systems are uniquely both local and global. Taken together, they are the source of important relationships and resources that enable students to create opportunities for learning and belonging. Abshir highlighted the structures that international agencies provided for education in Dadaab—Bronfenbrenner's exosystem—as a necessary but insufficient foundation upon which he was able to be successful in school. He made a connection between the school buildings in Dadaab and a distant public who did not know him but cared about him, envisioning in his mind the positive duty to strangers that Henry Shue (see Chapter 5) described. As Abshir said, the "world has assisted us." His friends talked about how international organizations "paid for [his] free primary education" and "facilitated [his] high school education," supplying materials needed for school that made school life easier in a context when home life was very hard.[13] Abshir and his friends were able to see clearly the role of international funding because they experienced the structures as they were being built. Upon their arrival in the camps from Somalia, there was no infrastructure, and they learned outside, under trees, and they did their writing in the soil. Later, they had notebooks, but they split them in half to share between two children. With these new possibilities, one student said, "I stopped the plan of going back to Somalia, and I studied from there [Dadaab] under the trees." When a Norwegian agency came, "they built two rooms" and, he said, "from there I completed my primary education."[14]

These structures, created and augmented over time by UNHCR, NGOs, and refugee community groups, provided the possibility that children in Dadaab could attend school. Yet it was relationships with the Dadaab-based staff members of these organizations—Bronfenbrenner's mesosystem—that were key for young people like Abshir in transforming access into opportunities. These relationships, that bridged across refugee, national, and international status, provided motivation, served as deterrents to dropping out, and, through information and guidance, created openings for further study.

Teachers also played these roles, through both bonding and bridging relationships. Refugee young people described the connections, the bonding relationships, they built with refugee teachers from their own communities, who had experienced being refugees in Dadaab and been educated in the same schools. One student described how differently she could interact with them, as compared to the predominantly male Kenyan teachers from outside the camp. "If I cannot just understand from the [Kenyan] teacher," she said, "I usually go to them [the refugee teachers]."[15] Refugee teachers were "aware of the condition at home," and they thus understood what students needed and they "sometimes provided material support, buying materials such as books, papers, and writing materials that were not available from the district with their own funds."[16] One student expressed surprise that some of her teachers cared enough to notice when things were not going well for her. "When they see I'm not doing well this time, some of them used to call me," and, using her name, which was rare, they would say, "'What's wrong? What's the problem?'"[17] Another student explained that he trusted his refugee teachers more than his Kenyan teachers "because I can tell them everything and they will understand." He emphasized the role of language in addition to trust, "the fact that they can explain to me . . . [in a] combination of Somali, English and everything, how I understand."[18] Having "teachers who know me," one student noted, was essential to her academic performance: "I had to perform better because it will be shame for you when you perform poorly when you are expected [to do well]."[19]

Teachers combined this interest with encouragement: one teacher used to say, "'You . . . can perform better. Try it.'"[20] One student described the specific encouragement his physics teacher provided: "He always helped me, like I remember . . . I applied several times for this DAFI scholarship, and I was often left [not awarded the scholarship]."[21] This process of applying for scholarships, perceived as the only way for young people to geographically leave the camps, felt to young people as the epitome of their dependence on global and national systems that did not make space for them. They apply for these very few scholarships again and again, year after year, waiting and waiting, their futures in the balance of someone else's decision making.[22] Teachers supported students in trying to navigate this flawed system. One said about his teacher and his process of seeking a scholarship, "I used him to give me the courage— [he would say,] 'Proceed, go for it. Don't just lose courage.'"[23] Teachers did more than use their words to support their students' education. They often served as tutors, especially for subjects that were particularly challenging, such as "extra classes during the week and Saturdays and Sundays . . . like practicals [of] chemistry and biology."[24]

Practices of hiring refugee or Kenyan national teachers in Dadaab shifted over time, with implications for the types of relationships between students and teachers. Until 1997, students followed the Somali curriculum with Somali refugees as their teachers. After 1997, refugee students began to follow the Kenyan curriculum and to sit for the Kenyan national exams at both primary and secondary levels, coming into more contact with Kenyan institutions and norms. This change also entailed a shift in the language of instruction and examination, from Somali to English, which meant that the success of refugee students then additionally depended on acquiring a new language. Concurrent with this shift was the new hiring of Kenyan teachers in Dadaab schools. Abshir emphasized how important this shift was, saying, "Now, the teachers are trained. We have even some teachers who have gone to university and they have attained their degree," pointing to a form of social capital that Kenyan teachers enabled, previously unavailable in the camps.[25]

Refugee teachers also enabled their students to create a new form of social capital. Relationships with refugee teachers did not end with graduation from secondary school or at the borders of the camp. The nature of these relationships shifted over time from local to global. Refugee students and recent secondary-school graduates in Dadaab were connected on Facebook to their former teachers, many of whom had since left the camp through rare but not impossible resettlement or scholarships for university education in Canada or Nairobi. These virtual connections built on the previously existing in-person relationships that teachers and students had cultivated in schools in Dadaab to stretch across expanses of time and distance, shifting also the web of dependency that clung over the camps. One teacher who moved to Canada described how "when we see online each other, they will seek my advice to reach the WUSC [World University Service Canada higher education scholarship] goal, to perform well. . . . I just give counseling to students who are waiting to do their final exams, something like this."[26]

Refugee young people created these relationships in part through informal one-on-one mentoring-like experiences with older students and teachers and by forming both local and virtual study groups via online platforms, institutionalizing in a small way for each other the kinds of support they did not find readily in their schools. One student described sending her essays to a peer who studied in Canada who read them and provided feedback virtually.[27] Salim, the student who identified himself as "Dadaabian," described a Facebook group of thirty students from Dadaab, the purpose of which was to share past exam papers and to help each other, using the chat (Messenger) function.[28] The group was transnational, with eleven members remaining in Dadaab, six studying in North America, seven in East Africa, one in Somalia, and the location of the five others unknown. This group transformed what had been relationships of bonding social capital, helping refugee young people to get by in daily life in Dadaab, into relationships of bridging social capital, helping refugee young people to expand their opportunities to be successful in their education.

For refugee young people, the opportunity for educational success is integrally tied to belonging, in particular the kind of belonging that provides a sense of home.[29] "Home" for refugees can be a place filled both with memories of a longed-for past and suspicion and distrust of people and institutions that have caused deep harm. "Home" for refugees is also "deterritorialized" through processes of flight and exile.[30] Education can be a way through which to conceptualize home not as static or as some idealized place, but to re-create it. For all of what is lost in forcibly living outside one's country of origin, education can be what is gained, a peer of Abshir said. "One of my educational goals," he said, "is to become someone, then take part in the reconstruction of Somalia. The only way we can get out of these problems [is] through education."[31] As another put it, "I myself going to school was a contribution to my community."[32] The goal of contributing to the reconstruction of what they saw as their home was consistently on the minds of refugee young people in Dadaab as they pursued education. A student who completed his secondary schooling in Dadaab and was sponsored for a bachelor's degree in Nairobi expressed his thinking: "Why not . . . come back to Somalia and add a value on this tree that's growing called Somalia? It's very small and very delicate now."[33] Others echoed that the "burning issue is to go back to Somali country and construct that collapsed country."[34]

This purpose for refugee education, which synthesized the power of local and global relationships with an orientation toward contributing to "home," echoes the earlier Liberation era of refugee education. Despite a time horizon of those contributions that could seem impossible to imagine, students continued to focus on their present lives and educations in a host country as a means to meet the needs of a radically reimagined future of a home country.

The ways in which refugee young people are connecting local and global relationships also provides an example of how the notion of who is a stranger and who we each have responsibility to might shift. As Shue argued, unlike in previous eras when interactions among individuals living in geographically disparate places were nonexistent (or at least often invisible or unrecognized), we are now entwined in webs of interdependence. This interdependence brings with it a duty to others whom we may never meet in person.

As we see in the way sanctuary for refugees is offered or restricted and the ways in which power in refugee education is situated, the globalization of institutions remains caught within the old view where duty to "strangers" reduces to nil, confined by what is possible when the rigid organizing structures of states dominate. Refugee young people demonstrate that if we think about globalization both in terms of institutions *and* in terms of relationships, through which we are interdependent, we might begin to reimagine what our duties are to each other, and use these transformed relationships not only to navigate existing education systems but also to shift the kinds of learning and belonging they include.

Becoming Entwined

Renegotiating who belongs to an interdependent collective requires shifting how resources are allocated to disrupt resource-based inequalities. These kinds of shifts, however incomplete, are evident in formal, structural endeavors to include refugees in national education systems and in nonformal, relational endeavors through which refugees access resources to support their education through connecting local and global relationships. This linking of local and global relationships is one manner in which refugee young people work against the institutional ways that resource-based inequalities shape their lives in exile. These relationships expand their educational opportunities and, through those opportunities, forge a sense of belonging connected to possibilities of contributing to the re-creation of home. At the same time, refugee young people still live their daily lives within the less flexible limits of sanctuary that rest on exclusion from and within institutions and harmful encounters on the basis of legal status, race, language, and more. Disrupting these identity-based inequalities requires changing how each of us see ourselves in connection to others and redesigning our institutions to reflect that.

This kind of renegotiation requires conditions that encourage a linking of self and other that recognizes how we are entwined and allows us to practice *being* entwined. The idea of *ubuntu* embodies this kind of interdependence.[35] In the South African language isiXhosa, it means "I am because we are."[36] I cannot be human all by myself, as my humanity is inextricably connected to yours.[37]

African philosophers, theologians, and sociologists view ubuntu as something both practical and ethical, and it is in both of these dimensions that it holds relevance in the context of current mass migration and education. It is an empirical description of the "way things are" as well as a guiding principle for conduct. Steve Biko—whom Siyabulela longed to learn about—described the incomprehensibility of greeting a visitor with the phrase "What can I do for you?" Biko wrote, "We regard our living together not as an unfortunate mishap warranting endless competition among us but as a deliberate act of God to make us a community of brothers and sisters jointly involved in the quest for a composite answer to the varied problems of life."[38] This sense of belonging to an interconnected community is the core of ubuntu.[39] Importantly, ubuntu is not incompatible with individual identities. Nomonde Masina, a South African sociologist, explains that "neither is [the worldview of ubuntu] comfortable with collectivism where collectivism stresses the importance of the social unit to the point of depersonalizing the individual."[40] Indeed, achieving individual "personhood" is the purpose of ubuntu. This individual is not subjugated to the group but needs the group—the community—in order to realize their full potential. Individual personhood is achieved in the context of relationship.[41]

The idea of ubuntu has sometimes been characterized as "superficial and confusing."[42] It has certainly been co-opted in superficial and commercial ways both inside and outside of South Africa. A globally popular Linux-based open-source operating system is named Ubuntu. Ubuntu Cola made with fair-trade sugar from Malawi and Zambia is sold across Europe under the slogan "Ubuntu is ethical cola that tastes great."[43] And "Ubuntu!" was a cheer that fans of the Boston Red Sox took on in the 2007 World Series playoffs.

However, both the ethic and the practice of the ubuntu worldview are also deeply embedded in many modern African sociopolitical contexts and institutions. In Botswana, for example, *kgotla*, translated as "meeting place," embodies the principles of ubuntu, the Setswana word for which is *botho*. They are spaces of communal decision making where conflict resolution—the kind of productive conflict that Munir finds no space for in his school in Beirut—occurs through discussion.[44] In South Africa, the word "ubuntu" itself was inscribed in the 1993 South African Interim Constitution, and the concept formed the moral and legal foundation of the Truth and Reconciliation Commission (TRC).[45] Cynthia Ngewu, the mother of Christopher Piet who was murdered by the apartheid regime, spoke about the process of the TRC: "This thing called reconciliation . . . if I am understanding it correctly . . . if it means this perpetrator, this man who has killed Christopher Piet, if it means he becomes human again, this man, so that I, so that all of us, get our humanity back . . . then I agree, then I support it all."[46] The TRC was possible, Antjie Krog argues, because participants like Mrs. Ngewu knew and understood interdependence—ubuntu—from the "daily living of interconnectedness."[47]

Despite persistent evidence of the ubuntu worldview in some societies, there is no doubt that ubuntu has been eroded by social, economic, and political changes.[48] Colonialism, apartheid, and urbanization have all disrupted the "daily living of interconnectedness" that Krog described and have broken down bonds within families and communities, both those who share space and those who are geographically disparate.[49] In settings of exile, like Jacques experienced in Uganda and Munir experienced in Lebanon, laws, policies, and institutions encourage not interdependence but isolation and dependence. To experience my humanity tied up in yours requires experiences of being together and understanding how I am more with you than I am without you. What conditions—among young people, in classrooms, in schools, and in communities—can enable the practice of interdependence, experiences of which are so central to being able to build relationships of belonging?

Hassan and his family fled Somalia in 1994, just a few years after Abshir.[50] Unlike Abshir who fled to Dadaab, Hassan's family arrived as refugees in the United States. Seven years old at the time he left, Hassan remembers Somalia as a place of "mostly people dying because of warlords."[51] American public perceptions of Somalia, and by extension of Somalis, were framed less by this sense of anarchy than by a good guy–bad guy narrative. Like the photos of Alan Kurdi who had fled Syria, and of Phan Thi Kim Phuc and Hector Pietersen engulfed in conflict in Vietnam and South Africa, the 1993 photo of US army sergeant William David Cleveland's lifeless body being dragged through the streets of Mogadishu by a chanting mob provoked deep outrage in the United States. This moment, which later was the subject of the 2001 film *Black Hawk Down*, is widely held to be a turning point in US foreign policy, away from ground-based interventions toward inaction in conflicts such as Rwanda and Bosnia.[52]

Hassan arrived in the United States just a few months later. After living in a small town in New York State and in Boston, Hassan's family moved to Lewiston, Maine, a place where in winter people walked up the street with hats pulled down over their eyebrows and scarves pulled up above their noses. A place where as school let out for the day, traffic along the main street slowed to the mandated—and obeyed—fifteen miles an hour. A place where the ancient French of the Québecois, still spoken despite its ban in schools by the descendants of mill workers and canal diggers who came to the area over a hundred and fifty years ago, mixed with the slow and lilting English of the Irish of central Maine. The population of Lewiston at the time Hassan was growing up there was mostly White, mostly Catholic, mostly old, and mostly out of work.

Recall that in 2002, when Hassan was fifteen, a city hall administrator described a stack of complaints about Somalis from longtime residents that piled over a foot high on his desk, and that the mayor had published an open letter in the local newspaper asking Somali residents of the city to discourage other Somalis from relocating to the city.[53] This was the context—the ecology of history, sociocultural norms, institutions, and practices—in which Hassan, a Black, Muslim, and Somali teenager, and Michelle, a White, Catholic, and longtime resident Lewistonian teenager, developed a friendship that allowed them to experience interdependence.

Teenagers at their high school, of 1,250 students, crowded the front entrance, talking and laughing away their last minutes before the bell rang to start the school day. Every student I could see was White; the boys baggy-pant-clad and skateboard-toting, the girls had 2004-era flared jeans, puffy coats, and sneakers. Making my way through the swirl of students, I saw small groups of Somali students. All of the Somali girls wore hijab, some in muted colors and others in fuchsia and orange; their skirts were long, some with blue jeans underneath.

Hassan described himself as being in "mainstream" classes. Michelle quickly pointed out that there were not very many Somalis in these classes, that most were in English Language Learner classes that had only Somali students. When there was more than one Somali student in a class, which was rarely, they usually sat together. In English class, Hassan sat next to Michelle on one side and Jamelia, who is Somali, on the other.

When Somalis first started coming to Lewiston, Michelle recalled, she was in middle school. "When I first met them, I couldn't tell them apart. Like who are you? Why won't you say 'hi' to me?" At first, Hassan was "just another one of the Hassans."[54]

Hassan felt this sense of being seen as a stranger in the city and in school. Often he felt "looked at, treated like I don't know much. They think I just arrived, or something. You know what I mean? Like I don't know anything. Like they can take advantage of me. . . . Like the way they act toward us [Somalis], like I don't know what they're saying and stuff."[55] As they found themselves in more of the same classes, Hassan and Michelle began to hang out together, in a small group of Somali and White friends, and they quickly became each other's closest friends.

Both of them described the barriers and resistance they faced to their friendship.

"I was born here in Lewiston, Maine," Michelle explained, dressed in a fitted purple sweater and flared jeans, "lived in the same house all my life, never moved. Everybody thinks about Lewiston, they think about like, oh, crummy town." Michelle threw her hands up in the air. "People isolate themselves . . . the Whites are unknown to the Somalis and the Somalis are unknown to the Whites and some people are afraid of what they don't know."[56] Somalis and Whites "are scared to talk to each other," Hassan quietly agreed. "Scared is the most biggest thing."[57] Michelle pointed to the explicit racism she saw in each of these interactions. "Black and White treat each other as enemies," she said. Refusing to get caught up in generalities—"my teachers," she said, "tell me to use examples"—Michelle began to describe her family. "My dad . . . thinks that [having Somali friends] is just wrong"; he sees them as "completely different people," she said. He "loves his grandchild to death, but. . . ." Puzzled, Hassan interrupted: "He what?" Michelle paused for only a beat before explaining, "Loves his grandchild. She's Black, or part Black." "Well, that's not the part he loves, I guess," Hassan said quietly.[58]

Hassan and Michelle talked easily to each other about building relationships across the divides of race and nationality that split their town. These topics seemed common for them—"Remember when we talked about . . ." and "Michelle told me she thinks . . . , but I think. . . ." It was not only my questions that prompted them to think on and discuss issues of race, of migration, of belonging. Race and migration status were not subtexts for them, as they were in so many interactions in Lewiston. Through talk about the inequalities that defined their experiences, they defined themselves in opposition to this larger community while also using each other as touchstones, finding a kind of interconnectedness that allowed them to be more human with each other.

Hassan was clear that "for me to put myself in Michelle's position would be . . . very hard because I [can't] be doing what she be doing. . . . But if I was a White woman in this school, how would I feel? I could run

around! . . . Like actually just feel not looked upon. Like I feel that . . ."
Michelle cut him off: "But it's different because I'm White and I talk with
you guys and so the people who don't talk to you guys think I'm a ho
and I'm a slut and all that." "I didn't know that," Hassan laughed in a
self-conscious but break-the-tension kind of way. "Now I know. I'm
sorry."

"I don't think she can handle [being in my position either]," Hassan
said seriously, but not as a conversation-stopper. Michelle reflected, "I
think I'd feel kind of like an outcast, sort of. . . . There is some people
that, like, say, 'Oh My God, he's Black, he's Somalian and he's evil, like
don't come near me, and they're mooching off our taxes.'" Hassan
reached into his pocket: "I got my paycheck right now." He pointed to
where the paid taxes were, determined to combat the hurtful stereotype
that resulted in such articles as "The Great Somali Welfare Hunt" in
The American Conservative.[59] "If you ever were [in my shoes]," he said,
"just look down . . .'cause you're going to see things you're gonna hate
from other people."[60]

When coming to meet them after school, I found Michelle lying with
her head on her backpack, propped up against one of the endless bright
yellow lockers. Hassan was similarly slouched on the floor, his crooked
arm served as his pillow and his gangly legs rode halfway up the locker
beside Michelle. They were talking in low voices, sharing confidences
with each other in a way that adults wish they still could, as if there were
nothing else going on in the world, as if they were alive only to listen to
each other. I could look at Hassan and Michelle and see teenagers,
slouching and self-absorbed. They did care about themselves, but also
about others, about their community, and about a more just world that
they imagined creating for their respective children. When asked
about their hopes for the future, they did not talk of money and fame;
they described in detail the values that they wanted to teach these children.
And they were just as comfortable telling me about the thoughts of their
friend as about their own. "Michelle wants to tell her kids not to drink,
not to do drugs, and if they are having sex to tell her," Hassan said,

looking at Michelle for confirmation, and she nodded her head. "Not me," he continued, "I'd rather not have [my kids] do it at all. I'd rather not have them know what a condom is. Seriously . . . I'm just going to tell them that they can't date anyone until they're married."

"Yup, we're different," Michelle shrugged and gave Hassan a playful punch on the arm. But that was OK, Hassan responded, "because I'm a double-thinker," echoing the notion of ubuntu.[61] Through talk about race and divisions in this place that they both shared as home, Hassan and Michelle helped each other to understand the world not from but *through* each other's points of view, creating within their relationship recognition of their individual differences and strengths. Their interactions provide what critical race theorists call "counter-stories" to each other, stories that "challenge the perceived wisdom of those at society's center."[62] Hassan labeled as "double-think" his ability to receive a counter-story. Observing Hassan and Michelle, it was clear that they used skills of both storytelling and listening to do this effectively. Each of them explained how they felt in a given situation as well as the processes by which they made sense of the tensions all around them.

In these ways, they practiced what critical race theorists do: they embraced the "responsibility to demonstrate the complexities of people's lives and the contexts influencing the choices they make."[63] Hassan and Michelle also listened to each other in ways that were "deliberate, conscious, and open."[64] Listening with this open stance, they heard not only stories that defied stereotypes, but also stories of racism and xenophobia, of fitting in, of fighting for beliefs, and of dreams for the future that reminded them of themselves. They began to see themselves "as a collective or joint unit, to feel a sense of 'we-ness.'"[65] They showed, through their words and their body language, that they would take the time to explain their thinking and to expose their tensions because they cared that the other person understood. They learned from each other about the history of and ongoing embeddedness of racism and xenophobia in the institutions— school, family, city—that they inhabited and how they each experienced and made sense of the entrenched inequity that defined the country that was both of their permanent homes, where they could work to make individual and collective contributions, as citizens and without concern that their sanctuary would expire. While Hassan and Michelle may be transformed through their relationship, this interdependence did not exist apart from, or transcend, the social, political, and racial identities that were their own. The sense of belonging for Hassan and Michelle was not about becoming the same; it was about the mutual respect they had for each other and for their differences.

Michelle and Hassan nevertheless felt isolated and unique in building a friendship with each other in the face of inequalities inside and outside of school. The sense of belonging that they created on an individual level did not align with experiences that impeded a more widespread collective sense of belonging in their families, in their other school relationships, and in their city.[66] They experienced little in the way of institutional or collective support for groups of young people to practice building these relationships and expanding their repertoires to create spaces of belonging on a wider scale. How might we link the interdependence they developed as individuals to institutions and relationships that would influence if and how they could create the more just futures they imagined?

Munir, like Hassan and Michelle, listened and questioned. At age sixteen, he was confident in class, and he was ready and open to explain his experiences as a Syrian in Lebanon and how he understood them and their connection to the future he imagined. But he could find no one with whom to have these conversations. As a Syrian, the closest he could get to building relationships with Lebanese citizens was with his teachers. And although he asked them questions about why things were the way they were, why they taught about Lebanese society in the ways they did, his teachers were reluctant to engage. As Munir reflected on if and how he belonged in his school in Beirut, he emphasized the value of the structural barriers that were permeable to him, allowing him access to Lebanese national schools. "What's important is that they're [Lebanese] studying the same way we [Syrians] are," he said, "and we're all getting the same certificate, so I belong to this class." Yet he continued, reflecting on what was not permeable: "But if I think about relationships, loyalty, dedication, or love, there isn't much of those. No, I can't contribute but I have self-confidence. But contributing and helping, no."[67]

In Dadaab, Abshir experienced similar exclusions that prevented his freedom of movement, his right to work, and his ability to create relationships in Kenya outside of Dadaab. As he progressed in school and these exclusions became evident to him, he began to doubt the purposes of pursuing an education that, like for Munir, would not allow him to contribute in the ways he envisioned. Yet in linking local and global relationships, he was able to create a sense of belonging, and connection to his desires to contribute, that existed beyond the geographic confinement of Dadaab. The relationship he maintained with his teacher, whose ideas and support traveled to Dadaab virtually from Canada, represented to Abshir expanded possibilities for his future and motivated him to persist, applying to and gaining acceptance into a higher-education degree program. Through these types of relationships, Abshir and his peers found supports they needed to begin mobilizing together, in incremental ways, to create the kind of future that they could belong to and could belong to them.

The refugee teachers we observe supporting students in these processes used their shared identities and experiences to create curricula and relationships that opened spaces for new kinds of learning. They enabled their students to feel seen and recognized and to begin developing senses of how they might build their futures and contribute to society. Yet, like for Hassan and Michelle, the belonging students felt in those schools or relationships, like the sanctuary of their liminal status as refugees, often expired outside of those spaces. Countering identity-based inequities and redrawing maps of belonging requires the entwining of self and other not only in these individual and circumscribed experiences. If we learn to be interdependent by doing it, by being in situations of interconnectedness, how might we grow opportunities for these experiences? This requires engagement across the spheres of Bronfenbrenner's

ecological system, to synthesize small-scale experiences of belonging
with the national and global political contexts of migration.

Building a New Politics of Migration

I usually did not leave my accommodations at night in the Kyaka II refugee settlement in central Uganda, where I was doing research in 2003.
But one of the students in the school had spiked a sudden high fever and
was rushed to the clinic. I wanted to check on her. As I stood outside in
the pooled light from one of the clinic windows, a man came over to me.
He leaned his back against the wall and in a soft voice, and without much
preamble, he asked if I would be interested in trading firearms for some
of the diamonds he had. It would be a good deal, he insisted. Seeing my
confusion, he quickly explained, "Since you are Canadian, I thought you
might be interested."[68]

While I and those around me in my Toronto home could think of
this man and the 1,241 other refugees from DRC living in Kyaka II as
strangers, we were no strangers to him.[69] I was visibly connected to him
now through our shared geography, through our conversation. But we
were all connected to him through the minerals in our computers and cell
phones, through illegal mining by Canadian companies.[70] We were
connected through networks of geopolitical power that permitted actions
by and interests of Canadian companies that, though more than 11,500
kilometers away, were not isolated and disconnected from this man, but
tightly bound to him, to his experiences of conflict, and why he would
identify me as possibly interested in this deal. The fact that I was not
interested did not erase these connections that, made visible by his proposed deal, changed my understanding of the multiple scales at which action is needed to transform relationships of dependence into relationships
of interdependence.

Living in Uganda in 2002, Jacques needed to conduct himself like a
stranger to be safe. He needed to be unrecognizable as himself. There
were other moments in his life, spread geographically from Uganda to

Ottawa to Boston, when he also considered whether withdrawing to the role of stranger might not be the better option. After being denied a visa to enter the United States twice between 2011 and 2015, he was granted a visa to come to Boston for a conference at which we would co-present. As we made our way around the city, to the big, fancy hotel where the conference was taking place to the school our children attended to pick them up, I could see he was reading the world to determine how warm the welcome was for him. Maybe the visa this time was a mistake. He had his guard up as we entered the school, despite the excitement I knew he felt going into a new school, what everyone whose calling is to be a teacher feels. He smiled at children; he greeted teachers. Then I introduced him to Samantha, the principal, in the way one introduces a stranger, something like "This is my friend and colleague Jacques who is visiting from Ottawa." Instead of reflexively extending a hand to shake, the principal smiled warmly. I am not sure exactly what she said, but what she communicated was "I know you, I recognize you as connected to me."

The three of us quickly put the pieces together. When Jacques and his family arrived in Ottawa on December 8, 2011, a week after getting news of their resettlement from Uganda, I had worked with Samantha to mobilize the school community in gathering winter clothing for Jacques and his family. Warm clothing for December in Ottawa is one of many essential, but insufficient, steps to the longer and harder processes of building a new life. Four years earlier, Samantha had listened, she had heard, she had acted, and she had transformed an abstract idea of a refugee from DRC into the nonstranger of Jacques, a father, a husband, a teacher, someone seeking tools to create a new future, connected to a web of interdependence that she too felt part of. So when he stood before her, despite never having met, he was recognizable. And in that instant, Jacques felt that he belonged.[71]

As in Kampala, Uganda, Beirut, Lebanon, and Lewiston, Maine, so segregated are daily lives by migration status—and by race, class, religion, and other divisions—that if left to chance, it is likely that the kinds of relationships of belonging that span local and global, that connect nationals with refugees, that link self and other in interdependence will remain rare. To build a new politics of migration where structures of sanctuary function to create sanctuary, and relationships of belonging are possible, requires that these experiences not be rare but instead cultivated in intentional ways.

Who bears the responsibility for creating these opportunities? It can be individuals, like Abshir, who found ways to navigate distance and create the transnational relationships he needed, marshaling resources and supports that enabled pursuit of a future that feels purposeful. It can be individuals within institutions, like Hassan and Michelle who found in a school the opportunity to come to know each other—unlike Munir in Lebanon who was not able to connect with any Lebanese young people. It can be school leaders like Jacques who create conditions under which families interact with each other for a shared purpose and come to see their lives entwined one with the other. While so core to the sanctuary and belonging refugees seek, it is rare that institutions or governments take on responsibility for cultivating these kinds of relationships in systematic ways.

The Host Program is a "limit breaker" in this regard. Since 1985, it has partnered longtime resident Canadians with newcomer Canadians to foster "friendship" and "integration to Canadian society."[72] It is funded by the Canadian federal government. Newcomers, both immigrants and refugees, and longtime residents, who have lived in Canada for at least ten years, participate in six-month-long experiences in which they are expected to meet with each other at least once per week with a focus on cultural exchange and friendship. Reinforcing the tenets of the 1985 Canadian Multiculturalism Act and the 2001 Immigration and Refugee Protection Act, the Host Program was one of a set of federal programs designed to act on the idea that migration processes and settlement experiences are a "two-way street" between newcomers and longtime residents and that "integration involves mutual obligations for new immigrants and Canadian society."[73] In other words, it is premised on building interdependence.

Like for Jacques, Annette, Munir, Abshir, and others, these processes are experiences of changing natures of existing relationships and trying to learn the rules of the game to build new ones. Host Program participants described their motivation to participate as a way to overcome loneliness and to create bridges across the gulfs they saw developing in Canadian society. One participant recounted how he received his Permanent Residency card in the mail one day when he had gone home for lunch from his English class. This was a big moment, one he had been eagerly awaiting. He wanted to share his excitement with someone, and his language classmates were the only people he knew in Canada, even though he did not know them very well. He went to the store and bought a big crate of oranges to share with them. After this experience, he was actively looking for ways to build relationships and hoped that the Host Program would allow him to do this, so he could share his experiences in Canada and of his life in general.[74]

Meeting people in a new place, when others are going about their lives as they always have not looking for new relationships, is really hard, another newcomer participant explained. He said, "I don't know how to say something [to people I meet], I don't know the regulations, how to make friends with them."[75] The culture of meeting people and making friends can also be really different: "Canadians, they have private boundaries. They don't want to make a relationship with a newcomer or a stranger soon. Actually, it is impossible to meet them for a long time."[76] Santosh, who had fled conflict in Nepal, expressed the same frustration: "it's very hard to contact people, not like in Asia. There, for example, in a neighborhood, you can go knock. Here, you first phone and first get permission [to go visit]. Here, we need the place where we can meet people."[77]

Through the Host Program, several participants described figuring out the key to meeting Canadians: "I will say, 'Hi, can I invite you to have a cup of coffee?' . . . and then maybe you can sit and talk."[78] When one participant invited her Host Program partner back to her home after one of their first meetings, the longtime resident described being surprised and uncomfortable since she did not yet know her partner very well. She also began to question why she felt this discomfort and whether she might find ways to extend herself more readily.[79] One participant explained how important these invitations were, including to a dinner party: "Jonathan [my Host partner] invited us to his house, to join the party. That was a very great experience. Because usually the chance to join the party, this Canadian party, is hard for me, it is rare for me. So I went to Jonathan's house and I met some of Jonathan's friends and some of Jonathan's housemates' friends. We did some games and we talked to each other. We ate dinner." This experience led to having more shared moments with other longtime resident Canadians, in bars, at movies, at horse races, and during bowling games.[80]

Learning language in the midst of real-life experiences, in addition to through formal classes, also shaped a new sense of belonging. "She is my dictionary," one participant said of her partner, who had also migrated to Canada years before. "I am joking, but she tells me a lot. I have always my notebook where I write some new words, what she says. . . . She builds my vocabulary." One of the words she learned was "cheesy," as she and her partner watched people in the coffee shop and they were acting in overly lovey-dovey ways. While the definition in her printed dictionary was "like cheese in flavor, smell, or consistency," her partner was able to explain its meaning in common usage, which led to her realizing just how often she heard this word, both in casual settings and in the school where she volunteered and someday hoped to work. Through the partnership, she began to feel the comfort that comes when you understand not just the words but the meaning of what is being said.[81]

Longtime resident Jonathan explained that one of his reasons for inviting his Host partners to the dinner party at his home was to assure them that he did not only meet with them "when I had to, once a week, together as a group." "It is not like that at all," he said, and he hoped that by creating the opportunity for them to mix with his friends they would understand that he too felt a need to be interconnected.[82] Javier, who had fled conflict in Colombia, ran into one of Jonathan's friends from the dinner party again at the YMCA. He explained, amazed, that Jonathan's friend said, "'Hi Javier, how are you?' and we started to play soccer." Being recognized and engaged in building a new kind of space for interaction that he could help to define made Javier feel, for the first time, a sense of belonging in Canada.[83]

Like Hassan and Michelle and children and families at Jacques's school in Kampala, participants in the Host Program came to understand that they were contributing to a collective endeavor, that they were each invested in each other and the new kind of community they needed each other to build. Of course, it is not possible to standardize the processes of building relationships, but we can make more possible direct encounters among people who might be less likely to interact in the segregated spaces in which we live, be that in Toronto, Kampala, or Beirut, so that they might practice the synthesis of individual and collective. While Host Program participants at first felt some artificiality about the relationships they were building, they overcame that awkwardness and formality by listening to each other, opening themselves up to new learning, engaging in activities together, and cultivating a sense of reciprocity, each participant in the partnership both giving and receiving. With some small-scale institutional scaffolding to match newcomers and longtime residents and provide them with some guidance in beginning their interactions, participants were able to cultivate interdependence from there. They were able to blur the boundaries of belonging that had initially felt so unwelcoming and immovable and create relationships in which their individual and collective interests were entwined. Building on these examples can provide the foundation for a new politics of migration, transforming isolated and small-scale relationships that refugee teachers and students create in schools into widespread experiences of belonging and sanctuary outside of those school spaces as well.

Epilogue
Home

Jacques's apartment in Ottawa, Canada, was more than 11,000 kilometers from Kampala, Uganda, but it had a similar feel. The concrete of the walls was cool but, inside, the rooms radiated warmth. Every inch of the space was thoughtful, with brightly colored cloths draped over the backs of chairs and photos hand-carried from DRC to Uganda and now to Canada with pride of place. And books. The dictionaries brought from Kampala and the new Canadian school books of children and adults alike sit side by side, as Jacques's children quickly started school and childcare and Marie enrolled in government-provided language classes. As Jacques had taught his students in Kampala, when you are a refugee, "you must begin to *live* here [where you are], from the moment you arrive." Home, he taught them, is what you build, wherever you are.

Yet building home can feel like a Sisyphean task. It is circumscribed by practices of distant countries that seek to contain refugees' opportunities for movement in the name of protecting their own homes. And it is structured by daily encounters with power imbalances in laws, policies, curricula, pedagogy, and relationships in limited spaces of sanctuary where many of those who do consider themselves home also experience uncertainty, marginalization, and exclusion.

Abdi's small shed at the back of an office building in Kampala was just the space where he lived, staring constantly at the expiration date on his UNHCR-issued refugee papers, missing a sense of stability on which he could begin to build his future. As he wrote in his poem, "I have no place to go, I'm just like / The air blowing around, no stay . . ."[1]

As they searched for a place to be safe, Charity and Simone found walls erected all around them, against them, having no access to health care for their war trauma and HIV in Uganda, and deemed not to be worthy of public investment by the Australian government, and thus denied resettlement.

Annette watched her father plant long-to-mature bananas and stood daily in front of the Ugandan flag where, as in the anthem she sang each day, she "lay our future" in the hands of this host country. With access to national schools, Annette believed that her education in Uganda would be the foundation on which she would build her future. Yet building this future, educated as she became, was elusive, as she was barred from work in Uganda and her once-upon-a-time home of DRC remained unsafe and unreachable.

Henri, who lived his whole life as a refugee in Tanzania, was able to "return" to Burundi, which, in his mind and through his mother's stories, was home. Yet once there, he found that the languages he had been stockpiling through shifting education policies in exile did not permit him to continue his education or to work to contribute to the home he longed to be part of.

Manar's family navigated education through the prism of unknowable "if" decisions: If she would return to Syria, she would choose a nonformal school to allow her continuity in her education. If she would remain in exile in Egypt, she would choose to attend Egyptian schools to enable future livelihood prospects. She felt trapped as if within her own Choose Your Own Adventure book. Without much information, and faced with shifting forms of both geopolitical and everyday relational exclusions connected to her national origin and threatening her sense of belonging, she had to make a decision at the bottom of every page that was the highest of high stakes: her life, not a story, hinged on these decisions.

Khawla, also Syrian but living in Lebanon, sought to create certainty by planning, by trying to anticipate and then account for every contingency over the next twelve years of her education that would allow her, at the end, to become a surgeon to help people in need. Yet, like Annette, Henri, and Manar, Khawla also knew that her search for learning and belonging hung by a thread in a fragile balance of power between states and in the limits of sanctuary that could impose roadblocks on her future at any moment. Would she, a Syrian national, be allowed to enroll in school in Lebanon next year? She knew she had no power in that decision, which could go either way.

Each of these young people's lives is testament to how we—as researchers, teachers, policymakers, political leaders—have not got this figured out. When people must leave their homes, how do we go beyond the most basic protections and open space for young people, individually and collectively, to imagine and create their futures?

The vast majority of refugees—73 percent—live in countries that neighbor their conflict-affected countries of origin, like Abdi, Charity and Simone, Annette, Henri, Manar, and Khawla.[2] This is no accident of geography. Through distance and national laws and policies, countries in Europe, North America, and Australia build figurative and literal walls seeking to enforce strict limits on the numbers of refugees. Education decision making at all levels—by students, families, teachers, schools, communities, national and global actors—is entangled in these politics and power structures, and in the ever-shifting landscape of what kinds of sanctuary and belonging are possible for those who seek refuge.

In some spaces of refugee education, and the relationships within it, we see young people and their teachers discussing and taking actions, both explicitly and quietly, to counter the power structures that have created these roadblocks. These young people and teachers create conditions that stand in generative contrast to the many situations where young people threaten what grown-ups around them see as fine threads holding together what they know, what they experience, to be fragile peace—like Munir in Lebanon when he asked questions about historical causes of conflict, about current inequities, and about different possible futures. Some teachers, like Munir's, thus remain silent in the face of these questions, creating an even larger chasm between the purposes that refugee young people see for their education—in terms of belonging and contributing to society—and the learning they do in school. Often in precarious and risky situations themselves, teachers can come to see the purposes of education narrowly, within the bounds of temporary and limited sanctuary. They orient what they teach toward standardized and state-centric approaches that fail to meet the needs of their refugee students in the present or for the future. Syrian children learning about the ways in which Lebanese citizens can access rights may seem straightforward, simply what is included in the national curriculum and thus what "should" be taught in Lebanon. Yet the mismatch between what they learn in school about the value of these rights and their lived experiences outside of school, devoid of any such rights, exposes so very explicitly to Syrian young people the boundaries of exclusion and the limits of welcome.

The same night I stood outside the clinic in the Kyaka II refugee settlement in Uganda and was mistaken for an arms dealer, a woman who had brought food for her sick relative spoke without preamble, clearly needing to speak the words aloud. "Everyone doesn't have the same sickness," she said, "but everyone gets the same treatment."[3] Literally, the clinic had only one kind of medicine, so everyone received the same little pills, no matter their sickness. We can all imagine how absurd that is. The same is true for refugee education.

Research and policymaking in education has long engaged with this question of standardization across regions and schools or autonomy at local levels in the structures and content of schooling. Across time and context, we see how the purposes of education shape what kinds of standardization or autonomy are expected or possible in what and how children learn. In much of the recent history of refugee education, global strategies, national frameworks, and classrooms practices have tightly reflected how the purposes of education for refugees are understood: often as moment-in-time, temporary, stop-gap endeavors that are isolated from deep-seated inequities that refugee young people experience, along lines of nationality, race, class, caste, ethnicity, language, and colonization, both in home countries and host countries. With these purposes, refugee education has been standardized, focused on addressing immediate needs with goals of mass expansion of access to schooling and efficiency of delivering this service at scale.

Yet refugees are displaced for an average of ten to twenty-five years, and they do not view their education as temporary or stop-gap endeavors, nor as disconnected from their histories or their futures. Following periods of Liberation, Standardization, and Localization, in the current Nationalization era, refugee education policies orient toward including refugees in national education systems, creating possibilities of more stability and long-term planning. Yet while this approach addresses the length of displacement, it does not adequately grapple with the implications of submerging refugee young people in education systems that do not reflect their histories, their current experiences, or their imagined futures. The approach fails to engage with the structural barriers young people face both inside and outside of school, within the state and connected to global geopolitics. These structural barriers of exclusion influence their everyday lives in the present and constrain opportunities that could enable future social, civic, economic, and political participation.

The experiences of refugee young people demonstrate how the one-size-fits-all approaches of generations of refugee education policy, both outside of and inside of national education systems, have prioritized negative peace, the absence of direct violence, over positive peace, the absence of structural violence and the presence of opportunities for participation by all. Positive peace requires engagement with the structures of power, identity-based inequalities, and histories within which educational experiences are embedded.

While the field of refugee studies has long been concerned with the
ways in which individuals navigate structural barriers in settings of exile,
rarely are the interconnections of these barriers examined across local,
national, and global power structures and as pertains to the past, the present, and the future. The unique dataset I have collected over fifteen
years, with over 600 interviews from twenty-three countries, spans these
local, national, and global power structures and experiences and meaning
making within and across them; and it interweaves the history of refugee
education and where we are now, and with an orientation toward a future
of what could be.

What we see across time and place is that spaces of generativity open
when refugee young people and their teachers see these interconnections
as the foundation of learning. Their approaches are premised on *not* being
silent in the face of young people's search to understand the inequities
around them, including the disconnects between the promise of education within a country and the expiration of sanctuary in that same country.
Instead, they use curricula and pedagogies that support young people in
envisioning and creating spaces, small as they may be, where the often-
incomplete negative peace of getting by at the margins that they experience outside of school is recognized and understood as blatantly insufficient. They work to create conditions of learning and belonging that
orient toward positive peace, where the outcome to be measured against
is opportunity, not just for a set of individuals but for all. In taking incremental steps to build these radially reimagined futures, teachers and
students have learned to work outside of rigid state-centric conceptions
of where resources are located, what learning should look like, and who
belongs. Their visions are more expansive and often transnationally oriented, less limited by conditions of conflict and exile. At the same time,
the learning is deeply contextual, centered in histories and personal and
community experiences and relationships that make the learning meaningful and inclusive.

Learning to be interdependent emerges as the crux of these curricula
and pedagogies that work against the structural limits of sanctuary to

create spaces for learning and relationships of belonging. Young people like Hassan and Michelle in Maine and refugee and national children in Jacques's school in Uganda took this challenge head-on. They created friendships across race, religion, language, and refugee and national status in the face of direct animosity from the adults and communities around them. Others, like Munir, were more ambivalent about the risks of leading the charge to build relationships across lines of difference, when unsure of the expiration of their sanctuary in Lebanon and whether the hard work would be worth it. They also perceived a more acute possible tipping point for the tenuous presence Syrians had in Lebanon and what they risked if this tip happens. When Lebanese students at his school ripped his friends' beautifully made periodic table, Munir wanted to confront them. Yet he ultimately followed the lead of his teachers who chose to avoid possible conflict, asking their Syrian students not to leave any trace of themselves in the classrooms that were occupied by Lebanese students each morning. With these actions, the spaces for learning of interdependence for Munir, his Syrian peers, *and* the Lebanese peers they did not yet know closed. Like Hassan and Michelle, Munir was eager for and capable of receiving and understanding a counter-story, an experience that was different and even contrary to his own. But the spaces for him to engage in these kinds of activities were shut off, with refugees and nationals purposefully separated in schools to avoid conflict.

In Uganda, Jacques experienced spaces closed to belonging, and he sought to be unrecognizable as he moved about Kampala in order to protect himself. At the same time, he created spaces open to belonging through the school he founded. He learned Luganda; he visited his students, both refugee and national, at their homes; and he linked refugee and national families together through the opportunities he expanded for the education of their children, out of reach in government schools financially for nationals and by law for refugees. Yet despite practice at being part of and creating spaces for interdependence, Jacques arrived in Ottawa to live in a building that, like Munir's second-shift school, felt apart from possibilities for belonging.

At sixteen stories high, this building housed many newcomer families. As the Host Program participants felt, it was hard to build relationships in a new place when the spaces in which people lived were so isolated and so closed off. For Jacques it was the workplace where he began to build relationships with others, both newcomers and longtime resident Canadians. His first job in Ottawa was with a furniture company, working in a warehouse and delivering furniture to people's homes, a job my cousin's husband helped him to apply for. Jacques was a teacher, he had founded a school in Uganda, and he was looked up to as a community leader. Yet Jacques told me this job was the best first job he could have hoped for in Canada. He made "new ties with people I never met before," he wrote, "people with different background and culture completely different from mine."⁴ Importantly, as he explained, in delivering furniture inside their homes, it allowed him to see how Canadians lived. It had been the same for me when I visited his Kampala home more than a decade before, observing all of the books that he held dear. Jacques was now a researcher in a new place, reading the world around him to try to understand how he could create home in this place not apart from, but as part of, a collective.⁵

In schools, refugees like Annette and Henri and Manar find that their experiences and imagined futures don't fit neatly into the boxes of country borders and into the boxes of belonging. Learning from these experiences and those of hundreds of others across country contexts, refugee education is poised for a new era of Liberation—this time from these narrow boxes of limited and temporary sanctuary toward relationships of belonging and interdependence. How do we shift the shape of these boxes? As refugee teachers and students show us, these shifts take place in the practices of daily life and are incrementally built through our learning from relationships with individuals and our experiences with institutions.

The boxes that are all around us can, at times, help us to understand and even navigate the world, but they limit our abilities to imagine beyond the probable, "a dream deferred,"⁶ to the possible. Jacques had learned, through his experiences teaching refugee children in Uganda and creating a school where refugees and nationals could go to school together, that his role was larger and more important than preparing children to live in the world that they did live in, filled with the boxes into which they did not fit. His saw his role as teaching his students to build a future of differently shaped boxes. Refugee young people, and their teachers like Jacques, show us how what and how they learn in schools conveys the narrowness of these boxes. They show us how critical it is to have intentional support in navigating what they need to know to persist through daily lives within those boxes. But most importantly, they show us why and how we need to disrupt the boxes completely in order to create conditions of meaningful learning and belonging, including adapting to change, understanding historical and current inequities, and learning to build relationships across lines of difference, all oriented toward building equitable futures, unknowable as they may be, for all.

Educational policies and practices, building on the experiences of refugee teachers like Jacques, can help to create the conditions for conversations and actions that build interdependence, ones that are not just self-initiated between two teenagers or created within liminal, private, and hidden spaces, but in the public spaces of schools. Over the past decade, global and national refugee policies have importantly shifted in their structures, enabling inclusion of refugees in public services, like schools. These shifts address the protracted length of displacement, making room for the idea that refugee young people need long-term and dependable access to schools in host countries.

Yet there has been little room within the politics of policy negotiation for a focus on practices that address marginalization, equity, and justice. When we expand our lens from the policies of inclusion into the institutions of schools, we see that young people often experience physical harm; messages of unwelcome; not seeing themselves, or seeing themselves vilified, in the curriculum. They experience exclusions of being silenced in their questions; being resigned to taking up only enough space to learn a little and then retreating to private and isolated spaces; and being unable to find social, economic, or political space to imagine or create their futures. Though policies have shifted to focus on structural inclusion, what has not shifted is the idea that refugee young people themselves are rightful shapers of these institutions, of their education, and of their futures.

The global promise of education for all will be achieved not when all children are simply sitting in classrooms. It will be achieved when education helps each of us understand who we are individually and collectively, make sense of our experiences, and create the kinds of opportunities that enable participation and belonging.

Mowana trees are a natural world example of shifting the shape of the boxes to create the interdependence needed to meet collective goals. "Mowana" is the Setswana word for baobab tree. The massive trunk of this tree gives way to what appears to be a burst of roots that reach toward the sky. They look dead. But if only we could see inside, we would see it growing slowly but steadily, surviving, and thriving, in the harshest of conditions. A mowana can live to be 3,000 years old, be more than 150 meters around, and their wood is more than two-thirds water. Elephants in southern Africa, migrating to follow seasonal waters, would die in the desert if not for the water they find when they peel back the mowana's bark. Mowana trees draw in whatever water and nutrients are available and turn them—against all odds—into something solid on which everything around them depends.[7]

What would it take to turn our boxes upside down, like the mowana tree appears to do, its roots to the sky? In addition to roots growing down to the past, refugee young people and their teachers also cultivate roots growing up, building futures that provide something solid for all of us to stand on together. Learning from them provides opportunities to re-create education by re-envisioning the kinds of learning and belonging that can define a much more inclusive collective success.

In Uganda and Canada, South Africa and Botswana, the United States and Kenya, Lebanon and all of the places in between across which we build relationships, education is a space to raise children, collectively, to disrupt power structures and the drivers of conflict that tear apart communities, and to enable learning and cultivate belonging that enables young people to remake the boxes of the future. As Jacques came to realize when he arrived in the "forest" that was Kampala in the early 2000s, where refugees were not legally allowed to live and go to school, he could not leave for others the most important work of educating children. "You cannot leave the future of your children for others to take care of," he said. These futures, we must create together.

By 2004, ten years after the end of apartheid, Siyabulela had seen no tangible shift in his daily experiences. His life seemed no different. So all the reasons he had to learn about Steve Biko, to think that his education might disrupt the status quo of inequality that surrounded him, began to fade and dissipate. He said about the third elections since the end of apartheid, "We are not voting for democracy. Now, we are just voting for fun."[8] As Siyabulela feels the winds of the Cape Doctor blow across Cape Town; as Jacques watches the maple trees in Ottawa turn from green to fiery red; as Henri inhales the sweet smell of the purple jacarandas blooming across Bujumbura; and as Munir hears the pop of the pistachios ripening on the trees in Lebanon, years pass. Life can feel, for each of them, as if suspended, as if, like voting for Siyabulela, it just is. Yet season after season, year after year, in classrooms and communities, refugee young people and their teachers persist, together, as they seek and build the kinds of learning and belonging that can, piece by piece, enable more peaceful and equitable collective futures for us all.

Appendix
Doing the Work

Breakfast would have been as usual on a clear but below-freezing Sunday morning in late January 1991. Our kitchen, in Toronto, Canada, was dominated by two things: the heavy wood table around which the four of us sat and a map of the world that filled one wall. Around that table, our parents talked to us— my brother, Michael, and I—about every part of that map. As we learned about a place in school, we would find it on the map. As we heard about a place on the news, we would find it on the map. Over the past week, we had been focused on Iraq and Kuwait as a US-led coalition began airstrikes in what would come to be known by White North Americans, like me, as the first Persian Gulf War.

On this day, though, our eyes were glued on the Soviet Union. Today, a Russian family would join us around this table. We would be welcoming Igor, Natasha, and Zhenya to Canada. I had just turned sixteen, and what dominated my attention was getting my driver's license as soon as possible. In the midst of these self-centered teenager preoccupations, I remember a weightiness about the idea of welcoming a family to a new place, to a new home. My dad had gotten to know Igor in the USSR, a country accessible to him because sports opened Cold War borders in ways politics could not. My dad played hockey for Team Canada, Canada's national hockey team, and Igor was a hockey reporter, for a Soviet national sports newspaper with five million subscribers. They shared this love of hockey and, even on Igor's day of arrival, went straight from the airport to a rink, to watch my brother's game.[1]

Igor, Natasha, and Zhenya were, in 1991, stepping through an ideological curtain. It was hard for Igor to do his job as a hockey reporter, unable to criticize the Soviet players or teams lest he be accused of treason to the Soviet state.[2] It was also an immensely chaotic time in their hometown of Moscow, with food shortages and escalating crime. By the end of the year Igor had arrived in Canada, the walls erected by the Cold War would continue to crumble, and the map on our kitchen wall would need to change. The December 23, 1991, cover of *Time* magazine read, "Gorbachev Says He'll Fight on, but He's Already a Man without a Country."[3] The Soviet Union that Igor left in January would, twelve months later, be Russia again.

Yet on that cold January day, these changes to come were still hazy. That night, Whitney Houston performed the US national anthem at Super Bowl XXV, the American football championships, and it was the first time this sporting event was broadcast outside North America and the United Kingdom. A few months later, a teacher took a handful of students from my high school to the USSR. One of the boys returned to reveal that he had not showered the whole time, bathing himself only with Wet Wipes; he was afraid of what contamination might befall him if he used Soviet water. From my home in Toronto, during the time I was growing up, I could see only glimpses of a world emerging from a very us-against-them time.

Many years later, Igor told me that part of their luggage had been stolen at the Toronto airport on the day they arrived. As he talked, I could tell that Igor made sure this detail was glossed over at the time, unimportant to him and to his family, who were filled with an optimism of what Canada could be for them. As he recalls those early years in Canada, Igor focused on the opportunities of his new job with the Winnipeg Jets hockey team, and the ways in which the people around him went out of their way to help make him and his family feel welcome in their new home. In 1996, when the Winnipeg Jets team moved to Phoenix, Arizona, Igor was packing up the offices in Winnipeg and found in the files a memo that had been circulated before he and his family arrived. It outlined in detail what the Jets' staff could donate so his family could get set up: couches, utensils, sheets. "We did not have anything," he said. "They brought us everything for a home."

Yet being Russian in Canada in 1991 was not easy, even with this intentional material support. On the playground at school, children would run away from

Igor's then ten-year-old daughter. But Zhenya knew what spoke across lines of difference. As Igor recalls it, Zhenya, intent on building a friendship, had taken one of the signed hockey sticks from her father's prized collection. Her Russianness may have prompted some kids to run away from her, but she knew someone else Russian who would bring them running to her: Pavel Bure. "The Russian Rocket" had played with the USSR Central Red Army hockey team, and her father had covered him as a reporter when they lived in Moscow. Bure had just joined the Vancouver Canucks and was a sensation, winning the Calder Trophy as rookie of the year. She took Bure's signed stick from her basement and gifted it to a boy in her class. Some gestures are universal. Zhenya was figuring out how to belong by listening, by making connections across snippets of understanding, by figuring out who she was in this new place in connection to those around her.

I had grown up on stories of Canadian hockey players, my dad among them, in the USSR, a place that adults and kids around me talked about as a big unknown swath on the map and with great fear. The Cold War all around us, some of these hockey stories were of downright bewilderment at the way people lived—my dad recalled his teammates thinking they were being served horsemeat and blackbird as their pregame meals in Moscow.[4] The stories were also about hockey and not about hockey, one worldview battling the other on the ice. In between, there were stories of people like Igor, of experiences finding a connection like Zhenya did, of meals shared together around kitchen tables on snowy days that could as well have been Moscow or Toronto. These people, these stories, began to make the borders of that big unknown swath on the map in our kitchen feel less rigid to me, more fuzzy and porous.

This kind of excavation of the boxes we place around countries and understanding is core to the tools I use to do my work, and these methodological processes are defined by listening and talking freely, following the inquiry, and creating relationships and collaborations.

On Listening and Talking Freely

This book is the product of many years of my own commitment to listening and creating spaces to talk freely. I situate my discussion of the methods of this work in the context of a kitchen table in Toronto in 1991 as the questions that shape it and the approaches I take to research are rooted in my history, my identities, my preoccupations, and the ways I make meaning in relationships with others. The location and shape of the "kitchen table" vary from place to place and time to time. It can be a large piece of furniture, planted in a particular place, but it is also moveable and it changes shape over time, with chairs pulled up or placed to the side. It can be outside, inside, off the ground, a patch of ground, a milk crate turned over, a set of stones beside a football pitch (US audience read: soccer field). I have learned that when I find the space that it occupies for the teachers, students, parents, government officials, and agency staff members I seek to learn from, I find the spaces of their histories, identities, preoccupations, and meaning making as well.

My identities and experiences as a teacher and as someone continually engaged with policy and practice have shaped the ways I ask questions in my research and in the ways I listen to and make sense of data.[5] Our social positions—what social scientists call "positionality"—shape the ways we design research, build relationships and interact in field sites, and analyze data.[6] What does it mean for the researcher to be the instrument of the research? Just as the historical, political, social, and relational contexts of a setting are "used to place people and action in time and space and as a resource for understanding what they say and do," the identities and experiences of the researcher are essential contexts for the processes and outcomes of the research.[7] These identities and experiences are resources for asking questions, for developing relationships, for probing meaning, for pursuing silences, for making sense of contradictions. This conception of the researcher as instrument of the research shapes my commitment to transparency of process, in terms of why and how I do my research, and clarity about who I am in the research. It is why you see me in the classrooms, communities, offices, and conversations that make up the interview and observation data in this book.

As a teacher, I listened for what I came to realize were silenced stories of my refugee-origin students and their educational experiences in other places before they became my students. When I taught eighth grade in Massachusetts, a few of my students would come to school early, just to talk. I had a beautiful classroom, on the third floor of an old brick building. Jorge, who had moved to the United States as a child from Honduras, was not one for small talk. But one morning, he sat himself down at my desk and did begin to talk. This was an era, the early 2000s, where headphones were not nearly as ubiquitous as they are today. Jorge was preoccupied with them, though. He couldn't understand how his peers could choose that kind of isolation, inside their headphones and with loud music. Jorge told me that he would not use them. As he later wrote in a reflective piece of writing, "How will I become American if I don't listen to find out what this new place is all about?"

As a teacher in South Africa, Madagascar, and the United States, listening opened spaces for my students to teach me about how their pasts, presents, and futures were connected in ways that often shook my preconceptions. As their teacher, I tried to create conditions for the kind of learning and belonging that this book illuminates, and I learned how very hard this work is. As a professor, I focus on research that allows me to engage with schools, with teachers, and with young people over time, and I listen for how experiences change and how they are situated in shifting social and political contexts. I also work with national governments, UN agencies, and civil society organizations on policy and on strategy, for example with the United Nations High Commissioner for Refugees (UNHCR) on the development and writing of their 2012–2016 and 2019–2030 refugee education strategies. This work has allowed me to listen to how national and humanitarian and development actors grapple with the financial, political, and moral trade-offs of high-stakes decisions they make. It has also allowed me to insert questions in those conversations about both the resonance and the disconnects of these decisions with what I observe of school- and classroom-based experiences of teachers and students, including the protagonists of this book.

The gulfs between these worlds can be vast and demonstrate how the role of a listening researcher includes not only empathy but also risk, challenge, and the explicit confrontation of tensions and contradictions. I began doing research in the Kyaka II refugee settlement in Uganda in 2003. There was a guest house in this refugee camp, a simple brick building near the small brick homes of the staff of humanitarian agencies, almost all of whom were Ugandan nationals. These brick buildings contrasted with the mud and stick homes of the refugee families who lived, much more permanently, in the camp. The guest house, where I lived while doing research, was almost always empty. But my first afternoon there, a White woman from Geneva who was on a monitoring mission for an international agency was having tea in the common-room area, where I joined her. We both made polite conversation and talked some about each of our work. On her way out the door, she paused and said, "Don't talk to the refugees, they are liars."[8] And then she stepped up into the white Toyota 4x4 Land Cruiser that would take her back to Kampala, and her driver drove her away. I knew this woman gave me this advice because she perceived some kind of alliance between us—one White woman to another. I did not want this alliance, and yet I also did not want to shut her out. I wanted to understand how she was thinking and how this thinking, and her decisions (she had a great deal of power), connected to daily experiences of learning and teaching in schools that I was focused on. In order to situate my research across levels of power, I have come to see this fairly constant navigation as essential, particularly in enacting my ethical commitments to being explicit about how I disagree with positions expressed while not closing off openings to understanding, no matter how different the views shared are from my own.

To be explicit, my beliefs and practices are in opposition to this woman's notion of who I should talk to and listen to, and I regret not having that conversation with her before she drove away. My approach aligns with French sociologist Daniel Bertaux who argues, in his work on life history interviewing, that "if given the opportunity to talk freely, people appear to know a lot about what is going on."[9] Yet through listening, I have also come to see how rarely any refugee feels able to talk freely. Survival, while living as a refugee, can depend on navigating power politics, and details shared when talking freely can backlash in high-stakes decisions on resource allocation and migration status. I knew that if this woman who had just left in her Land Cruiser saw us as aligned based on our Whiteness, so too did the students, teachers, and families whom I wanted to be able to talk freely with, all of whom were Black and in need of the material resources her organization provided.

In humanitarian settings, I have found trust to be fleeting, if present at all, with implications for how listening, and talking freely, can happen. A staff member of the Ugandan Red Cross in the Kyaka II refugee settlement told me that she was unable to distribute sanitary materials to the women in a particular area of the camp she was to visit that day because she had not yet been able to cut the cloth into strips. I asked if this was something the women could do. "No," she said, "we cut the cloth so that they do not use it for table coverings or for baby carriers." I wondered out loud if it would be all right for the cloth to be used in these ways if the women wanted. I used wondering instead of overt dismissal of a harmful outsider-driven approach, in this instance, as in so many others, as a way to keep conversation open. The woman who planned to cut the cloth, who had grown up in this area of Uganda, explained the position she felt pinned within: "the donors," she said, meaning international agencies far away, "will not pay to buy cloth for that."[10]

Listening and asking questions have helped me to understand and make transparent for myself and my research participants the forms of power that stand in the way of building trust and creating possibilities for talking freely to each other. Core to this endeavor has been coming to understand the expectations each actor in the large constellation of relationships my research involves have for each other and disrupting the force fields of power that those expectations create. At times my disruptions are only small and symbolic. If outsiders are expected to drive, I walk. If White foreigners are expected to sit up front at community meetings in refugee camps and be served tea, I help teachers set up benches for parents to sit on.

I focus on disruptions that are sustained over time and through relationships. This relationship-building over years has allowed my participants and I to be more honest, more transparent, and more vulnerable with each other. In spending time in classrooms, for example, I listen for the moment when the immediate question from a teacher after a lesson is not "tell me how bad that was," but instead about ideas and decisions, as a shift from evaluation to meaning making. Sometimes feelings of trust and comfort in explicitly discussing issues of power happen in the middle of the first time I am in a classroom; sometimes they take months.

A common greeting I get from research participants is "You came back?" Sometimes this question is about coming back from one day to the next, sometimes about one year to the next, and sometimes about returning many years later. I have come to see in the surprise at my continued showing up not only the prevalent expectation that White foreigners, aid workers, and other outsiders will drop in and drop out, but another question, which has become critical to my understanding of the power dynamics I navigate. That generally unspoken question is "You still have time for me?" I try to preempt this feeling of transactional and momentary worth through sustained relationships over time and also in actions, where I schedule meetings with teachers, students, and families, for example, long in advance and do not expect them to be available to talk to me whenever it is that I show up (which is the general M.O. of so many development organizations). I seek that my stance communicates the question "Do *you* still have time to talk to me?" Seeking to disrupt these forms of power that surround research has been central to the ways I design my research studies and also build the methods, relationships, and collaborations that underpin them.

On Following the Inquiry

Refugee education is a relatively new field of academic inquiry. The historical analysis I present in Chapter 3 ("Power") demonstrates how education of refugee children has, since World War II, been a research lens through which to examine the construction of narratives of home, as, for example, among Burundians in Tanzania and Palestinians in Lebanon, or the preparation of leaders of postliberation states, as, for example, among South Africans in Angola and Zimbabweans in Botswana. Recently, there is a growing body of academic work that explores refugee education in single schools, communities, or countries, examining critical questions about access to education, the content and pedagogies of what refugees learn, and how refugee children and their teachers experience education, of which my work is a part.

Out of this growing body of work have emerged questions that are not easily answered with single studies, about experiences in schools that enable young people to learn, to feel a sense of belonging, and to be prepared to help build more peaceful and equitable futures. To answer these questions in this book, I needed to look across countries, across time, and across political, social, and economic contexts. I also needed to shift the shape of the boxes that we usually place around research studies, precisely because refugees' lives, experiences, and education do not fit neatly within these boxes. In line with emerging transnational social science, my approach has been to "follow the inquiry" across the artificial lines that typically bound our research designs, sites, and samples.[11]

The data in this book comprise observations and interviews from nine discrete studies that I conducted between 1998 and 2020 and from a set of smaller projects from which I also draw insights, involving more than 600 research participants situated in twenty-three countries.[12] From across these studies, I have identified essential components of what refugee teachers and students are doing to remake the future through education. The kinds of observations and interviews I have used have varied between studies, to align with the purposes of the research, the research questions, the context of the research, and the participants involved.[13]

My study in Uganda followed sixty refugee and national children and their families over three years, and it included four school sites, representing different models of education that refugees accessed. Two were located in refugee camps and one was in a city.[14] The research involved interviews with children to understand how they thought about school, what they were learning, and how it connected to their visions for the future. In these interviews, I asked children to draw and tell me about what they drew, often while sitting under a tree in the schoolyard after we had worked together to bring the school benches outside to create our own place to sit. Private, enclosed spaces are not often ones where refugees can speak freely, similar as they are to spaces of detainment and interrogation. The best conversations often happened when we were walking, sometimes for almost two hours, to children's homes after school, and when translation came to feel less like a barrier as relationships developed over three years between myself, the children, and two consistent research assistants. I watched volleyball games (only boys could play) and learned how to weave rope, situations that did not connect directly to my research questions but to the important work of building relationships. This study included two months of classroom observations at each school, as well as interviews with teachers, students, and their families. These sources of data aimed to put in conversation what I saw in the classroom with how teachers thought about their teaching and made decisions and how students thought about what they were learning. By design, I used interviews to probe what is "not visible in everyday life."[15]

In Uganda, as in much of my research, relationships are core not only to my methodological approach but also to what I am studying. One of the most challenging processes for children in these schools was building relationships across lines of difference, particularly across refugee and national status and when social, economic, and political tensions were heightening within their families and communities. To narrow in on these processes of building relationships, I conducted two studies, one in the United States and one in Canada, examining the processes of building these types of relationships among young people and adults, in a school and through an intentional relationship-building program. In Lewiston, Maine, I focused on one Somali refugee and one White American student to dive deeply into how and why they developed their friendship, especially in a time of heightened racial and political tensions and as it was so different from other relationships in that place at that time.[16] The interviews with the two teenagers in this study were not once-off encounters. They were a set of four interviews with each one, with the subsequent interviews building off ideas raised in the last as well as questions that emerged from classroom and community observations and interviews with their teachers and community leaders. A final interview brought the two participants together to talk with each other and for me to learn both from the content of what they said and the ways in which they engaged in conversation with each other. The study in Canada used these same methods but in a setting where the relationships were created by a program, not chosen by individuals within a school site, a decision I made to follow this inquiry to understand different starting points and processes of relationship creation.[17] It also leveraged comparison across newcomers and longtime residents who brought to these relationships different histories of migration and racialized positions in Canada.

After authoring a review of the state of the field of refugee education and being invited to collaborate in the development of the 2012–2016 UNHCR Refugee Education Strategy (see Chapter 4, "Purpose"), I had the opportunity to study the processes of implementing this new strategy. Over three years, I worked with a team to study in what ways and for what reasons refugees were integrated into national education systems in fourteen country sites (Bangladesh, Chad, Egypt, Ethiopia, Iran, Kenya, Lebanon, Malaysia, Pakistan, Rwanda, South Sudan, Sudan, Uganda, and Yemen).[18] The study was undertaken as part of a research-practice partnership between UNHCR and Harvard University, a relationship that enabled access to documents, interviews, meetings, conference calls, and real-time reflection on the processes under study, which would otherwise have remained opaque. We retained independence in our data collection and analysis, but we purposefully incorporated dimensions of the implementation process that were of interest to UNHCR, in line with our partnership and our commitment to research that can usefully inform practice and policy. As part of a for-credit graduate course I teach, we conducted interviews with regional, national, and global actors working on refugee education, across the fourteen countries. Working with a team of three then doctoral students, Elizabeth Adelman, Michelle J. Bellino, and Vidur Chopra, we also conducted field-based cases of three of these countries, Egypt, Kenya, and Rwanda, to examine in more depth and from more perspectives the processes of integration of refugees in national schools through additional interviews and observations in schools and community spaces.

Through analysis of these data from fourteen countries, questions about how to foster not only structural inclusion but also learning and belonging in refugee education persisted and, following this inquiry, led to five new studies that explored promising dimensions and spaces of this kind of education. In partnership with Negin Dahya and Elizabeth Adelman, and building on the learning of our colleagues at York University (Toronto) and Kenyatta University (Nairobi) in the Borderless Higher Education for Refugees initiative, we asked what supports refugee young people draw on to be successful in their education, with a sample of students who had pursued their education in the Dadaab refugee camp in Kenya.[19] Rather than adding to a growing body of work that documented the failure of schools and lack of opportunities, we wanted to understand what kinds of support enabled students to learn and graduate from secondary school.[20] Some of these findings did not surprise us, such as the role of teachers and peers and the importance of books and quiet places to study. We also began hearing from refugee young people that they were accessing resources both locally in the camp and globally, most notably through relationships with refugees who had moved elsewhere. As we realized the phenomena of learning in refugee education that we were observing were not geographically bounded, we needed to ensure that our methods aligned with the globalization of relationships we were observing, and we included interviews and surveys with Somali refugees in other locations globally.

Our study in Dadaab documented how refugees who had been able to access opportunities for movement, further study, and work were supporting individual refugee students who remained confined within limited opportunities through their advice, mentorship, and academic tutoring. It also pointed to patterns evident across my other studies, in particular how teachers and community leaders with refugee backgrounds, like Jacques (see Chapter 1, "Teacher"), were re-envisioning what and how refugee children learn. A concurrent study of teachers and education leaders who had settled geographically at a distance now engaged in education work in their conflict-affected countries of origin explored these ideas in greater detail.[21] In collaboration with Irene Liefshitz, we conducted three-hour life-history interviews with twenty-eight participants, with origins in Afghanistan, Haiti, South Sudan, and Zimbabwe. We learned through these interviews how education development led by those who experienced and fled from conflict is distinct from the kind of international education development that I had observed to be implemented by global actors, which often reinforces inequalities. In collaborative analysis with Celia Reddick, we found that these actors embraced learning goals, pedagogies, and relationships that focused on systematic transformation of conflict trajectories and opportunity structures of education.

Growing understanding from these studies of the ways in which addressing conflict, identity development, and future opportunities in schools shaped learning and belonging for refugee young people led to two adjacent studies that examined conflict transformation and mitigation in nonrefugee settings. In 1998 and 1999, I conducted in-depth ethnographic work in four high schools in Cape Town, South Africa, which focused on Grades 8 and 9, and included classroom observations and interviews with history teachers and students.[22] Reanalysis of these data for this book project allowed me to examine a postconflict setting of mass migration. The absence of direct violence was incomplete (what Galtung calls "negative peace"; see Chapter 3, "Power") and schools, still de facto racially segregated, took very different approaches to education aimed at structural transformation and conflict resolution, echoing the range of approaches I observed in refugee settings. Twenty years later, in 2019, I returned to these schools and, in collaboration with Natasha Robinson, conducted similar classroom observations and interviews with teachers and students.[23] This return to the same sites offered a chance to look at the ways in which history teaching and learning had changed during an extended postconflict period, as related to the overarching focus of my inquiry, including conflict dynamics, identities, senses of belonging, and understandings of inequalities.

A set of studies in Botswana, in collaboration with Bethany Mulimbi, provided the opportunity for another adjacent analysis, in this case of how schools engage in conflict mitigation.[24] Botswana, a country that has remained politically and economically stable despite many of the same predictors of conflict as the countries that the refugee protagonists in this book have fled, allowed us to examine ways in which education disrupts and mitigates conflict. In this context of national education policies and funding that reduced resource-based inequalities, we were able to examine classroom pedagogy and curricular content in connection to the identity-based inequalities that emerged as salient in our other studies of refugee education.

The findings of each of these studies—connected to how students, teachers and school leaders, and national and global education actors understood and acted on refugees' learning, belonging, and possible futures—led to another study bringing these elements together and focused on the experiences and perspectives of refugee young people, in particular Syrian refugees in Lebanon. In collaboration with Vidur Chopra, Joumana Talhouk, and Carmen Geha, we studied the daily experiences of curriculum, pedagogy, and relationships for Syrian refugees in Grade 9 in Beirut. We selected different types of schools, including both public and private, building on what we had learned about how young people build relationships across lines of difference, connect local and global resources, experience resource- and identity-based inequalities, conceive of their futures as connected to their education, and interact with and learn from both refugee-origin and Lebanese teachers. As in the other studies, we observed in classrooms, focused on the content of the lessons, the pedagogies used, and relationships among teachers and students. We did interviews with teachers, school leaders, and national and global education actors working on refugee education in Lebanon. We also conducted a series of three in-depth interviews with six students in each school, as well as an interview with each student's parent(s).[25] Each of the three interviews lasted between one and three hours, in spaces of young people's choosing, including their schools, homes, local cafés, and public parks. We asked about specific situations of inclusion and exclusion they had experienced and we had observed in schools, engaged them in an identity-map drawing activity, and posed questions about the relationships of support and constraint in their education. Over the course of the interviews, as our relationships with students grew, we were able to have more in-depth and nuanced discussions, often returning in later interviews to probe in more detail themes covered in earlier conversations.

Through these nine discrete studies emerged questions that were not easily answered within them. As I looked across country contexts, across time, and across individuals' and communities' experiences, comparisons opened new ways of thinking about the kinds of education that enable young people to learn, to feel a sense of belonging, and to be prepared to help build more peaceful and equitable futures. This process involved revisiting all of the data from each study and all of the previous analyses. These data and analyses were in many forms. They were in field notebooks of all different sizes and colors of the kinds available in local stationary shops, hand-written and later typed, on what I observed in classrooms, community spaces, and during interviews, accompanied by my own in-the-moment notes on how I was making meaning of these observations. They were in listening notes, written while listening to the recording of each interview and including a narrative rendering of the content of the interview and emerging analysis and questions on themes connected to the research questions of the particular study. They were in transcripts of interviews and classroom observation notes, coded with the Atlas.ti software using codebooks developed to reflect the particular research questions of each study. In many cases, this coding was a collaborative process, using a process of "consensus coding" with my research collaborators, in which we discussed each instance where there was a difference in coding to come to consensus on the code to be applied.[26] They were in analytic memos that synthesized findings on a particular theme or question within a particular study.

For the analysis across the studies, I read and re-read all of the data and analyses described above while making notes and writing analytic memos across each dataset. I purposefully did not develop a new codebook for the analysis in this book, as I wanted to preserve the integrity of the design, research questions, methods, and analytic processes of each one. For this book, the analytic process was one I conducted alone, situating myself as an instrument of research who could traverse the distances, geographic and conceptual, between contexts, institutions, and individuals. I focused throughout this analytic memoing process on the main question that drives this book, the kinds of education that enable young people (1) to learn, (2) to feel a sense of belonging, and (3) to be prepared to help build more peaceful and equitable futures, in each instance focused on explanatory factors.

As within each of the studies, my overall analysis was comparative at multiple levels, drawing on case methods; focusing on mechanism-based explanations; and following the logic of "multiscalar" research, which includes comparisons on three axes.[27] One axis of comparison is horizontal across countries, including influences of policies, actors, ideas, and histories of conflict between and within states. The second axis is vertical, comparing policies, practices, and experiences of refugee education within that country as connected to global, national, school, and individual levels and actors. The third axis is "transversal," situating refugee education in historical contexts as well as examining changes and developments over time.

I do not conceive of these levels as hierarchical, but instead as mutually influential through relationships, institutions, and ideas that interact across the axes, with meaning working across what are often artificial boundaries.[28] As I considered data from specific moments in time and particular places, I set them within broader social and political contexts. Massive changes—such as globalization and polarization, refugee encampment and urbanization—both punctuate and surround these investigations and have influenced selecting what to study and how to study it. Studying history teaching and its relation to reconciliation and peacebuilding in South Africa just after the end of apartheid took on different contours than it did twenty years later. Studying relationships that bridge across national origin, race, and religion in Lewiston took place in the context of public conversations in that moment in time, about where Somali refugees were welcome in the United States. Comparing educational experiences of refugees in camps and urban areas in Uganda was set in the context of rapid urbanization of refugee populations combined with lack of freedom of movement in cities. Comparing learning and belonging in schools in national systems and outside of them in Kenya and Lebanon necessarily included an understanding of the rapid expansion of refugees' access to national schools globally. Studying educational resources that exist across borders required new methodological and analytic tools as we learned more about the types of relationships and activities that refugee students and teachers engaged in. Within and across contexts and over time, my analysis has focused on understanding how refugee education is experienced, understood, and created by national and global actors, community leaders, families, teachers, and students.

Across this body of work and through the analytic memos emerged themes that reflect this multiscalar approach and a focus on meaning making in contextual space and historical time. In the prologue, I discuss how I arrived analytically at the main themes, around which the book is organized: "Teacher," "Sanctuary," "Power," "Purpose," "Learning," and "Belonging." In my analysis, I drew on conceptual tools in sociology, political science, anthropology, and education. I needed to draw on theories about navigating uncertainty and how futures are created, but I also needed to unbound them from geographies, given refugees' mobilities. I thus linked them with theories of migration, particularly as related to the boundaries and possibilities of citizenship, state sovereignty, and transnationalism. While theories of globalization and global governance in education, including humanitarian governance, were useful in thinking about institutions, they came up short when thinking about relationships in schools and communities that were shaped by global and national power structures as well as transnationalism both in fact and in aspiration. In this case, theories of human development, connected to ideas about social capital, helped to traverse the conceptual spaces between individuals and institutions, linking together micro- and macro-processes. Theories of conflict, peace, and justice allowed me to examine curricula, pedagogies, and relationships in schools in connection with the economic, political, and social contexts of both countries of origin and host countries, and with a lens toward the educational processes that might mitigate conflict and create peace and justice.

Each of these concepts, while useful, showed their limits. Their synthesis also exposed some of the limitations of the theories we have to understand the purposes of education, the processes of education, and the outcomes of education. These purposes, processes, and outcomes are typically conceptualized bundled together and as related to an individual or within a bounded country. When we examine diverse experiences, along lines of marginalization, or as related to mobility, it exposes misalignments among the three, with consequences for young people's future opportunities. My analysis of refugee education shows this misalignment explicitly, pointing us in new conceptual directions as we think about questions of marginalization, equity, and justice in the field of education.

On Creating Relationships and Collaborations

Just as listening shapes the questions I ask and the way I hear and make meaning of data and follow the inquiry, the relationships with research participants and collaborations with students and colleagues that stem from these practices are defining, if often under-discussed, elements of this research. These relationships and collaborations occur during all phases of the research process.

Ideas for research often stem from many years of listening and conversations in all kinds of spaces. I had lived in Botswana for two years before I realized that where I was would be a productive site to examine questions that had emerged from my research in refugee settings. Though our family was in Gaborone, the site of my husband Scott's medical work, I had been living there with my research energies focused in other places. As I continued to observe ways that education was failing young people who had experienced conflict, I felt my research questions pulled toward understanding processes of peacebuilding, a *what would it take?* orientation. I had been inspired and intellectually primed on the relevance of these ideas to Botswana by years of interactions with others. The research itself, however, began in Botswana, as in all other sites of data collection described in this book, with negotiating an understanding between myself and my school and community sites. This process involves coming to shared understanding of why I am doing research and how the research takes place, including why and how I document situations, actions, words, and perceptions and how I analyze what I see, hear, and understand to answer sets of questions. In many research sites, not only in Botswana, these research questions were constructed with students, teachers, and government leaders, as we together talked over what each of us thought was interesting, important, and actionable.

Always, the research was formally permitted, using the mechanisms of each context. I engaged in ethical reviews and research permission processes through the universities with which I have been affiliated, including Harvard University, the University of Toronto, and the University of Cape Town, and partner universities, such as the American University of Beirut and the University of Botswana; in national reviews such as through the Uganda National Council of Science and Technology, the National Council for Science and Technology of Kenya, the Republic of Botswana and the Permanent Secretary Ministry of Education, the Western Cape (South Africa) Education Department, and the Ministry of Education and Higher Education of Lebanon; in other organizational reviews and permission processes, such as through national government refugee authorities in Uganda and Kenya, UNHCR at global, national, and local levels, and nonprofits, community organizations, and schools in each site. Especially at local levels, these processes were distinct from each other, at times in school leaders' offices, school district meetings, through emails and handwritten notes to families, in community leaders' homes, and at outdoor parent gatherings of several hundred people. In all cases, I saw the processes as about the relationships at the core of the research and how we could come to understand each other's goals, hesitations, and ways of working.

I always carried paper copies of my research permits and offered copies of them to participants. More importantly, I tried to show who I was and what I was doing as a way both to make the process of research understandable to people who often had little experience doing or consuming research and to remind those around me that I was documenting and analyzing and would eventually share with a larger audience what I was learning from these settings. I take up writer John McPhee's commitment to "display your notebook as if it were a fishing license," a physical reminder of my role as researcher.[29] I did not try to hide the notes I made in these notebooks, and I shared them when research participants were curious, as often happens in classrooms. This openness about my process and meaning making on numerous occasions enriched the observations and interviews that made up data collection, as children, for example, shared with me their thoughts on the questions I asked myself in my notes and also corrected factual errors.

My students are often wary of this practice. Exposing one's observations and thoughts can be disconcerting and make the researcher feel vulnerable. In one Cape Town classroom, a student leaned over and pointed to the notebook where Natasha Robinson, a doctoral student and my collaborator, was making notes on the lesson. He pointed to a letter, "T," in her notes, asking what it meant. She explained that it was her reminder to herself of his name, so she could properly trace the dialogue that was happening between him and the teacher. He smiled, took her pen, crossed it out, and carefully wrote his name in the notebook. The teacher does not know my name, he explained. This detail was critical, opening conversations about relationships among teachers and students and about disconnects between the ways in which naming was used to discipline, with lists of names on chalkboards, on papers posted in hallways, and in teachers' notebooks, yet misidentification through names was rampant in teaching and learning interactions in classrooms.

Despite these orientations toward openness and transparency, the role of researcher and the relationships that make up engagement in any research project were, of course, not always so clear. They were embedded in the power relations of each broader social and political context as well as my own positions of power in each one. In most cases, I was a clear outsider—a White, highly educated, relatively affluent, not always language-proficient, contextual newcomer. Trust across lines of race, class, religion, education level, and gender is tenuous, especially in the settings of both latent and acute conflict and violence that make up this book. And yet they were all lines I needed to navigate and negotiate continuously in each of my research sites. I needed to actively ensure that teachers and students knew I was not a "spy for the education department" in 1998 postapartheid South Africa or in 2018 Lebanon; that teachers and students who participated in my research in the Kyaka II refugee settlement in Uganda did not think I was an arms dealer as the man outside the clinic there did (see Chapter 6, "Belonging"); that I did not bring added risk to my participants by virtue of being there, calling attention to them in places where they were safer unnoticed; that Somali young people in the Dadaab refugee camps did not think that a research interview would bring them a step closer to resettlement to Canada; that teachers, who knew I had been a teacher, did not see my role in their classrooms as teacher. Building relationships with research participants involved clarifying for each other who we were in those relationships and what our expectations were for each other in those settings and beyond.

Yet these lines are often blurred. When a teacher in a class I was observing needed to leave the room to address an urgent need of one student, did I take on the role of teacher? I did (many times), feeling myself exactly what teachers described to me: the immense powerlessness of how to foster learning in classrooms of more than 100 students and a tendency toward control when faced with chaos. When I was mistaken for an arms dealer, did I bring the issue to the camp authorities, knowing it could compromise all of my relationships in the camp? I did, and I was surprised at how little interest they took in the possible harm these activities could cause. When asked by students for information about scholarships and where they could get legal advice on their refugee status, I shared what information I had access to and made connections to legal clinics and individual advocates when possible. When a student in my study in Uganda showed signs of AIDS despite not knowing he had been HIV+ since birth, I drove him to the hospital each week for the only treatment that was then available in Uganda. When Jacques asked me to write a letter for the application he and his family were submitting for resettlement, describing that I knew him and what I had observed of his and his family's experiences as refugees in Uganda, I did, knowing that I was in a position that might influence the outcome of a deeply flawed process designed to identify who of the few among millions might find a way out of the dangers and persecution of exile.

The processes of my analyses included sharing pieces of analysis and writing with research participants. For example, in South Africa, I was prompted by questions from teachers about how history was taught in other schools in Cape Town to engage teachers from across the school sites in conversations with each other about the research findings. These conversations deepened my analysis, particularly connected to comparisons across schools. In Uganda, I planned workshops in each research site to get feedback from students, teachers, NGO staff, and agency and government policymakers on emerging themes. I then followed the lead of participants in extending that work to community action plans on educational issues they identified as most salient. In Botswana, we formed and facilitated research clubs in three of the four case-study schools. We worked with students, analyzing research data together and supporting them in collecting their own data about questions that emerged for them in that analytic process. We also aligned our teaching of research skills to the national curriculum used in their schools. This depth of engagement with research participants in analytic phases was not always possible. It was constrained, for example, by security regulations that closed the Dadaab refugee camps to outsiders for months at a time during the research period, eliminating the possibility to return for these kinds of conversations; by shifting political and economic conditions in Lebanon that coincided with plans for workshops to discuss data and our analysis with groups of teachers, students, and policymakers. It has also been constrained by my time and presence, with deeper engagement in places where I lived over years and less in places where research took place over years but when my home base was far away, in Boston.

For every study, I shared draft manuscripts or sections of manuscripts with participants, if they were still contactable (some of my research participants became no longer reachable or passed away). At times, this sharing received no response. Sometimes this sharing resulted in changes to my work, where mistakes of fact were pointed out or where ethical issues of identification and political consequences became clear. A colleague at UNHCR asked a question about the need to use in published work a certain quotation from a senior government official in a refugee-hosting country. She asked the question, she explained, since her experience working in this context suggested that the political backlash from such a comment could lead to drastically limiting opportunities for refugees to access national schools. We looked back at the data, the analysis, and the draft manuscript and decided that deleting the quote itself would not change our written findings, allowing us to meet the dual ethical imperatives of doing no harm and independence in our research. Yet it was a reminder that independence in research does not mean doing work alone: we needed to be asked that question in order to avoid this type of harm.

Divergent interpretations also emerged in these conversations and always pushed my thinking and analysis further, even if in the end I did not agree with the proposed interpretations. One participant asked us to consider how we frame flows of resources, especially in the context of Haiti "given the prevailing narrative of the one-way flow of resources—from outside to inside Haiti—rather than bringing attention to the resources *within* Haiti."[30] While continuing to document the resources our research participants were bringing from outside their conflict-affected countries of origin to these countries, we took care to recognize the dominant political and humanitarian framing that often overlooked local resources.

At times, I shared emerging analysis with those involved in the research or working on similar issues, even when I was not finished with the analysis. One participant used a metaphor to describe the use of research in real-time moments of decision making, saying, "Research is like a flashlight. You shine it in front of you so that you do not step in a hole."[31] Writing and publication do not always, or even often, happen on the timeline of when decisions need to be made. With teachers and school leaders, these conversations are ongoing. The head teacher in a school in Uganda wrote a three-page handwritten letter to me a short time after I had spent one month in his school. He told me that the population of the refugee settlement had grown from 2,000 to over 8,000 and that there were now 1,196 students in his school, almost three times as large as before, and with almost 350 children in Primary 1 (Grade 1). Most of these students are from Congo, he explained, where they learned in French. "I know my children struggle in English," he wrote. "What shall I do is my question."[32] I sent him an SMS message to arrange a time to talk by phone—he needed to walk up to the highest rocky outcropping in the area to get a cell signal—and I shared with him what I had heard from families and students in his school about their struggles with language and what they found helpful in their learning; I also sent him by mail some articles on teaching in multilingual environments (which I later found had been carefully catalogued in the school library, which was the size of a small closet). Ongoing relationships with people working in government and in policy and practice have allowed me to share what I am learning when that information, even in its early form, matters to their work. These interactions come in the form of Skype messages that say "hoping all is well with you? also that you might be available for a spontaneous question . . . ," connected to a policy decision that needs to be made within an organization that day, and WhatsApp notes that ask to "discuss the policy implications of the research" to inform planning for a professional development activity by a ministry.[33] These types of ongoing interactions, and the listening and speaking freely involved, have been central to my decisions as to how I follow the inquiry, shaping next steps of each discrete study and the body of work as a whole.

Relationships with collaborators have also shaped all phases of the research process. While data collection and analysis are often conceived of as rote tasks that can be hired out, I see them as integrally connected to the intellectual work of research, particularly qualitative research. Each of the studies in this book has benefited from teamwork that embraces co-constructed ideas, joint participation in ongoing analysis during data collection, and continuous dialogue about questions, insights, and challenges that make the work stronger. These types of collaborations are more than acknowledgments: they are part of the methodological and intellectual contributions of each study that is part of this book. These collaborators are Elizabeth Adelman, Michelle J. Bellino, Vidur Chopra, Negin Dahya, Carmen Geha, Irene Liefshitz, Bethany Mulimbi, Nkobi Owen Pansiri, Celia Reddick, Natasha Robinson, Rob Siebörger, Kyohairwe Sylvia, and Joumana Talhouk.

In practice, collaboration looks different, depending on the site and the type of research. It involves being in classrooms together and negotiating the relationships of collaboration with the relationships with participants. In a classroom in Cape Town, Natasha and I sat at the front of the room, tucked amid papers and books. I had spent a year in this classroom twenty years prior in 1998. In 2019, Natasha had spent time in this classroom with this teacher and this set of students for a few months at that point, but I was new. After quietly getting out her books, a girl in the front row posed a question to Natasha: "Is she your

Mummy?" Natasha and I looked at each other and then at the girl and smiled. "No," Natasha said gently and then explained, not for the first time, how she and I were connected to each other and the reason why we were in this classroom. Laughable as the idea seemed to Natasha and me—she with her jet-black hair and Indian and Northern Ireland roots and me with my red hair and too-White skin, showing I had, at this time of year, come from winter—it was not absurd. By age, I could almost be her mother, and I am a parent, albeit to two children two decades younger.

Collaboration involves doing interviews together, listening to recordings of interviews that each of us have done and discussing strategies for follow-up interviews and / or next interviews, being analytic partners on listening notes through dialogue in writing on emerging themes and methodological choice, creating daily recorded voice memos to each other that raise questions and propose emerging ideas, conducting transnational phone calls and team meetings, collaboratively coding data, and writing analytic memos to share and discuss. After reading notes on one interview I had done in Botswana, Bethany noted a direction of inquiry to follow: "Thinking about the 'spaces' where young people might express dissent: I don't know whether we are just interested in how they express dissent with the intention of changing something, versus just talking about what they disagree with. . . . [Let's think more about this research participant's idea] that peer groups might be among the most important spaces, rather than more organized spaces or activities."[34] On an interview that Elizabeth did, I noted a description of how a teacher navigated a class situation that might help us think across the data about teachers "trying to do best by their students, but not really knowing what best is in a new and changing environment."[35] Vidur Chopra, Joumana Talhouk, and I had conversations many time zones apart, open with each other about what was arising each day in our work in schools, such as "Just got out of Futures School, faced a slightly tough situation."[36] Together, we navigated ethical dilemmas, knowing each of us had a different relationship with any given participant but being thought partners for each other throughout.

Collaboration involves some letting go, of being the only relationship builder and meaning maker. For many qualitative researchers, including for me, this sharing of power is hard. I love collecting data, I love being in schools and classrooms, and I love writing about the schools and classrooms that I have been in. I find it challenging to be on the other end of a WhatsApp message sitting at my desk in Boston while Vidur and Joumana are saying goodbye to students in Lebanon, who have been research participants for about a year. I love seeing the photos of handwritten notes in English and in Arabic that thank each student for "welcoming us into your class" and letting us learn from them, but I wish I was there with them.[37]

The opportunities created by these research collaborations have been good for me and good for the work. Essential have been collaborations with people who are based in and have longtime, if not lifetime, experiences in these contexts. In so many moments, collaborators like Rob in South Africa, Sylvia in Uganda, Owen in Botswana, and Carmen and Joumana in Lebanon have helped me to be in the generative "wait, what?" stance toward what we were seeking to understand.[38] Other collaborations have been with my students and postdoctoral fellows, who have over time become colleagues. These collaborations have originated in my commitment to apprenticeship models of learning, particularly in research that involves meaning making while collecting data and in-the-moment decisions about building relationships and navigating ethical dilemmas. They are also rooted in a commitment to building and expanding this field of research.

As in relationships we navigate with research participants, student-faculty relationships are also rife with unequal power. One way we seek to disrupt these dynamics together is through long-term collaboration processes. As Michelle noted, these collaborations can become unique spaces for collective learning: "we all benefit in the process—you as researcher, teacher, and mentor, us as collaborators, mentees, students, how the work itself improves, and how we all teach and learn from one another in the process."[39] Across all of these collaborations, the work is strengthened by each individual's deep commitment to the research questions, to the participants, to the ethics, and to the implications. It is also strengthened by our own learning from each other and making visible that, like this book argues, the collective is more than the sum of its parts.

Crediting work and ideas is part of these collaborations and is typical for scholarly work. I have coauthored, or am in the process of coauthoring, publications, related to the discrete studies with each of these collaborators. In this book, I have noted any instance where I did not conduct an observation or an interview, naming the collaborator who did and the collaborative project of which it was a part; I have not seen this done before in team-based research projects. In addition, on our research teams, we think about collaboration as a process and not only an outcome, which I find to be less readily recognized in academic work. As Negin puts it, "the whole is more important . . . than right at the end. . . . The whole being the understanding of how research happens, of how ideas come together, and in some ways of how who conducted each thing is not actually the point—that working together to make meaningful understanding out of 'data' that alone could mean anything or nothing is what matters most."[40]

In taking time to build relationships and collaborations, I have found they can embody both genuine care and clear understanding about who I am and what I am doing as a researcher, allowing me and even further enabling me to maintain a questioning stance and discerning analytic lens. Within these relationships, I have found that my research participants, collaborators, and I can ask hard questions of each other because we know and trust that we are not out to get each other and that we care deeply about understanding what the other person thinks, what they are experiencing, and how they are making sense of it. After reading a draft of an earlier journal article, Jacques responded, via email, "This work almost made me shade [sic] tears! Quite a loooooong and painful past! . . . This [is] exactly me. . . ."[41] As a researcher, it feels like a great success to have a participant read analysis and feel this resonance with their experiences, despite the ways in which it reflects pain, tensions, and hard decisions. Yet Jacques did not leave his response at that. He followed with two corrections of fact and a reminder that we were not done here: "On another note," he wrote, "I always wonder whether we could get an opportunity of briefly focusing on what happens to those refugee children who complete primary education at our school . . . for me what they become later in life (as a result of their stay at our school) is either the fruitage of my labor or a highlight of what is missing in the whole process. (I hope that makes sense)."

Research done in connection with others, in relationship with others, does not end; it leads only to more questions and the imperative to continue the work together. The nature of our fast-paced, interconnected, transnational world means that each of us is constantly in the process of one form of exit or another, from one place to another, from one job to another; from one virtual world to another. The methods that I have developed in the studies that make up this book center on what can be learned when we stay and trace the connections between places, among people, and over time.

Notes

Prologue

1. UNHCR, "Global Trends: Forced Displacement in 2019" (Geneva: UNHCR, 2020); UNHCR, "Global Trends: Forced Displacement in 2020" (Geneva: UNHCR, 2021).

2. Zachary Wagner et al., "Women and Children Living in Areas of Armed Conflict in Africa: A Geospatial Analysis of Mortality and Orphanhood," *Lancet Global Health* 7, no. 12 (2019).

3. Xavier Devictor and Quy-Toan Do, "How Many Years Have Refugees Been in Exile?" *Population and Development Review* 43, no. 2 (2017); James Milner and Gil Loescher, "Responding to Protracted Refugee Situations: Lessons from a Decade of Discussion" (Oxford: Refugee Studies Centre, University of Oxford, 2011).

4. Of the sixty-two million children globally who do not have access to education, more than half of them live in conflict settings. UNESCO, "2019 Global Education Monitoring Report, Migration, Displacement and Education: Building Bridges Not Walls" (Paris: UNESCO, Global Education Monitoring Report, 2018), 114.

1. Teacher

1. This portrait of Jacques draws on multiple sources of original data that I collected, including twelve hours of life history interviews; three one-hour semi-structured interviews in the context of Jacques's work as a teacher at a school research site; seventeen interviews with Jacques's students and their families; and participant observation at Jacques's schools over six years. These research endeavors

have also grown into a nineteen-year relationship between Jacques's family and my family. Most of the interviews and conversations between Jacques and me were in French, although some were in English; I have done all of my own translations to English, yet I have included certain short fragments of text in French, with English translations that follow, in order to signal the language of the setting. Interviews with students and families were conducted in several Bantu languages, with the assistance of a long-term translator and research assistant. In earlier writings, I referred to Jacques using a pseudonym, Bauma. It is a name he chose for himself, to protect his identity when he continued to live in exile in Uganda and, later, without permanent status in Canada. As of June 26, 2017, Jacques, his wife, and their five children are citizens of Canada. With this legal security, Jacques and I decided together that the benefits of being identified by his real name—rather than remaining invisible as he needed to do for so long—far outweigh any lasting risks. We have elected to change the names of his family members for their privacy.

2. Council on Foreign Relations, "The Eastern Congo" (Washington, DC: Council on Foreign Relations, 2015).

3. UNHCR, "The State of the World's Refugees 2000: Fifty Years of Humanitarian Action" (Geneva: UNHCR, 2000).

4. UNHCR, "The 1951 Convention Relating to the Status of Refugees and Its 1967 Protocol" (Geneva: UNHCR, 2011).

5. Interview with Zachary Lomo, then director of the Refugee Law Project in Kampala, Uganda, September 28, 2005.

6. A. Kiapi, "The Legal Status of Refugees in Uganda: A Critical Study of Legislative Instruments," in *Uganda and the Problem of Refugees*, ed. A. G. G. Gingyera Pinycwa (Kampala: Makerere University Press, 1998); Charles Mwalimu, "The Legal Framework on Admission and Resettlement of African Refugees with an Emphasis on Kenya, Tanzania, and Uganda," *Emory International Law Review* 18, no. 2 (2004): 464. A professor at Makerere University described these refugee settlements in a class and explained how they were places where refugees needed to stay, without freedom of movement. A student raised his hand and asked, "Doesn't this infringe on human rights?" The professor replied: "Nothing we can do about it until the Parliament wakes up and amends the Control of Alien Refugees Act." Observation of undergraduate course at Makerere University, Kampala, November 4, 2002.

7. Fieldnotes, November 11, 2002, Kampala, Uganda.

8. Human Rights Watch, "Hidden in Plain View: Refugees Living without Protection in Nairobi and Kampala" (New York: Human Rights Watch, 2002); Jason K. Stearns, *Dancing in the Glory of Monsters: The Collapse of the Congo and the Great War of Africa*, 1st ed. (New York: PublicAffairs, 2011).

9. A further result of the conflict was the barring of students with educational credentials from DRC from enrolling in university studies in Uganda. The Uganda National Examinations Bureau and the state-run newspaper claimed that this was an attempt to avoid a massive forgery of documents. Even those students with authentic documents, however, could not pursue university studies. Despite a full scholarship to study for his bachelor's degree, Jacques was unable to have his documents translated and certified for admission to a Ugandan university. The quotation here is from Human Rights Watch, "Hidden in Plain View."

10. UNHCR, "Global Trends: Forced Displacement in 2018" (Geneva: UNHCR, 2019), 57.

11. Uganda introduced Universal Primary Education in 1997, eliminating school fees for primary school. While school enrollment increased dramatically at that time, children from families with few resources remained out of school, unable to pay the hidden costs of school, such as uniforms, notebooks, pens, and Parent-Teacher Association fees. In my observations in government schools in Kampala and in rural areas of Uganda at the time when Jacques started his school, many head teachers did not allow children to attend school if they did not have these materials or pay these fees.

12. For more on pedagogy in low- and middle-income countries, see, among many, Michele Schweisfurth, "Learner-Centred Pedagogy: Towards a Post-2015 Agenda for Teaching and Learning," *International Journal of Educational Development* 40, no. 1 (2015); Michele Schweisfurth, Matthew A. M. Thomas, and Amy Smail, "Revisiting Comparative Pedagogy: Methodologies, Themes and Research Communities since 2000," *Compare* (2020; online); Alejandro J. Ganimian and Richard J. Murnane, "Improving Education in Developing Countries: Lessons from Rigorous Impact Evaluations," *Review of Educational Research* 86, no. 3 (2016); and Frances Vavrus and Lesley Bartlett, *Teaching in Tension: International Pedagogies, National Policies, and Teachers' Practices in Tanzania* (Rotterdam: Sense Publishers, 2013).

13. There is a growing literature on education in uncertainty, unrelated to refugee experiences. See, for example, Amy Stambach and Kathleen Hall, *Anthropological Perspectives on Student Futures: Youth and the Politics of Possibility,* Anthropological Studies of Education (New York: Palgrave Macmillan, 2017); Elizabeth Cooper and David Pratten, *Ethnographies of Uncertainty in Africa* (Houndmills, UK: Palgrave Macmillan, 2015); and Frances Vavrus, *Schooling as Uncertainty: An Ethnographic Memoir in Comparative Education* (New York: Bloomsbury Academic, 2021). See also UNESCO's work on "Futures Literacy" at https://en.unesco.org/futuresliteracy.

14. Fieldnotes, July 11, 2004, Nakivale refugee settlement, Uganda.

15. UNHCR, "Convention and Protocol Relating to the Status of Refugees" (Geneva: UNHCR, 2010), Article 1A(2) of the 1951 Refugee Convention and Article I(2) of the 1967 Protocol Relating to the Status of Refugees.

16. David Eltis and David Richardson, *Atlas of the Transatlantic Slave Trade*, Lewis Walpole Series in Eighteenth-Century Culture and History (New Haven, CT: Yale University Press, 2010).

17. See, for example, Louise W. Holborn, "International Organizations for Migration of European Nationals and Refugees," *International Journal* 20, no. 3 (1965): 333; Randall Hansen, "Constrained by Its Roots: How the Origins of the Global Asylum System Limit Contemporary Protection" (Washington, DC: Migration Policy Institute, 2017), 5; and Terje Einarnsen, "Part One Background, Drafting History of the 1951 Convention and the 1967 Protocol," in *The 1951 Convention Relating to the Status of Refugees and Its 1967 Protocol: A Commentary*, ed. Andreas Zimmermann, Felix Machts, and Jonas Dörschner, Oxford Commentaries on International Law (Oxford: Oxford University Press, 2011), 12.

18. UNHCR, "The State of the World's Refugees 2000," 51, 52, 59.

19. C. Zambakari, "South Sudan and the Nation-Building Project: Lessons and Challenges," *International Journal of African Renaissance Studies—Multi-, Inter- and Transdisciplinarity* 8, no. 1 (2013); Marc Sommers, "Island of Education: Schooling, Civil War and Southern Sudanese" (Paris: International Institute for Educational Planning, 2005).

20. UNHCR, "Population Statistics, Time Series, Uganda 2000," https://www.unhcr.org/refugee-statistics-uat/download/?url=L2sM.

21. Republic of South Sudan, "General Education Strategic Plan, 2012–2017: Promoting Learning for All," ed. Ministry of General Education and Instruction (Juba: Ministry of General Education and Instruction, 2012).

22. UNHCR, "East Horn of Africa and the Great Leaks Region Refugees and Asylum Seekers by Country of Asylum as of 30 September 2017," https://data2.unhcr.org/es/documents/download/60678.

23. UNHCR, "Global Trends: Forced Displacement in 2019" (Geneva: UNHCR, 2020), 3.

24. Langston Hughes, "Montage of a Dream Deferred," in *The Collected Poems of Langston Hughes*, ed. David Roessel and Arnold Rampersad (New York: A.A. Knopf, 1995), 387–388.

25. Susan Nicolai and Carl Triplehorn, "The Role of Education in Protecting Children in Conflict" (London: Humanitarian Practice Institute, 2003); Interagency Network for Education in Emergencies, *Minimum Standards for Education in Emergencies, Chronic Crises and Early Reconstruction* (Paris: UNESCO, 2004).

2. Sanctuary

1. I was not familiar with this story when Abdi referred to it in our conversation. I recognized it when I read it years later in a children's book. As told here, this folk story is based on that retelling, in Kathleen Moriarty and Amin Amir, *Wiil Waal: A Somali Folktale* (Saint Paul, MN: Minnesota Humanities Center / Somali Bilingual Book Project, 2007).

2. Ibid.

3. Poem by Abdi, given to me in hard copy, dated March 28, 2003, time 3:07 a.m.

4. Poem by Abdi, given to me in hard copy, dated April 14, 2002.

5. Letter, dated May 15, 2003, shown to me by Abdi and recorded in my fieldnotes.

6. This meal took place on October 17, 2005.

7. Bob Dylan, "Blowin' in the Wind," Sony Music Entertainment, 2018. https://www.bobdylan.com/songs/blowin-wind.

8. Fieldnotes and lesson plans, March 12, 2003.

9. Dylan, "Blowin' in the Wind."

10. United Nations General Assembly, "Final Act of the United Nations Conference of Plenipotentiaries on the Status of Refugees and Stateless Persons. Held at Geneva from 2 July 1951 to 25 July 1951" (Geneva: United Nations, 1951). The governments of the following twenty-six states were present with the right to vote: Australia, Austria, Belgium, Brazil, Canada, Colombia, Denmark, Egypt, France, Federal Republic of Germany, Greece, Holy See, Iraq, Israel, Italy, Luxembourg, Monaco, Netherlands, Norway, Sweden, Switzerland, Turkey, United Kingdom of Great Britain and Northern Ireland, United States of America, Venezuela, and Yugoslavia. The governments of the following two states were present as observers: Cuba and Iran.

11. See, for example, Louise W. Holborn, "International Organizations for Migration of European Nationals and Refugees," *International Journal* 20, no. 3 (1965): 333; Randall Hansen, "Constrained by Its Roots: How the Origins of the Global Asylum System Limit Contemporary Protection" (Washington, DC: Migration Policy Institute, 2017), 5.

12. UNHCR, "The 1951 Convention Relating to the Status of Refugees and Its 1967 Protocol" (Geneva: UNHCR, 2011).

13. Ibid.

14. UNHCR, "States Parties to the 1951 Convention Relating to the Status of Refugees and the 1967 Protocol" (Geneva: UNHCR, 2015).

15. Bonaventure Rutinwa, "Prima Facie Status and Refugee Protection," in *New Issues in Refugee Research* (Geneva: UNHCR, 2002).

16. For a global view of these developments, see, B. S. Chimni, "The Geopolitics of Refugee Studies: A View from the South," *Journal of Refugee Studies* 11, no. 4 (1998); for an analysis of the implementation of these practices in Uganda, see Human Rights Watch, "Hidden in Plain View: Refugees Living without Protection in Nairobi and Kampala" (New York: Human Rights Watch, 2002).

17. Hannah Arendt, *The Origins of Totalitarianism* (New York: Schocken Books, 2004), 370.

18. Ibid., 370.

19. Ibid., 371, 372, emphasis added.

20. Mark Goodale, "Introduction: Locating Rights, Envisioning Law between the Global and the Local," in *The Practice of Human Rights: Tracking Law between the Global and the Local*, ed. Mark Goodale and Sally Engle Merry (Cambridge: Cambridge University Press, 2007).

21. Yasemin Nuhoğlu Soysal, *Limits of Citizenship: Migrants and Postnational Membership in Europe* (Chicago: University of Chicago Press, 1994), 142.

22. UNHCR, "Population Statistics, Time Series, Uganda 2002," https://www.unhcr.org/refugee-statistics-uat/download/?url=8BSh; World Bank, "World Bank Databank, Population Total, Uganda, 2002," https://data.worldbank.org/indicator/SP.POP.TOTL?end=2017&locations=UG&start=2002; World Bank, "World Bank Databank GDP Per Capita PPP (Current International $), Uganda 2002," https://data.worldbank.org/indicator/NY.GDP.PCAP.PP.CD?end=2014&locations=UG&start=2002.

23. UNHCR, "Resettlement Data Finder, Canada 2005," http://rsq.unhcr.org/en/#B2Dt; World Bank, "World Bank Databank, Population Total, Canada, 2005," https://data.worldbank.org/indicator/SP.POP.TOTL?end=2005&locations=CA&start=2002&view=chart; World Bank, "World Bank Databank GDP Per Capita PPP (Current International $), Canada 2005," https://data.worldbank.org/indicator/NY.GDP.PCAP.PP.CD?end=2014&locations=CA&start=2002.

24. "Global Trends: Forced Displacement in 2020" (Geneva: UNHCR, 2021), 2.

25. "Global Trends: Forced Displacement in 2019" (Geneva: UNHCR, 2020), 3. The legal status of Venezuelans who have been displaced from Venezuela by violence, economic collapse, and limitations on human rights varies among host countries. To encompass the many terms and legal statues, UNHCR uses a category of "Venezuelans displaced abroad" in lieu of the term "refugee."

26. Jennifer Hyndman and Wenona Giles, "Waiting for What? The Feminization of Asylum in Protracted Situations," *Gender, Place and Culture: A Journal of Feminist Geography* 18, no. 3 (2011).

27. Jason K. Stearns, "North Kivu: The Background to Conflict in North Kivu Province of Eastern Congo" (London: Rift Valley Institute, 2012).

28. Interview, July 16, 2004, Nakivale refugee settlement, Uganda. One of the research participants in my longitudinal research study in Uganda died in this manner, as described by her parents in an interview.

29. James C. Hathaway, "A Global Solution to a Global Refugee Crisis," *European Papers: A Journal on Law and Integration*, no. 1 (2016); Sarah Dryden-Peterson, "Refugee Education in Countries of First Asylum: Breaking Open the Black Box of Pre-resettlement Experiences," *Theory and Research in Education* 14, no. 2 (2015).

30. Lucy Hovil, *Refugees, Conflict and the Search for Belonging* (Cham, NY: Springer International, 2016); Roger Zetter and Héloïse Ruaudel, "Refugees' Right to Work and Access to Labor Markets—an Assessment," in *KNOMAD Working Paper and Study Series* (Washington, DC: Global Knowledge Partnership on Migration and Development [KNOMAD], 2016).

31. See Hovil, *Refugees, Conflict and the Search for Belonging*, 51; Caitlin Nunn et al., "Mobility and Security: The Perceived Benefits of Citizenship for Resettled Young People from Refugee Backgrounds," *Journal of Ethnic and Migration Studies* (2015). Ecuador is another example of where citizenship for refugees is possible. In 2008, Ecuador introduced the concept of "universal citizenship" through a constitutional amendment, which grants the rights of citizens to all people of any nationality living in the country, including as related to education. In addition, refugees in Ecuador are eligible to apply for citizenship after living in Ecuador for three years, and all children of refugees born in Ecuador are citizens by birth. Despite these legal frameworks, bureaucratic obstacles and high costs prevent most refugees from accessing birth certificates and other documentation that formally establish citizenship. See Diana Rodríguez-Gómez, "Bureaucratic Encounters and the Quest for Educational Access among Colombian Refugees in Ecuador," *Journal on Education in Emergencies* 5, no. 1 (2019); Manuel Eduardo Góngora-Mera, Gioconda Herrera, and Conrad Müller, "The Frontiers of Universal Citizenship: Transnational Social Spaces and the Legal Status of Migrants in Ecuador" (Berlin: International Research Network on Interdependent Inequalities in Latin America, 2014); and Elizabeth Donger et al., "Protecting Refugee Youth in Ecuador: An Evaluation of Health and Wellbeing" (UNHCR; Harvard FXB Center for Health and Human Rights, 2017).

32. Parliament of Canada and Borys Wrzesnewskyj, "Distress Call: How Canada's Immigration Program Can Respond to Reach the Displaced and Most Vulnerable, Report of the Standing Committee on Citizenship and Immigration" (Ottawa: Parliament of Canada, House of Commons, 2016); in the United States and in the United Kingdom, there are limited provisions—Temporary Protected Status in the US and Humanitarian Leave in the UK—to grant temporary asylum at a group level related to a particular risk but only for those already within the borders of these countries. For example, Haitians in the United States at the time of the 2010 earthquake were granted TPS.

33. UNHCR, "Resettlement Fact Sheet 2014," https://www.refworld.org/docid/55aca2614.html.

34. Ibid.; UNHCR, "Global Trends: Forced Displacement in 2018" (Geneva: UNHCR, 2019).

35. Germany Federal Ministry of the Interior, "The Number of Refugees Must Be Substantially Reduced on a Permanent Basis," http://www.bmi.bund.de/SharedDocs/Kurzmeldungen/EN/2016/02/meeting-with-morgan-johansson.html;jsessionid=6E0305629BBED0BE2752A179EA6451DA.2_cid287.

36. UNHCR, "Global Trends: Forced Displacement in 2015" (Geneva: UNHCR, 2016).

37. UNHCR, "Global Trends: Forced Displacement in 2019," 73.

38. World Bank, "GDP Per Capita (Current US$), 2018 Germany, Lebanon, Uganda," https://databank.worldbank.org/source/world-development-indicators.

39. International Rescue Committee (IRC), "New IRC Analysis of US Refugee Resettlement Shows Vastly Reduced Arrivals at a Time of Record Global Need and Consistent Popular Support; Refugees Targeted by Country-of-Origin, Muslim Arrivals Facing Sharpest Decline" (New York: International Rescue Committee, 2019).

40. Letters shown to me by Charity and recorded in my fieldnotes, May 21, 2003.

41. US Census Bureau, "U.S. and World Population Clock," https://www.census.gov/popclock/; UNHCR, "Population Statistics, Time Series, United States of America, 2017," https://www.unhcr.org/refugee-statistics-uat/download/?url=9G28Rk.

42. Email from Jacques to me, dated December 1, 2011.

43. For more on different kinds of permanence and opportunities, see Michael Jackson, "Migrant Imaginaries," in *Excursions* (Durham, NC: Duke University Press, 2007).

44. Email from Jacques to me, dated February 22, 2017.

45. Telephone conversation with Jacques documented in my fieldnotes, November 16, 2020.

46. Gonzalo Sánchez-Terán, "Humanism and the Forced Confinement Crisis. Paper presented at the Workshop on Humanitarianism and Mass Migration, University of California, Los Angeles, January 18–19.

47. Alexander Betts, *Protection by Persuasion: International Cooperation in the Refugee Regime* (Ithaca, NY: Cornell University Press, 2009); E. Tendayi Achiume, "Syria, Cost-Sharing, and the Responsibility to Protect Refugees," *Minnesota Law Review* 100 (2015).

48. Chimni, "The Geopolitics of Refugee Studies," 362–63.

49. Carmen Geha and Joumana Talhouk, "From Recipients of Aid to Shapers of Policies: Conceptualizing Government–United Nations Relations during the Syrian Refugee Crisis in Lebanon," *Journal of Refugee Studies* 32, no. 4 (2018): 660.

50. Vidur Chopra, "Learning to Belong, Belonging to Learn: Syrian Refugee Youths' Pursuits of Education, Membership and Stability in Lebanon" (PhD diss., Harvard University, 2018), 96.

51. The boy's name was Alan Shenu, but I use here the name ascribed to him by the Turkish media at the time and thereafter in media reports.

52. Liz Sly, "The Ruins of Kobane: What One Small Town Says about the Destruction of Syria," *Washington Post*, November 13, 2015.

53. F. Vis and O. Goriunova, "The Iconic Image on Social Media: A Rapid Research Response to the Death of Aylan Kurdi" (London: Visual Social Media Lab, 2015), 10.

54. This simulation, called Forced from Home, was designed by Médecins sans Frontières and designed to encourage empathy for displaced people. The exhibit was in Boston in October 2016. See Alison Baitz, "Inside the Refugee Camp at the Foot of the Washington Monument," October 4, 2016, https://www.npr.org/sections /goatsandsoda/2016/10/04/496565028/inside-the-refugee-camp-at-the-foot-of -the-washington-monument.

55. A version of this poem was first published as "Conversations About Home (at the Deportation Centre)," in Warsan Shire, *Teaching My Mother How to Give Birth* (Manchester: Flipped Eye Publishing, 2011). The words as quoted here are as spoken by the author in the retitled poem "Home," accessible as audio (https://www .youtube.com/watch?v=nI9D92Xiygo) and as transcribed (https://www.facing history.org/standing-up-hatred-intolerance/warsan-shire-home).

56. Paul Slovic et al., "Iconic Photographs and the Ebb and Flow of Empathic Response to Humanitarian Disasters," *Proceedings of the National Academy of Sciences of the United States of America* 114, no. 4 (2017): 640.

57. Ibid., 641–42.

58. Vis and Goriunova, "The Iconic Image on Social Media," 11.

59. See the Dublin II Council Regulation, "establishing the criteria and mechanisms for determining the Member State responsible for examining an asylum application lodged in one of the Member States by a third-country national." European Union, "Council Regulation (EC) No. 343 / 2003," ed. European Union (2003).

60. "'Germany! Germany!' Ordinary Germans, Not Their Politicians, Have Taken the Lead in Welcoming Syria's Refugees," *The Economist*, September 12, 2015.

61. Spiegel Staff, "Two Weeks in September: The Makings of Merkel's Decision to Accept Refugees," *Spiegel Online*, August 24, 2016.

62. Jack Moore, "The Journey of Two Syrian Brothers That Ended on a Turkish Beach," *Newsweek*, September 3, 2015.

63. Dylan, "Blowin' in the Wind."

64. Barack Obama, "Remarks by President Obama at Leaders Summit on Refugees," news release, 2016, https://obamawhitehouse.archives.gov/the-press-office/2016/09/20/remarks-president-obama-leaders-summit-refugees.

65. Ibid.

66. United Nations General Assembly, "New York Declaration for Refugees and Migrants" (New York: United Nations, 2016).

67. Ibid., Articles 68, 77.

68. European Commission, "EU-Turkey Joint Action Plan," news release, October 15, 2015, http://europa.eu/rapid/press-release_MEMO-15-5860_en.htm.

69. Office of the Prime Minister and UNHCR Uganda, "Strategy Paper: Self-Reliance for Refugee Hosting Areas in Moyo, Arua, and Adjumani Districts, 1999–2006," ed. Office of the Prime Minister / UNHCR Uganda (Kampala: Government of Uganda, 1999), 10.

70. See, for example, Jeff Crisp, "Mind the Gap! UNHCR, Humanitarian Assistance and the Development Process," *New Issues in Refugee Research*, no. 43 (2001); UNHCR, "Convention Plus: Issues Paper on Targeting of Development Assistance" (Geneva: UNHCR, 2004); Gaim Kibreab, *African Refugees: Reflections on the African Refugee Problem* (Trenton, NJ: African World Press, 1983); and Robert F. Gorman, ed., *Coping with Africa's Refugee Burden: A Time for Solutions* (Dordrecht, The Netherlands: Brill, 1987).

71. Yolamu Rufunda Barongo, "Problems of Integrating Banyarwanda Refugees among Local Communities in Uganda," in *Uganda and the Problem of Refugees*, ed. A. G. G. Gingyera Pinycwa (Kampala: Makerere University Press, 1998);

Katy Long, "Rwanda's First Refugees: Tutsi Exile and International Response 1959–64," *Journal of Eastern African Studies* 6, no. 2 (2012).

72. Long, "Rwanda's First Refugees."

73. Interview with inspector of schools, Kyaka County, Kampala, April 4, 2003.

74. Interview with district education officer, Kyenjojo District, Kampala, April 25, 2003.

75. Hovil, *Refugees, Conflict and the Search for Belonging.* In urban South Africa, Loren Landau also documents the kinds of belonging that are "the products of street level pragmatism and tactics potentially framed by supra-local discursive currents and perceived opportunities" (p. 364), what he calls "estuaries" (I discuss liquid metaphors later in this chapter). He writes, "I argue that much as we must reconsider our language of migrants and hosts, in the face of fluidity and the frailty of formal institutions so too should we our language of civic, national, or municipal belonging—cultural, economic, or political—as the basis of meaningful membership and rights. At a spatial level, we must at once pan more widely and focus more locally to reveal forms of multi-sited belonging and the complex dynamics and engagements of specific sites where people negotiate multiple, and often conflicting histories and social positions" (pp. 360–61). Loren B. Landau, "Conviviality, Rights, and Conflict in Africa's Urban Estuaries," *Politics and Society* 42, no. 3 (2014).

76. Vidur Chopra and Sarah Dryden-Peterson, "Borders and Belonging: Displaced Syrian Youth Navigating Symbolic Boundaries in Lebanon," *Globalisation, Societies and Education* 18, no. 4 (2020).

77. Peggy Levitt et al., "Transnational Social Protection: Setting the Agenda," *Oxford Development Studies* 45, no. 1 (2017).

78. These interviews were conducted as follows: thirty-six in the spring of 2015; forty-nine in the fall of 2015; thirty-two in the fall of 2016; fifty-one in the fall of 2017; thirty-nine in the spring of 2019; and eighteen in the spring of 2020.

79. Interview, January 14, 2005, Lewiston, Maine.

80. Interview, October 27, 2004, Lewiston, Maine.

81. Laurier Raymond, "Mayor Appeals to Somalis to Stem Immigration," *Lewiston Sun Journal*, October 1, 2002.

82. Anna Chase Hogeland, "A City Divided: Lewiston's Acceptance and Resistance to the Somali Refugees in Lewiston, Maine from 2000 to 2011," *Maine History* 49, no. 1 (2015).

83. Interview, January 14, 2004, Lewiston, Maine.

84. CBC News, "Full Text of Justin Trudeau's Remarks Ahead of Refugees' Arrival" (2015).

85. Emails from the sponsorship group to me, on December 15, 2015, and February 28, 2018. See also Shauna Labman and Geoffrey Cameron, "What Joe Biden Can Learn from Canada's Private Refugee Sponsorship Program," *The Conversation* (2021); Michaela Hynie et al., "What Role Does Type of Sponsorship Play in Early Integration Outcomes? Syrian Refugees Resettled in Six Canadian Cities," *Refuge* 35, no. 2 (2019); and Lisa Kaida, Feng Hou, and Max Stick, "The Long-Term Economic Integration of Resettled Refugees in Canada: A Comparison of Privately Sponsored Refugees and Government-Assisted Refugees," *Journal of Ethnic and Migration Studies* 46, no. 9 (2020).

86. Julia Zorthian, "Canada Prepares to Accept First Plane of Syrian Refugees," *Time*, December 10, 2015.

87. Jennifer Ivanov, "Prime Minister Trudeau Responds to Racist, Hateful Graffiti Sprayed on Calgary School," *Global News*, February 14, 2016.

88. Mary Catherine Bateson, *Willing to Learn: Passages of Personal Discovery* (Hanover, NH: Steerforth Press, 2004), 86.

89. Liisa H. Malkki, *Purity and Exile: Violence, Memory, and National Cosmology among Hutu Refugees in Tanzania* (Chicago: University of Chicago Press, 1995), 15–16.

3. Power

1. Interview, December 13, 2013, Bujumbura, Burundi. This interview was conducted by Vidur Chopra for a collaborative project. See also Vidur Chopra and Sarah Dryden-Peterson, "More Than Words: Language as a Tool to Move from Refugee to Returnee to Citizen in Burundi?," in *Teaching Cases* (Cambridge, MA: Harvard Education Press, 2015).

2. Peter Uvin, *Life after Violence: A People's Story of Burundi*, African Arguments (London: Zed, 2009); Marc Sommers, *Fear in Bongoland: Burundi Refugees in Urban Tanzania*, Refugee and Forced Migration Studies Vol. 8 (New York: Berghahn Books, 2001); Lucy Hovil, *Refugees, Conflict and the Search for Belonging* (Cham, NY: Springer International, 2016).

3. Edward Mogire, "Refugee Realities: Refugee Rights versus State Security in Kenya and Tanzania," *Transformation* 26, no. 1 (2009): 7.

4. Barbara E. Harrell-Bond, *Imposing Aid: Emergency Assistance to Refugees* (Oxford: Oxford University Press, 1986); Guglielmo Verdirame and Barbara E. Harrell-Bond, *Rights in Exile: Janus-Faced Humanitarianism*, Studies in Forced Migration Vol. 17 (New York: Berghahn Books, 2005).

5. Mogire, "Refugee Realities," 8.

6. Ibid.

7. Interview, October 23, 2013, Ruyigi Province, Burundi. This interview was conducted by Vidur Chopra for a collaborative project.

8. Loren B. Landau, *The Humanitarian Hangover: Displacement, Aid, and Transformation in Western Tanzania* (Johannesburg: Wits University Press, 2008); Human Rights Watch, "In the Name of Security: Forced Round-Ups of Refugees in Tanzania" (New York: Human Rights Watch, 1999).

9. See also, Human Rights Watch, "Tanzania / Uganda: Prevent Forced Return of Refugees" (New York: Human Rights Watch, 2009).

10. World Bank, "World Bank Databank, School Enrollment, Secondary (% Gross), Burundi 2007," https://data.worldbank.org/indicator/SE.SEC.ENRR ?locations=BI.

11. Mark Bray, "Community Partnerships in Education: Dimensions, Variations and Implications," in *UNESCO International Consultative Forum on Education for All 2000* (Paris: UNESCO, 2000); Joel Samoff, "Institutionalizing International Influence," *Safundi: The Journal of South African and American Studies* 4, no. 1 (2007); Everard Weber, "Globalization, 'Glocal' Development, and Teachers' Work: A Research Agenda," *Review of Educational Research* 77, no. 3 (2007).

12. Keith Darden and Anna Grzymala-Busse, "The Great Divide: Literacy, Nationalism, and the Communist Collapse," *World Politics* 59, no. 1 (2006): 100.

13. Francisco O. Ramirez and John Boli, "The Political Construction of Mass Schooling: European Origins and Worldwide Institutionalization," *Sociology of Education* 60, no. 1 (1987).

14. Julia C. Lerch, S. Garnett Russell, and Francisco O. Ramirez, "Whither the Nation-State? A Comparative Analysis of Nationalism in Textbooks," *Social Forces* 96, no. 1 (2017).

15. Government of Southern Sudan, "The Transitional Constitution of the Republic of South Sudan, 2011" (Juba: Government of Southern Sudan, 2011), 3.

16. Mario Novelli et al., "Exploring the Linkages between Education Sector Governance, Inequity, Conflict, and Peacebuilding in South Sudan, Research Report Prepared for UNICEF Eastern and Southern Africa Regional Office (ESARO)" (Sussex: University of Sussex, 2016).

17. Republic of South Sudan, "Curriculum Framework South Sudan" (Juba: Republic of South Sudan, 2015), 2.

18. Between 2013 and 2017, Bethany Mulimbi and I engaged in a set of embedded research projects, including key informant interviews, observations, and interviews in four case-study schools and also participatory action research with students in three of these schools. For more on each of the studies and our findings,

see Sarah Dryden-Peterson and Bethany Mulimbi, "Pathways toward Peace? Negotiating National Unity and Ethnic Diversity through Education in Botswana," *Comparative Education Review* 61, no. 1 (2017); Bethany Mulimbi and Sarah Dryden-Peterson, "'There Is Still Peace. There Are No Wars': Prioritizing Unity over Diversity in Botswana's Social Studies Policies and Practices and the Implications for Positive Peace," *International Journal of Educational Development* 61 (2018); Bethany Mulimbi and Sarah Dryden-Peterson, "Experiences of (Dis)Unity: Students' Negotiation of Ethnic and National Identities in Botswana Schools," *Anthropology & Education Quarterly* 50, no. 4 (2019); and Bethany Mulimbi and Sarah Dryden-Peterson, "Responses to Cultural Diversity in Botswana's Schools: Links between National Policy, School Actions and Students' Civic Equality," *Journal of Curriculum Studies* (2017).

19. Sarah Dryden-Peterson et al., "In Search of Learning for All in Botswana: Equality of Opportunities, Inequity of Outcomes" (under review).

20. Dryden-Peterson and Mulimbi, "Pathways toward Peace?; Mulimbi and Dryden-Peterson, "'There Is Still Peace. There Are No Wars.'"

21. NCE, "Kagisano Ka Thuto: Education for Kagisano, Report of the National Commission on Education" (Gaborone: Government of Botswana, 1977), 210.

22. Daron Acemoglu and James A. Robinson, *Why Nations Fail: The Origins of Power, Prosperity and Poverty* (New York: Crown, 2012).

23. David Tyack, "Forming the National Character: Paradox in the Educational Thought of the Revolutionary Generation," *Harvard Educational Review* 36, no. 1 (1966): 30.

24. Mario, Novelli, "Education and Countering Violent Extremism: Western Logics from South to North?," *Compare: A Journal of Comparative and International Education* 47, no. 6 (2017): 835–851; Rodney Muhumuza, "Uganda Shuts Down 5 Madrassas over Training Extremists," *AP News* (Kampala, Uganda), 2015; Alexis Okeowo, "Teaching Anti-Extremism in Kenya," *The New Yorker*, May 26, 2016.

25. Tyack, "Forming the National Character: Paradox in the Educational Thought of the Revolutionary Generation," 31.

26. Ibid., 32.

27. Ibid., 31.

28. Curriculum outline, Massachusetts School, 2001–2002.

29. Curriculum outline, Massachusetts School, 2001–2002.

30. Letter to parents from my colleague and me, dated January 2002.

31. Written reflection to parents from my colleague and me, dated June 24, 2002.

32. This conversation took place on July 17, 2019. Hadee reviewed this text to check my reconstruction of the conversation.

33. Jal Mehta, *The Allure of Order: High Hopes, Dashed Expectations, and the Troubled Quest to Remake American Schooling*, Studies in Postwar American Political Development (New York: Oxford University Press, 2013).

34. A large body of literature critiques provisions of NCLB that hindered equity in education, including as related to teacher recruitment and retention, assessment, and military recruitment in schools. See among many, Linda Darling-Hammond, "No Child Left Behind and High School Reform," *Harvard Educational Review* 76, no. 4 (2006): 642–667; Rosa Furumoto, "No Poor Child Left Unrecruited: How NCLB Codifies and Perpetuates Urban School Militarism," *Equity & Excellence in Education* 38, no. 3 (2005): 200–210.

35. Lerch, Russell, and Ramirez, "Whither the Nation-State?"

36. Elisabeth King, *From Classrooms to Conflict in Rwanda* (New York: Cambridge University Press, 2014).

37. Sarah Warshauer Freedman et al., "Teaching History after Identity-Based Conflicts: The Rwanda Experience," *Comparative Education Review* 52, no. 4 (2008): 674–675.

38. Mulimbi and Dryden-Peterson, "Experiences of (Dis)Unity." This research in Botswana was a three-year collaborative study with Bethany Mulimbi.

39. Anne Ríos-Rojas, "Managing and Disciplining Diversity: The Politics of Conditional Belonging in a Catalonian Institut," *Anthropology & Education Quarterly* 45, no. 1 (2014): 3.

40. Dryden-Peterson and Mulimbi, "Pathways toward Peace?"

41. Interview, September 13, 2015, Kgatleng District, Botswana.

42. Mulimbi and Dryden-Peterson, "'There Is Still Peace. There Are No Wars.'"

43. Ibid.

44. Focus group, April 30, 2015, Northwest District, Botswana.

45. Ørnulf Gulbrandsen, *The State and the Social: State Formation in Botswana and Its Pre-colonial and Colonial Genealogies* (New York: Berghahn Books, 2012); Mulimbi and Dryden-Peterson, "Experiences of (Dis)Unity."

46. Statistics Botswana, "Secondary Education Statistics Brief 2014" (Gaborone, Botswana: Statistics Botswana, 2014).

47. Paul Collier and Anke Hoeffler, "Greed and Grievance in Civil War," *Oxford Economic Papers* 56, no. 4 (2004); Paul Collier, "Implications of Ethnic Diversity" (Washington, DC: World Bank, 2001); Alberto Alesina et al., "Fractionalization," *Journal of Economic Growth* 8, no. 2 (2003); Benn Eifert, Edward

Miguel, and Daniel N. Posner, "Political Competition and Ethnic Identification in Africa," *American Journal of Political Science* 54, no. 2 (2010); Acemoglu and Robinson, *Why Nations Fail;* Robin Shields and Julia Paulson, "'Development in Reverse'? A Longitudinal Analysis of Armed Conflict, Fragility and School Enrolment," *Comparative Education* (2014).

48. Institute for Economics and Peace, *Global Peace Index 2017: Measuring Peace in a Complex World* (Sydney, Australia: Institute for Economics and Peace, 2017).

49. Martin Luther King Jr., *Letter from the Birmingham Jail* (San Francisco: Harper San Francisco, 1994).

50. Johan Galtung, "Violence, Peace, and Peace Research," *Journal of Peace Research* 3 (1969).

51. On resource-based inequalities, identity-based inequalities, and parity of participation, see Nancy Fraser, "Injustice at Intersecting Scales: On 'Social Exclusion' and the 'Global Poor,'" *European Journal of Social Theory* 13, no. 3 (2010); and Nancy Fraser, "Reframing Justice in a Globalized World," in *Global Inequality,* ed. David Held and Ayse Kaya (Oxford: Oxford University Press, 2007). In connection to "relational inequalities" in institutional contexts in the field of sociology, see, for example, Donald Tomaskovic-Devey and Dustin Robert Avent-Holt, *Relational Inequalities: An Organizational Approach* (New York: Oxford University Press, 2019). On these concepts in education as connected to conflict, see Dryden-Peterson and Mulimbi, "Pathways toward Peace?"; King, *From Classrooms to Conflict in Rwanda;* and Mario Novelli, Mieke T. A. Lopes Cardozo, and Alan Smith, "The 4Rs Framework: Analyzing Education's Contribution to Sustainable Peacebuilding with Social Justice in Conflict-Affected Contexts," *Journal on Education in Emergencies* 3, no. 1 (2017).

52. Will Kymlicka and Wayne J. Norman, "Citizenship in Diverse Societies: Issues, Contexts, Concepts," in *Citizenship in Diverse Societies,* ed. W. J. Norman and Will Kymlicka (Oxford: Oxford University Press, 2000), 10.

53. Fieldnotes, November 15, 2018, Beirut, Lebanon.

54. Phillip W. Jones and David Coleman, *The United Nations and Education: Multilateralism, Development and Globalisation* (London: RoutledgeFalmer, 2005).

55. *Statute of the Office of the United Nations High Commissioner for Refugees,* chapter 1, section 1.

56. Will Ross, "Uganda Kicks out UN Man," *BBC News,* April 14, 2003.

57. John Gerard Ruggie, "The United Nations and Globalization: Patterns and Limits of Institutional Adaptation," *Global Governance* 9, no. 3 (2003).

58. See UNESCO and UNHCR, "Memorandum of Understanding between UNESCO and UNHCR on Education for Refugees" (Paris: UNESCO / UNHCR, 1984).

59. UNHCR, "Convention and Protocol Relating to the Status of Refugees" (Geneva: UNHCR, 2010).

60. Christian Morrisson and Fabrice Murtin, "The Kuznets Curve of Human Capital Inequality: 1870–2010," *Journal of Economic Inequality* 11, no. 3 (2013): 287.

61. UNHCR Inspection and Evaluation Service, "Review of UNHCR's Refugee Education Activities" (Geneva: UNHCR, 1997), 5.

62. See, for example, T. Dodds and S. Inquai, "Education in Exile: The Educational Needs of Refugees" (Cambridge: International Extension College, 1983); Margaret Sinclair, "Education in Emergencies," in *Learning for a Future: Refugee Education in Developing Countries*, ed. Jeff Crisp, Christopher Talbot, and D. B. Cipollone (Geneva: UNESCO, 2001); Kilemi Mwiria, "Kenya's Harambee Secondary School Movement: The Contradictions of Public Policy," *Comparative Education Review* 34, no. 3 (1990); and Bernard Moswela, "From Decentralisation to Centralisation of Community Secondary Schools in Botswana: A Community Disenfranchisement in Education," *International Education Journal* 8, no. 1 (2007).

63. Jo Kelcey, "Lessons Not Learned. The AFSC School Program for Palestinian Refugees in Gaza, 1949 to 1950," *Journal on Education in Emergencies* (forthcoming); Dodds and Inquai, "Education in Exile," 11; Pilar Aguilar and Gonzalo Retamal, "Protective Environments and Quality Education in Humanitarian Contexts," *International Journal of Educational Development* 29 (2009); Pethu Serote, "Solomon Mahlangu Freedom College: A Unique South African Educational Experience in Tanzania," *Transformation* 20 (1992): 49.

64. Oliver Tambo, "President O.R. Tambo's Opening Address" (paper presented at the ANC 48th National Conference, Durban, South Africa, 1991).

65. Dominic Pasura, "A Fractured Transnational Diaspora: The Case of Zimbabweans in Britain," *International Migration* 50, no. 1 (2012): 147–148.

66. Stella Tendai Makanya, "The Desire to Return: Effects of Experiences of Exile on Refugees Repatriating to Zimbabwe in the Early 1980s," in *When Refugees Go Home*, ed. Tim Allen and Hubert Morsink (Trenton, NJ: Africa World Press, 1994), 107.

67. Ibid., 113.

68. Tichatonga J. Nhundu, "The Effects of Policy Marginalization on the Implementation of a Curriculum Innovation: A Case Study of the Implementation of Education with Production in Zimbabwe," *Journal of Curriculum Studies* 29 (1997): 50; Jeremy Jackson, "Repatriation and Reconstruction in Zimbabwe during the 1980s," in *When Refugees Go Home*, ed. Tim Allen and Hubert Morsink (Trenton, NJ: Africa World Press, 1994), 150.

69. Rosemary Sayigh, *Too Many Enemies* (London: Zed Books, 1994), 17.

70. Kelcey, "Lessons Not Learned."

71. Sayigh, *Too Many Enemies,* 23, 80.

72. Sarah Dryden-Peterson, "Refugee Education: A Global Review" (Geneva: UNHCR, 2011), 37.

73. Kelcey, "Lessons Not Learned."

74. Khalil Mahshi and Kim Bush, "The Palestinian Uprising and Education for the Future," *Harvard Educational Review* 59, no. 4 (1989): 472.

75. Philipp O. Amour, "The Evolution and Implementation of a National Curriculum under Conditions of Resistance: The Case of the Palestinians (1970–1982)," *International Journal of Middle East Studies* 51, no. 1 (2019).

76. Ibid.

77. *Statute of the Office of the United Nations High Commissioner for Refugees,* chapter 1, section 2.

78. Karen Mundy, "Education for All and the New Development Compact," *International Review of Education* 52, no. 1 / 2 (2006); "Global Governance, Educational Change," *Comparative Education* 43, no. 3 (2007): 346.

79. Mundy, "Education for All and the New Development Compact," 28.

80. Ibid., 29, 35; Karen Mundy and Lynn Murphy, "Transnational Advocacy, Global Civil Society? Emerging Evidence from the Field of Education," *Comparative Education Review* 45, no. 1 (2001).

81. Roger Dale, "Globalization and Education: Demonstrating a 'Common World Educational Culture' or Locating a 'Globally Structured Educational Agenda'?," *Educational Theory* 50, no. 4 (2000): 441.

82. Joel Spring, "Research on Globalization and Education," *Review of Educational Research* 78, no. 2 (2008); Stephen Carney, Jeremy Rappleye, and Iveta Silova, "Between Faith and Science: World Culture Theory and Comparative Education," *Comparative Education Review* 56, no. 3 (2012).

83. Roger Dale, "Specifying Globalization Effects on National Policy: A Focus on the Mechanisms," *Journal of Education Policy* 14, no. 1 (1999); Roger Dale and Susan Robertson, "Toward a Critical Grammar of Education Policy Movements," in *World Yearbook of Education 2012: Policy Borrowing and Lending,* ed. Gita Steiner-Khamsi and Florian Waldow (London: Routledge, 2012).

84. Dale, "Specifying Globalization Effects on National Policy."

85. For more on structural adjustment in education and critiques, see, among many, Lawrence Summers and Lant H. Pritchett, "The Structural-Adjustment Debate," *American Economic Review* 83, no. 2 (1993); Frances Vavrus, "Adjusting Inequality: Education and Structural Adjustment Policies in Tanzania," *Harvard Educational Review* 75, no. 2 (2005); and Karen Mundy and Antoni Verger, "The

World Bank and the Global Governance of Education in a Changing World Order," *International Journal of Educational Development* 40 (2015). On connections between international aid and security interests, particularly in conflict settings, see Mario Novelli, "Education, Conflict and Social (In)Justice: Insights from Colombia," *Educational Review* 62, no. 3 (2010); Mario Novelli, "The Role of Education in Peacebuilding: Case Study—Sierra Leone" (New York: UNICEF, 2011); and Dana Burde, *Schools for Conflict or for Peace in Afghanistan* (New York: Columbia University Press, 2014).

86. John W. Meyer et al., "World Society and the Nation-State," *American Journal of Sociology* 103, no. 1 (1997).

87. Gita Steiner-Khamsi, "Understanding Policy Borrowing and Lending: Building Comparative Policy Studies," in *Policy Borrowing and Lending: World Yearbook of Education 2012*, ed. Gita Steiner-Khamsi and Florian Waldow (London: Routledge, 2012).

88. Ibid.

89. UNHCR, "Review of Upper Level Education: Assistance in Four African Countries" (Geneva: UNHCR, 1985).

90. UNHCR, "Organizing Primary Education for Refugee Children in Emergency Situations: Guidelines for Field Managers" (Geneva: UNHCR, 1988).

91. United Nations, "Convention on the Rights of the Child" (1989), Article 28.

92. World Conference on Education for All, "World Declaration on Education for All" (Jomtien, Thailand: World Conference on Education for All, 1990).

93. United Nations Treaty Collection, "Status of Treaties. Chapter V Refugees and Stateless Persons, 2. Convention Relating to the Status of Refugees, Geneva, 28 July 1951," in *United Nations Treaty Collection* (New York: United Nations, 2017).

94. Pierre Centlivres and Micheline Centlivres-Demont, "The Afghan Refugees in Pakistan: A Nation in Exile," *Current Sociology* 36, no. 88 (1988): 72.

95. Rüdiger Schöch, "Afghan Refugees in Pakistan during the 1980s: Cold War Politics and Registration Practice," in *New Issues in Refugee Research* (Geneva: UNHCR, 2008).

96. Centlivres and Centlivres-Demont, "The Afghan Refugees in Pakistan," 75.

97. For further discussion of the origins of and accountability for refugee camps, see UNHCR, "The State of the World's Refugees 2000: Fifty Years of Humanitarian Action" (Geneva: UNHCR, 2000); Verdirame and Harrell-Bond, *Rights in Exile*; Gil Loescher, *The UNHCR and World Politics: A Perilous Path* (Oxford: Oxford University Press, 2001); and Zachary Lomo, "Refugee Camps: In Search of the Locus of the Accountability of the United Nations High Commissioner for

Refugees (UNHCR) under International Law" (PhD diss., Osgoode Hall Law School, York University, 2020).

98. Alex de Waal, "The Humanitarians' Tragedy: Escapable and Inescapable Cruelties," *Disasters* 34, no. S2 (2010): S136.

99. Alexander Betts, *Protection by Persuasion: International Cooperation in the Refugee Regime* (Ithaca, NY: Cornell University Press, 2009); Alexander Betts, *Survival Migration: Failed Governance and the Crisis of Displacement* (Ithaca, NY: Cornell University Press, 2013).

100. UNHCR, "Education Field Guidelines" (Geneva: UNHCR, 2003).

101. Centlivres and Centlivres-Demont, "The Afghan Refugees in Pakistan."

102. Ibid., 88–89.

103. Adele Jones, "Curriculum and Civil Society in Afghanistan," *Harvard Educational Review* 79, no. 1 (2009): 115.

104. Tony Waters and Kim Leblanc, "Refugees and Education: Mass Public Schooling without a Nation-State," *Comparative Education Review* 49, no. 2 (2005).

105. UNHCR, "Revised Guidelines for Educational Assistance to Refugees" (Geneva: UNHCR, 1995); UNHCR, "Refugee Children: Guidelines on Protection and Care" (Geneva: UNHCR, 1994); UNHCR, "Guidelines for Educational Assistance to Refugees" (Geneva: UNHCR, 1992); UNHCR, "Organizing Primary Education for Refugee Children in Emergency Situations."

106. UNHCR, "Refugee Children," chapter 1.

107. Interview, April 13, 2011, by Skype.

108. Tom Kuhlman, "Responding to Protracted Refugee Situations: A Case Study of Liberian Refugees in Cote d'Ivoire" (Geneva: UNHCR, 2002), 3.

109. Ninette Kelley, Peta Sandison, and Simon Lawry-White, "Enhancing UNHCR's Capacity to Monitor the Protection, Rights and Well-Being of Refugees, Main Report" (Geneva: UNHCR Evaluation and Policy Analysis Unit, 2004), 27.

110. Interview, April 7, 2011, by Skype.

111. UNHCR Inspection and Evaluation Service, "Review of UNHCR's Refugee Education Activities," 1.

112. Interviews, 7 April 2011, 13 April 2011, 19 April 2011, all by Skype.

113. UNHCR Inspection and Evaluation Service, "Review of UNHCR's Refugee Education Activities," 1.

114. UNHCR Education Unit, "Report on Statistics of UNHCR-Assisted Refugee Education 2000" (Geneva: UNHCR Education Unit, Health and Community Development Section, 2002).

115. UNHCR, "Revised Guidelines for Educational Assistance to Refugees."

116. Xavier Devictor and Quy-Toan Do, "How Many Years Have Refugees Been in Exile?" *Population and Development Review* 43, no. 2 (2017); James Milner

and Gil Loescher, "Responding to Protracted Refugee Situations: Lessons from a Decade of Discussion" (Oxford: Refugee Studies Centre, University of Oxford, 2011); N. Crawford et al., "Protracted Displacement: Uncertain Paths to Self-Reliance in Exile" (London: Overseas Development Institute, 2015).

117. Jonny Steinberg, *A Man of Good Hope* (New York: Alfred A. Knopf, 2014), 25–26.

118. UNHCR and UNICEF, "Joint Strategy for Education in Dadaab, 2012–2015" (Dadaab, Kenya: UNHCR, UNICEF, CARE, Windle Trust, AVSI, ADEO, NRC, National Council of Churches Kenya, Save the Children, Handicap International, GiZ, FilmAid, 2011), 6.

119. Interview, June 25, 2014, Kakuma, Kenya. This interview was conducted by Michelle J. Bellino for a collaborative project.

120. Njogu Marangu, Josephine Gitome, and Irene Njogu, "Background of Education in Dadaab," in *Borderless Higher Education for Refugees Workshop* (Kampala, Uganda, 2011).

121. Sarah Dryden-Peterson, Negin Dahya, and Elizabeth Adelman, "Pathways to Educational Success among Refugees: Connecting Local and Global Resources," *American Educational Research Journal* 54, no. 6 (2017).

122. Christine Monaghan, "Educating for Durable Solutions? Histories of Schooling in Kenya's Dadaab and Kakuma Reufgee Camps" (PhD diss., University of Virginia, 2015); Christine Monaghan, *Educating for Durable Solutions: Histories of Schooling in Kenya's Dadaab and Kakuma Refugee Camps* (New York: Bloomsbury Academic, 2021).

123. Office of the Prime Minister / UNHCR Uganda, "Strategy Paper: Self Reliance for Refugee Hosting Areas in Moyo, Arua, and Adjumani Districts, 1999–2005" (Kampala: Government of Uganda / UNHCR, 1999).

124. Interview, April 1, 2003, UNHCR Community Services / Education Coordination Meeting, Entebbe, Uganda.

125. Office of the Prime Minister (Directorate of Refugees), Planning and Economic Development Ministry of Finance, Ministry of Education and Sports, and UNHCR, "Consultative Workshop for Integration of Education Service Delivery" (Kampala, 2001), 5.

126. Office of the United Nations Resident Co-ordinator in Uganda, "Uganda: Promise, Performance and Future Challenges (Common Country Assessment of the United Nations Agencies Working in Uganda)" (Kampala: United Nations System in Uganda, 2000), 27.

127. Office of the Prime Minister / UNHCR Uganda, "Strategy Paper," 32.

128. Dorothy Jobolingo, "Mid Year Progress Report: Education 2002" (Kampala: UNHCR BO-Kampala, 2002).

129. Office of the Prime Minister (Directorate of Refugees), Planning and Economic Development Ministry of Finance, Ministry of Education and Sports, and UNHCR, "Consultative Workshop," annex 1, p. 30.

130. Interview, April 1, 2003, UNHCR Community Services / Education Coordination Meeting, Entebbe, Uganda.

131. Office of the Prime Minister (Directorate of Refugees), Planning and Economic Development Ministry of Finance, Ministry of Education and Sports, and UNHCR, "Consultative Workshop," annex 1, p. 30.

132. Interview, July 3, 2004, Kyaka II refugee settlement, Uganda.

133. Interviews, April 9, 2003 and July 22, 2005, Kyaka II refugee settlement, Uganda

134. Interview, July 1, 2004, Kyaka II refugee settlement, Uganda.

135. Letter to me, dated March 22, 2005.

136. Conversation, documented in fieldnotes, June 21, 2004, Kampala, Uganda.

137. Conversations, documented in fieldnotes, June 28, 2004, Kyaka II refugee settlement, Uganda.

138. Interview, July 1, 2004, Kyaka II refugee settlement, Uganda.

139. Class observation, June 22, 2005, Kyaka II refugee settlement, Uganda.

140. Interview, July 1, 2004, Kyaka II refugee settlement, Uganda.

141. With thanks to Zachary Lomo for pointing out that there is a connection to God in the Ugandan anthem that is important to many Ugandans. Annette did not interpret the anthem in this way. As she explained it, she was putting her future in the hands of the state, of Uganda.

4. Purpose

1. Aliyah participated in a comparative case-study project, conducted as a research-practice partnership between UNHCR and Harvard University. This research took place over three years (2012 to 2014) in collaboration with my then doctoral students Elizabeth Adelman, Michelle J. Bellino, and Vidur Chopra, as well as students in for-credit graduate courses on education in armed conflict. Our dataset comprised global refugee education-policy documents, as well as interviews (n = 147) and observations related to policy and practice in fourteen refugee-hosting countries: Bangladesh, Chad, Egypt, Ethiopia, Iran, Kenya, Lebanon, Malaysia, Pakistan, Rwanda, South Sudan, Sudan, Uganda, and Yemen. For more on the methods of this project, see Sarah Dryden-Peterson et al., "The Purposes of Refugee Education: Policy and Practice of Including Refugees in National Education Systems," *Sociology of Education* (2019), including the online appendix.

2. L. Scott Mills et al., "Camouflage Mismatch in Seasonal Coat Color Due to Decreased Snow Duration," *Proceedings of the National Academy of Sciences* (2013).

3. Interview, August 19, 2019, Cairo, Egypt. This interview was conducted by Elizabeth Adelman for a collaborative project.

4. United Nations, "The Global Compact on Refugees" (New York: United Nations, 2018), 13; UNHCR, "Refugee Education 2030: A Strategy for Inclusion" (Geneva: UNHCR, 2019).

5. Email to me, dated September 23, 2011.

6. Ibid.

7. The UNHCR Executive Committee is a body of UN member-states that meets once a year to advise the UN High Commissioner on Refugees on priorities, approve budgets, and plan yearly programs of work.

8. Email to me, dated October 2, 2011.

9. António Guterres, "High Commissioner's Closing Remarks to 62nd Session of Excom" (Geneva: UNHCR, 2011).

10. UNHCR, "Education Strategy 2012–2016" (Geneva: UNHCR, 2012), 8.

11. Email to me, dated November 16, 2011.

12. Ibid.

13. Interview, April 2014, by Skype. Interview conducted by Brian Dooley under my supervision in the context of a for-credit class at the Harvard Graduate School of Education.

14. Fieldnotes, November 14, 2013, UNHCR Strategy coordination meeting, Kuala Lumpur, Malaysia. Observation conducted by Vidur Chopra for a collaborative project.

15. UNHCR, "Part II: Guidance for the Preparation of National-Level Refugee Education Strategies and the Consultative Process" (Geneva: UNHCR, 2013).

16. For a more detailed discussion of this shift in rhetoric, see Sarah Dryden-Peterson et al., "Integrating Education for Refugees in National Systems," in *Global Education Monitoring Report 2019: Migration, Education, and Displacement* (Paris: UNESCO, 2018).

17. In early 2020, the refugee education policies in Bangladesh changed to include possibilities of small-scale pilots of access to the national curriculum, yet these plans were stalled with the onset of the Covid-19 pandemic. See Amnesty International, "Bangladesh: Rohingya Children Get Access to Education" (Amnesty International, 2020).

18. Fieldnotes, November 14, 2013, UNHCR Strategy coordination meeting, Kuala Lumpur, Malaysia. Observation conducted by Vidur Chopra for a collaborative project.

19. Ibid.

20. UNHCR, "Global Trends: Forced Displacement in 2016" (Geneva: UNHCR, 2017), 135–139.

21. United Nations General Assembly, "New York Declaration for Refugees and Migrants," 1, 2.

22. UNHCR, "Resettlement Fact Sheet 2014," https://www.refworld.org /docid/55aca2614.html.

23. UNHCR, "Resettlement Data Finder," https://rsq.unhcr.org/en/#Ou8A.

24. Interview, October 2010, Kuala Lumpur, Malaysia. This interview was conducted by Joanna Rahman for a collaborative project, also with Marion Fresia.

25. Interviews with student and family and observations at his home, November 29, 2002, June 26, 2004, and August 9, 2005.

26. This conversation took place on April 26, 2018, in Oslo, Norway. The student reviewed this text to check my reconstruction of the conversation.

27. Interview, July 1, 2004, Kyaka II refugee settlement, Uganda.

28. Ibid.

29. Interview and observation, June 20, 2005, Kyaka II refugee settlement, Uganda.

30. Interview, July 1, 2004, Kyaka II refugee settlement, Uganda.

31. Interview, July 17, 2014, Kigeme refugee camp, Rwanda. This interview was conducted by Vidur Chopra for a collaborative project

32. Interview by Elizabeth Adelman, October 26, 2015, Beqaa, Lebanon. Used with permission.

33. Interview, July 28, 2013, Toronto, Canada.

34. Ibid.

35. UNHCR, "Operations Plan: Kenya" (Nairobi: UNHCR, 2014).

36. Interview, November 1, 2013, Toronto, Canada. This interview was conducted by Negin Dahya for a collaborative project.

37. Interview, July 27, 2013, Nairobi, Kenya. This interview was conducted by Negin Dahya for a collaborative project.

38. Interview, August 13, 2013, Nairobi, Kenya. This interview was conducted by Negin Dahya for a collaborative project.

39. Interview, August 6, 2013, Dadaab, Kenya. This interview was conducted by Negin Dahya for a collaborative project.

40. Interview, August 12, 2013, Dadaab, Kenya. This interview was conducted by Negin Dahya for a collaborative project.

41. Interview by Elizabeth Adelman, December 15, 2015, Beqaa, Lebanon. Used with permission.

42. Interview, June 25, 2014, Kakuma, Kenya. This interview was conducted by Michelle J. Bellino for a collaborative project.

43. Email to me, dated November 10, 2015.

44. UNHCR, "Refugee Education 2030."

45. Ibid., 10.

46. Interview, July 23, 2014, Kigali, Rwanda. This interview was conducted by Vidur Chopra for a collaborative project.

47. Interview, July 22, 2014, Kigali, Rwanda. This interview was conducted by Vidur Chopra for a collaborative project.

48. Interview, July 17, 2014, Kigeme, Rwanda. This interview was conducted by Vidur Chopra for a collaborative project.

49. Interview, July 22, 2014, Kigali, Rwanda. This interview was conducted by Vidur Chopra for a collaborative project.

50. Interview, July 15, 2014, Gihembe, Rwanda. This interview was conducted by Vidur Chopra for a collaborative project.

51. Interview, June 30, 2014, Nairobi, Kenya. This interview was conducted by Michelle J. Bellino for a collaborative project.

52. Interview, July 7, 2014, Nairobi, Kenya. This interview was conducted by Michelle J. Bellino for a collaborative project.

53. Interview, June 30, 2014, Nairobi, Kenya. This interview was conducted by Michelle J. Bellino for a collaborative project.

54. Interview, June 26, 2014, Kakuma, Kenya. This interview was conducted by Michelle J. Bellino for a collaborative project.

55. Interview, July 22, 2005, Kyaka II refugee settlement, Uganda.

56. Michael Barnett, "Humanitarian Governance," *Annual Review of Political Science* 16 (2013).

57. Ibid.; Barbara E. Harrell-Bond, *Imposing Aid: Emergency Assistance to Refugees* (Oxford: Oxford University Press, 1986).

58. Patricia Buck and Rachel Silver, *Educated for Change? Muslim Refugee Women in the West*, Education Policy in Practice: Critical Cultural Studies (Charlotte, NC: Information Age, 2012), 306; Tony Waters and Kim Leblanc, "Refugees and Education: Mass Public Schooling without a Nation-State," *Comparative Education Review* 49, no. 2 (2005); Alexander de Waal, *Famine Crimes: Politics and the Disaster Relief Industry in Africa*, African Issues (Bloomington: Indiana University Press, 1997).

59. Sarah Dryden-Peterson, "Refugee Education: The Crossroads of Globalization," *Educational Researcher* 45, no. 9 (2016).

60. Barnett, "Humanitarian Governance," 391, 383.

61. Ibid., 385–386.

62. Sarah Dryden-Peterson et al., "The Purposes of Refugee Education: Policy and Practice of Including Refugees in National Education Systems," *Sociology of Education* 92, no. 4 (2019).

63. Global Education Monitoring Report, "Aid to Education Is Stagnating and Not Going to Countries Most in Need" (Paris: UNESCO, 2017), 7–8.

64. Interview, July 18, 2014, Kigeme, Rwanda. This interview was conducted by Vidur Chopra for a collaborative project.

65. Interview, August 12, 2014, Cairo, Egypt. This interview was conducted by Elizabeth Adelman for a collaborative project.

66. Lebanon Ministry of Education and Higher Education, "RACE II Fact Sheet" (Beirut: Ministry of Education and Higher Education, 2018), 5.

67. UNICEF, UNHCR, and UNESCO, "2018–2019 Out of School Mapping" (Beirut: UNHCR, UNICEF, and UNESCO, 2018).

68. Lebanon Ministry of Education and Higher Education, "RACE II Fact Sheet," 2.

69. "Memo No. 136/2018: Standard Operating Procedures of Second Shift Schools' Administration—General Illustrative Instructions and Guidelines (English Translation)" (Beirut: Ministry of Education and Higher Education, 2018), 1–2.

70. United Nations, "The Global Compact on Refugees."

71. E. Tendayi Achiume, "The Postcolonial Case for Rethinking Borders," *Dissent Magazine* Summer (2019); Dryden-Peterson et al., "The Purposes of Refugee Education."

72. Dryden-Peterson et al., "The Purposes of Refugee Education"; Lucy Hovil, *Refugees, Conflict and the Search for Belonging* (Cham: Springer International, 2016); Katy Long, *The Point of No Return: Refugees, Rights, and Repatriation* (Oxford: Oxford University Press, 2013).

73. Roger Zetter and Héloïse Ruaudel, "Refugees' Right to Work and Access to Labor Markets—an Assessment," in *KNOMAD Working Paper and Study Series* (Washington, DC: Global Knowledge Partnership on Migration and Development [KNOMAD], 2016)

74. Interview by Elizabeth Adelman, December 12, 2015, Beqaa, Lebanon. Used with permission.

75. Interview, February 15, 2019, Beirut, Lebanon. This interview was conducted by Vidur Chopra and Joumana Talhouk for a collaborative project.

76. Interview, February 5, 2019, Beirut, Lebanon. This interview was conducted by Joumana Talhouk for a collaborative project.

77. Ibid.

78. Interview, March 20, 2019, Beirut, Lebanon. This interview was conducted by Joumana Talhouk for a collaborative project.

79. Interview, February 13, 2019, Beirut, Lebanon. This interview was conducted by Joumana Talhouk for a collaborative project.

80. Interview, February 5, 2019, Beirut, Lebanon. This interview was conducted by Joumana Talhouk for a collaborative project.

81. Michelle J. Bellino and Sarah Dryden-Peterson, "Inclusion and Exclusion within a Policy of National Integration: Refugee Education in Kenya's Kakuma Refugee Camp," *British Journal of Sociology of Education* 40, no. 2 (2018).

82. Ibid.

83. Kenya National Bureau of Statistics and Society for International Development—East Africa, "Exploring Kenya's Inequality Pulling Apart or Pooling Together?" (Nairobi: Kenya National Bureau of Statistics and Society for International Development—East Africa, 2013).

84. Benjamin Piper et al., "Are Refugees Learning? Early Grade Literacy Outcomes in a Refugee Camp in Kenya," *Journal on Education in Emergencies* 5, no. 2 (2020).

85. Interview, June 24, 2014, Kakuma, Kenya. This interview was conducted by Michelle J. Bellino for a collaborative project.

86. Interview, July 17, 2014, Kigeme, Rwanda. This interview was conducted by Vidur Chopra for a collaborative project.

87. Interview, August 20, 2014, Cairo, Egypt. This interview was conducted by Elizabeth Adelman for a collaborative project.

88. Interview, February 27, 2014, by Skype. Interview conducted by Zohra Manjee under my supervision in the context of a for-credit class at the Harvard Graduate School of Education.

89. Interview, April 16, 2014, by Skype. Interview conducted by Chris Del Vecchio under my supervision in the context of a for-credit class at the Harvard Graduate School of Education.

90. CERD, "Statistical Bulletin for the Academic Year" (Beirut: CERD, 2016); Lebanon Ministry of Education and Higher Education, "Race Lebanon: Presentation to Education Partners Meeting" (Beirut: MEHE, 2017).

91. Francisco O. Ramirez and John Boli, "The Political Construction of Mass Schooling: European Origins and Worldwide Institutionalization," *Sociology of Education* 60, no. 1 (1987).

92. Julia C. Lerch, S. Garnett Russell, and Francisco O. Ramirez, "Whither the Nation-State? A Comparative Analysis of Nationalism in Textbooks," *Social Forces* 96, no. 1 (2017).

93. Ibid.

94. Anthony Appiah, *Cosmopolitanism: Ethics in a World of Strangers*, Issues of Our Time (New York: W. W. Norton, 2006); Jeffrey S. Dill, *The Longings*

and Limits of Global Citizenship Education: The Moral Pedagogy of Schooling in a Cosmopolitan Age, Routledge Advances in Sociology (New York: Routledge, 2013); Rubén Gaztambide-Fernández and Dennis Thiessen, "Fomenting Flows and Internationalizing Curriculum Studies," *Curriculum Inquiry* 42, no. 1 (2012).

95. James A. Banks, "Diversity, Group Identity, and Citizenship Education in a Global Age," *Educational Researcher* 37, no. 3 (2008); Heela Goren and Miri Yemini, "Citizenship Education Redefined—a Systematic Review of Empirical Studies on Global Citizenship Education," *International Journal of Educational Research* 82 (2017).

96. This research in Lebanon was a partnership among the Peace Research Institute of Oslo, the American University of Beirut, and the Harvard Graduate School of Education, funded by the Research Council of Norway (project number 274650). The research, conducted between October 2018 and May 2019, included collaboration with Cindy Horst, Carmen Geha, Joumana Talhouk, and Vidur Chopra, and ongoing conversations with NGOs working on refugee education in Lebanon and with the Ministry of Education and Higher Education and their teacher coaches. The data includes 101 classroom observations in three schools (2 public and 1 private), 3 interviews each with 18 Syrian students, including an identity-mapping exercise (54 total interviews), interviews with 15 parents and 18 teachers, a focus group with 5 students, and 75 student writing prompts.

97. For further discussion of the response of Arab Gulf NGOs' engagement with Syrian refugees in Lebanon, see Estella Carpi, "Different Shades of 'Neutrality': Arab Gulf NGO Responses to Syrian Refugees in Northern Lebanon," in *Refuge in a Moving World: Tracing Refugee and Migrant Journeys across Disciplines,* ed. Elena Fiddian-Qasmiyeh (London: UCL Press, 2020).

98. Interview, February 14, 2019, Beirut, Lebanon. This interview was conducted by Vidur Chopra and Joumana Talhouk for a collaborative project.

99. Interview, February 12, 2019, Beirut, Lebanon. This interview was conducted by Vidur Chopra and Joumana Talhouk for a collaborative project.

100. Class observation, February 2, 2019, Beirut, Lebanon. This observation was conducted by Vidur Chopra and Joumana Talhouk for a collaborative project and documented in fieldnotes.

101. Class observation, February 6, 2019, Beirut, Lebanon. This observation was conducted by Vidur Chopra and Joumana Talhouk for a collaborative project and documented in fieldnotes.

102. Class observation, January 26, 2019, Beirut, Lebanon. This observation was conducted by Joumana Talhouk for a collaborative project and documented in fieldnotes.

103. School observation, November 12, 2018, documented in fieldnotes.

104. Interview, February 8, 2019, Beirut, Lebanon. This interview was conducted by Vidur Chopra and Joumana Talhouk for a collaborative project.

105. Ibid.

106. Jenny Erpenbeck, *Go, Went, Gone* (New York: New Directions, 2017), 241.

5. Learning

1. This quote is from Steve Biko and Aelred Stubbs, *I Write What I Like* (San Francisco: Harper and Row, 1986).

2. I reconstructed this portrait based on interviews, informal conversations, and observations with Siyabulela and his grandmother in their home, between July 1998 and September 2002. During this time, Siyabulela attended two schools: one was part of my larger research project on history teaching in South African schools, the site of data collection in 1998 and in 2019; the other school I know about only from conversations with Siyabulela.

3. This book was originally published in 1988 and sold 85,000 copies in South Africa. Its market success has been described as a "publishing coup" and reflective of the public demand for new versions of South African history; I have found no documentation on how widespread its use was in schools. See Leslie Witz and Carolyn Hamilton, "Reaping the Whirlwind: The *Reader's Digest Illustrated History of South Africa* and Changing Popular Perceptions of History," *South African Historical Journal* 24, no. 1 (1991).

4. Specific references to history content are derived from the *Interim Syllabus for History Ordinary Grade, Standards 5, 6 and 7*. This was an unpublished document from the Department of Education, Western Cape, in January 1995. Other interactions are drawn from fieldnotes made during my ethnographic observations at Siyabulela's school and in his home between 1998 and 2002.

5. Pam Christie, *The Right to Learn: The Struggle for Education in South Africa*, A People's College Book (Braamfontein, South Africa / Johannesburg: Ravan Press / Sached Trust, 1985).

6. Peter Kallaway, *The History of Education under Apartheid, 1948–1994: The Doors of Learning and Culture Shall Be Opened*, History of Schools and Schooling (New York: Peter Lang, 2002).

7. For more on the history and impacts of this photo, see Aryn Baker and *Time* Staff, "This Photo Galvanized the World against Apartheid. Here's the Story Behind It," *Time Magazine*, June 15, 2016.

8. African National Congress, "A Policy Framework for Education and Training" (Johannesburg: African National Congress, 1994).

9. Interview, July 29, 1998, Cape Town, South Africa.

10. Interview, July 29, 1998, Cape Town, South Africa.

11. H. A. Mocke and H. C. Wallis, *Exploring History 7*, 5th ed. (Pretoria: Via Afrika, 1993), 79–80.

12. This conversation took place on July 29, 1998.

13. Nancy Fraser, "Injustice at Intersecting Scales: On 'Social Exclusion' and the 'Global Poor,'" *European Journal of Social Theory* 13, no. 3 (2010).

14. James A. Banks, "Diversity, Group Identity, and Citizenship Education in a Global Age," *Educational Researcher* 37, no. 3 (2008).

15. Amy Gutmann, "Unity and Diversity in Democratic Multicultural Education: Creative and Destructive Tensions," in *Diversity and Citizenship Education: Global Perspectives*, ed. James A. Banks (San Francisco: Jossey-Bass, 2004), 80. See also, Sarah Warshauer Freedman et al., "Teaching History after Identity-Based Conflicts: The Rwanda Experience," *Comparative Education Review* 52, no. 4 (2008); Julia Paulson, "'Whether and How?' History Education about Recent and Ongoing Conflict: A Review of Reseach," *Journal on Education in Emergencies* 1, no. 1 (2015).

16. Julia C. Lerch, S. Garnett Russell, and Francisco O. Ramirez, "Whither the Nation-State? A Comparative Analysis of Nationalism in Textbooks," *Social Forces* 96, no. 1 (2017).

17. Chana Teeger, "'Both Sides of the Story': History Education in Post-apartheid South Africa," *American Sociological Review* 80, no. 6 (2015).

18. Johan Galtung, "Violence, Peace, and Peace Research," *Journal of Peace Research* 3 (1969): 170–171.

19. Interview, February 6, 2006, Kyaka II refugee settlement, Uganda.

20. UNHCR, "Refugee Education 2030: A Strategy for Inclusion" (Geneva: UNHCR, 2019).

21. Consultation meeting, September 14, 2018, by WebEx, documented in fieldnotes.

22. Consultation meeting, September 5, 2018, by WebEx, documented in fieldnotes.

23. Consultation meeting, September 14, 2018, by WebEx, documented in fieldnotes.

24. Consultation meeting, September 5, 2018, by WebEx, documented in fieldnotes.

25. Ibid.

26. Ibid.

27. Interview, March 14, 2019, Beirut, Lebanon. This interview was conducted by Joumana Talhouk for a collaborative project.

28. For a summary related to refugees, see Celia Reddick and Sarah Dryden-Peterson, "Refugee Education and Medium of Instruction: Tensions in Theory, Policy and Practice," in *Language Issues in Comparative Education*, ed. Carolyn Benson and Kimmo Kosonen (Boston: Sense Publishers, 2021).

29. Comment on draft report coauthored with Celia Reddick, January 2, 2018, by email.

30. For more on practices of productive conflict in schools and community settings, see, among many, John Paul Lederach, "Beyond Violence: Building Sustainable Peace," in *The Handbook of Interethnic Coexistence*, ed. Eugene Weiner (New York: Continuum, 1998); Kathy Bickmore, Ahmed Salehin Kaderi, and Ángela Guerra-Sua, "Creating Capacities for Peacebuilding Citizenship: History and Social Studies Curricula in Bangladesh, Canada, Colombia, and México," *Journal of Peace Education* 14, no. 3 (2017); Monisha Bajaj, "'Pedagogies of Resistance' and Critical Peace Education Praxis," *Journal of Peace Education* 12, no. 2 (2015); Michelle J. Bellino, "So That We Do Not Fall Again: History Education and Citizenship in 'Postwar' Guatemala," *Comparative Education Review* 60, no. 1 (2016); Sean Higgins and Mario Novelli, "Rethinking Peace Education: A Cultural Political Economy Approach," *Comparative Education Review* 64 (2020); Tejendra Pherali, Mai Abu Moghli, and Elaine Chase, "Educators for Change: Supporting the Transformative Role of Teachers in Contexts of Mass Displacement," *Journal on Education in Emergencies* 5 (2020).

31. Elisabeth King, *From Classrooms to Conflict in Rwanda* (New York: Cambridge University Press, 2014).

32. Freedman et al., "Teaching History after Identity-Based Conflicts."

33. Ibid., 674–675.

34. Interview, April 28, 1998, Cape Town, South Africa.

35. Ibid.

36. Ibid.

37. On the changing nature of history curriculum and teaching in South Africa, see Department of Basic Education, "Curriculum and Assessment Policy Statement Grades 10–12: History" (Pretoria: Department of Basic Education, 2011); Daniel Hammett and Lynn Staeheli, "Transition and the Education of the New South African Citizen," *Comparative Education Review* 57, no. 2 (2013); Teeger, "'Both Sides of the Story.'"

38. Sarah Dryden-Peterson and Natasha Robinson, "Post-Conflict History Education and Social Transformation: Continuity and Change in a South African School, 1998 and 2019" (under review).

39. Observation, February 11, 2019, documented in fieldnotes. This interview was conducted by Natasha Robinson for a collaborative project.

40. Interview, December 20, 2018, Beirut, Lebanon. This interview was conducted by Joumana Talhouk for a collaborative project.

41. Class observation, November 19, 2018, Beirut, Lebanon. This observation was conducted by Vidur Chopra and Joumana Talhouk for a collaborative project and documented in fieldnotes.

42. Class observation, December 6, 2018, Beirut, Lebanon. This observation was conducted by Vidur Chopra and Joumana Talhouk for a collaborative project and documented in fieldnotes.

43. Interview, December 20, 2018, Beirut, Lebanon. This interview was conducted by Joumana Talhouk for a collaborative project.

44. Interview, February 8, 2019, Beirut, Lebanon. This interview was conducted by Vidur Chopra and Joumana Talhouk for a collaborative project.

45. This conversation took place on July 17, 2019. Hadee reviewed the text to check my reconstruction of the conversation.

46. Alex Hutchinson, *Endure: Mind, Body, and the Curiously Elastic Limits of Human Performance* (New York: William Morrow, 2018).

47. Terrence Lyons, "Conflict-Generated Diasporas and Transnational Politics in Ethiopia," *Conflict, Security and Development* 7, no. 4 (2007); Jennifer M. Brinkerhoff, "Diasporas and Conflict Societies: Conflict Entrepreneurs, Competing Interests or Contributors to Stability and Development?," *Conflict, Security and Development* 11, no. 2 (2011); Nauja Kleist, "Mobilising 'the Diaspora': Somali Transnational Political Engagement," *Journal of Ethnic and Migration Studies* 34, no. 2 (2008).

48. Amartya Kumar Sen, *Development as Freedom* (New York: Oxford University Press, 1999); Brinkerhoff, "Diasporas and Conflict Societies."

49. Interview, December 12, 2013, by telephone.

50. Ibid.

51. See also Dana Burde, *Schools for Conflict or for Peace in Afghanistan* (New York: Columbia University Press, 2014).

52. Ibid.

53. Interviews, May 13, 2014, and May 19, 2014, by telephone. These interviews were conducted by Irene Liefshitz for a collaborative project.

54. Ibid.

55. See Haiti Constitution of 1806, Article 36.

56. Interview, November 6, 2013, Cambridge, Massachusetts. This interview was conducted by Irene Liefshitz for a collaborative project.

57. See also USAID, "Haiti Education Fact Sheet," in *Education Fact Sheet* (2016).

58. Interview, July 16, 2014, by telephone. This interview was conducted by Irene Liefshitz for a collaborative project.

59. Interview, December 12, 2013, by telephone.

60. Assata Shakur, *Assata: An Autobiography* (Chicago: L. Hill Books, 2001).

61. Burde, *Schools for Conflict or for Peace in Afghanistan;* King, *From Classrooms to Conflict in Rwanda;* Keith Takayama, Arathi Sriprakash, and Raewyn Connell, "Toward a Postcolonial Comparative and International Education," *Comparative Education Review* 61 (2017).

62. Michael Barnett, "Humanitarian Governance," *Annual Review of Political Science* 16 (2013).

63. Benjamin Piper, "International Education Is a Broken Field: Can Ubuntu Education Bring Solutions?," *International Review of Education* (2016); Francine Menashy, "Multi-stakeholder Aid to Education: Power in the Context of Partnership," *Globalisation, Societies and Education* (2017); Susan Cotts Watkins, Ann Swidler, and Thomas Hannan, "Outsourcing Social Transformation: Development NGOs as Organizations," *Annual Review of Sociology* 38 (2012).

64. Henry Shue, "Mediating Duties," *Ethics* 98, no. 4 (1988): 689.

65. Ibid., 689–690.

66. Ibid., 690.

67. Ibid., 702.

68. Maxine Greene, "Public Education and the Public Space," *Educational Researcher* 11, no. 6 (1982): 9.

69. "Curriculum and Consciousness," *Teachers College Record* 73, no. 2 (1971).

6. Belonging

1. Interview, August 1, 2013, Dadaab, Kenya. This interview was conducted by Negin Dahya for a collaborative project.

2. UNHCR, "Dadaab: World's Biggest Refugee Camp 20 Years Old" (Geneva: UNHCR, 2012).

3. UNHCR, "Operations Plan: Kenya" (Nairobi: UNHCR, 2014).

4. The Student Refugee Program of World University Service Canada resettles about 130 refugee students each year to Canada and, in partnership with student groups on university campuses, supports their university education. See www .srp.wusc.ca.

5. Turner documents how a group of refugees established public authority in the Lukole refugee camp in Tanzania in 1997–1998 and shows the ways in which humanitarian governance creates logics of dependence including through the

narrative that "UNHCR can create pure victims in need of help" (761). Simon Turner, "Negotiating Authority between UNHCR and 'the People,'" *Development and Change* 37, no. 4 (2006).

6. Poem by Adbi, given to me in hard copy, dated March 28, 2003, time 3:07 a.m.

7. Barbara E. Harrell-Bond, *Imposing Aid: Emergency Assistance to Refugees* (Oxford: Oxford University Press, 1986); Roger Zetter, "Protection in Crisis: Forced Migration and Protection in a Global Era" (Washington, DC: Migration Policy Institute, 2015); Neil Boothby, "Political Violence and Development: An Ecologic Approach to Children in War Zones," *Child and Adolescent Psychiatric Clinics of North America* 17, no. 3 (2008).

8. Robert D. Putnam, *Bowling Alone: The Collapse and Renewal of American Community* (New York: Simon and Schuster, 2000); Pierre Bourdieu, "The Forms of Capital," in *Handbook for the Theory and Research for the Sociology of Education,* ed. John G. Richardson (New York: Greenwood Press, 1986).

9. In addition to work in anthropology, like that of Anna Tsing, which focuses on transnational relationships, there is a well-developed sociology of migration focused on economic, social, and political processes of transnationalism among migrants living in North America and Europe and the ties they maintain with their communities of origin. See, for example, Douglas S. Massey et al., *Return to Aztlan: The Social Processes of International Migration from Western Mexico* (Berkeley: University of California Press, 1987); Thomas Faist and Margit Fauser, "The Migration–Development Nexus: Toward a Transnational Perspective," in *The Migration-Development Nexus: A Transnational Perspective,* ed. Thomas Faist, Margit Fauser, and Peter Kivisto (New York: Palgrave Macmillan, 2011); and Peggy Levitt, *The Transnational Villagers* (Berkeley: University of California Press, 2001). And as related to education, see, for example, Gabrielle Oliveira, *Motherhood across Borders: Immigrants and Their Children in Mexico and New York* (New York: New York University Press, 2018); Alejandra Cox Edwards and Manuelita Ureta, "International Migration, Remittances, and Schooling: Evidence from El Salvador," *Journal of Development Economics* 72, no. 2 (2003). There is a smaller literature on refugee transnationalism and diasporic ties, see, for example, Jennifer M. Brinkerhoff, "Diasporas and Conflict Societies: Conflict Entrepreneurs, Competing Interests or Contributors to Stability and Development?," *Conflict, Security and Development* 11, no. 2 (2011); Cindy Horst, *Transnational Nomads* (Oxford: Berghahn, 2006); and Nicholas Van Hear, "Refugees, Diasporas, and Transnationalism," in *The Oxford Handbook of Refugee and Forced Migration Studies,* ed. Elena Fiddian-Qasmiyeh et al. (Oxford: Oxford University Press, 2014). And as related to refugee transnation-

alism and education, see, for example, Sarah Dryden-Peterson and Celia Reddick, "'What I Believe Can Rescue That Nation': Diaspora Working Transnationally to Transform Education in Fragility and Conflict," *Comparative Education Review* (2019).

10. Anna Lowenhaupt Tsing, *Friction: An Ethnography of Global Connection* (Princeton, NJ: Princeton University Press, 2005).

11. Ibid., 271.

12. Urie Bronfenbrenner, *The Ecology of Human Development: Experiments by Nature and Design* (Cambridge, MA: Harvard University Press, 1979).

13. Interview, November 1, 2013, Ottawa, Canada. This interview was conducted by Negin Dahya for a collaborative project.

14. Interview, August 6, 2013, Dadaab, Kenya. This interview was conducted by Negin Dahya for a collaborative project.

15. Interview, November 2, 2013, Ottawa, Canada. This interview was conducted by Negin Dahya for a collaborative project.

16. Interview, August 7, 2013, Dadaab, Kenya. This interview was conducted by Negin Dahya for a collaborative project.

17. Interview, November 2, 2013, Ottawa, Canada. This interview was conducted by Negin Dahya for a collaborative project.

18. Interview, June 28, 2013, Toronto, Canada. This interview was conducted by Negin Dahya for a collaborative project.

19. Interview, November 2, 2013, Ottawa, Canada. This interview was conducted by Negin Dahya for a collaborative project.

20. Ibid.

21. Interview, August 13, 2013, Nairobi, Kenya. This interview was conducted by Negin Dahya for a collaborative project. "DAFI," the short and commonly used name for the Albert Einstein German Academic Refugee Initiative, supports higher education scholarships for refugees and returned refugees in their country of origin or host country.

22. See, for example, Michelle J. Bellino, "Youth Aspirations in Kakuma Refugee Camp: Education as a Means for Social, Spatial, and Economic (Im)Mobility," *Globalisation, Societies and Education* (2018); Patricia Buck and Rachel Silver, *Educated for Change? Muslim Refugee Women in the West*, Education Policy in Practice: Critical Cultural Studies (Charlotte, NC: Information Age, 2012).

23. Interview, August 13, 2013, Nairobi, Kenya. This interview was conducted by Negin Dahya for a collaborative project.

24. Interview, August 3, 2013, Dadaab, Kenya. This interview was conducted by Negin Dahya for a collaborative project. While there is a growing literature on

tutoring and its role in the privatization of education, students described that these tutoring and support relationships were free. For more on private tutoring, often called "extra tuition," in Kenya and beyond, see Will Brehm, *Cambodia for Sale: Everyday Privatization in Education and Beyond* (Milton: Taylor and Francis, 2021); Laura Paviot, Nina Heinsohn, and Julia Korkman, "Extra Tuition in Southern and Eastern Africa: Coverage, Growth, and Linkages with Pupil Achievement," *International Journal of Educational Development* 28, no. 2 (2008).

25. Interview, August 1, 2013, Dadaab, Kenya. This interview was conducted by Negin Dahya for a collaborative project.

26. Interview, November 1, 2013, Ottawa, Canada. This interview was conducted by Negin Dahya for a collaborative project.

27. Interview, July 12, 2013, Toronto, Canada. This interview was conducted by Negin Dahya for a collaborative project.

28. Interview, June 28, 2013, Toronto, Canada. This interview was conducted by Negin Dahya for a collaborative project.

29. Marco Antonsich, "Searching for Belonging—an Analytical Framework," *Geography Compass* 4, no. 6 (2010); N. Yuval-Davis, "Belonging and the Politics of Belonging," *Patterns of Prejudice* 40, no. 3 (2006).

30. Liisa H. Malkki, *Purity and Exile: Violence, Memory, and National Cosmology among Hutu Refugees in Tanzania* (Chicago: University of Chicago Press, 1995), 35.

31. Interview, November 1, 2013, Ottawa, Canada. This interview was conducted by Negin Dahya for a collaborative project.

32. Interview, November 2, 2013, Ottawa, Canada. This interview was conducted by Negin Dahya for a collaborative project.

33. Interview, August 13, 2013, Nairobi, Kenya. This interview was conducted by Negin Dahya for a collaborative project.

34. Interview, July 27, 2013, Nairobi, Kenya. This interview was conducted by Negin Dahya for a collaborative project.

35. Ubuntu is stressed in African philosophy, African theology, and African sociology. See, for example, Kwame Gyekye, *Tradition and Modernity: Philosophical Reflections on the African Experience* (New York: Oxford University Press, 1997); Paulin J. Hountondji, *African Philosophy: Myth and Reality*, 2nd ed., African Systems of Thought (Bloomington: Indiana University Press, 1996); Kwasi Wiredu, *Philosophy and an African Culture* (Cambridge: Cambridge University Press, 1980); G. M. Setiloane, *The Image of God among the Sotho-Tswana* (Rotterdam: A. A. Balkema, 1976); Desmond Tutu, *No Future without Forgiveness* (London: Rider and Random House, 1999); Placide Tempels, *Bantu Philosophy* (Paris: Présence Afric-

aine, 1959); John S. Mbiti, *African Religions and Philosophy* (Oxford: Heinemann, 1990); Kopano Ratele, *Inter-group Relations: South African Perspectives* (Cape Town: Juta, 2006); P. Gobodo-Madikizela, *A Human Being Died That Night—a Story of Forgiveness* (Cape Town: David Philip, 2003); and I. N. M Goduka and E. B. Swadenar, *Affirming Unity in Diversity in Education: Healing with Ubuntu* (Cape Town: Juta Academic, 1999).

36. Nomonde Masina, "Xhosa Practices of Ubuntu for South Africa," in *Traditional Cures for Modern Conflicts: African Conflict "Medicine,"* ed. I. William Zartman (Boulder, CO: Lynne Rienner, 2000).

37. See Tim Murithi, "A Local Response to the Global Human Rights Standard: The Ubuntu Perspective on Human Dignity," *Globalisation, Societies and Education* 5, no. 3 (2007): 281.

38. Steve Biko and Aelred Stubbs, *I Write What I Like* (San Francisco: Harper and Row, 1986), 42.

39. Mluleki Mnyaka and Mokgethi Motlhabi, "The African Concept of Ubuntu / Botho and Its Socio-moral Significance," *Black Theology: An International Journal* 3, no. 2 (2005).

40. Masina, "Xhosa Practices of Ubuntu for South Africa," 170.

41. Julius Mutugi Gathogo, "The Challenge and Reconstructive Impact of African Religion in South Africa Today," *Journal of Ecumenical Studies* 43, no. 4 (2008).

42. Antjie Krog, "'This Thing Called Reconciliation': Forgiveness as Part of an Interconnectedness-towards-Wholeness," *South African Journal of Philosophy* 27, no. 4 (2008): 354.

43. See http://www.ubuntucola.com.

44. Ørnulf Gulbrandsen, *The State and the Social: State Formation in Botswana and Its Pre-colonial and Colonial Genealogies* (New York: Berghahn, 2012). While kgotla are originally Tswana institutions, other ethnic groups have participated in them, in varying capacities, since precolonial times. Yet, like in all institutions, there are limits to who is included in the collective and with what power; women, for example, were historically excluded from kgotla. See, for example, Lily Mafela, "Batswana Women and Law: Society, Education and Migration (C. 1840–C. 1980)," *Cahiers d'études africaines* (2007).

45. Truth and Reconciliation Commission, "Truth and Reconciliation Commission of South Africa Report" (Truth and Reconciliation Commission of South Africa, 1998).

46. Leonhard Praeg, "An Answer to the Question: What Is [Ubuntu]?," *South African Journal of Philosophy* 27, no. 4 (2008).

47. Krog, "'This Thing Called Reconciliation,'" 357.

48. For more on how communalism has evolved and changed in the United States, see, among many, Putnam, *Bowling Alone*.

49. Mnyaka and Motlhabi, "The African Concept of Ubuntu / Botho and Its Socio-moral Significance."

50. I collected data in Lewiston, Maine, between October 2004 and May 2005, including eight interviews with public officials and school and civic leaders (October 27, 2004; November 1, 2004; January 12, 2005; January 14, 2005), school observations (November 8, 2004; November 16, 2004; November 18, 2004; November 23, 2004) and interviews with Hassan and Michelle, both individually and together (November 16, 2004; November 18, 2004; November 23, 2004).

51. Interview, November 16, 2004, Lewiston, Maine.

52. Samantha Power, *A Problem from Hell: America and the Age of Genocide* (New York: Basic Books, 2002).

53. See Chapter 2, "Sanctuary," for more context on Somali migration to Lewiston.

54. Interview, November 18, 2004, Lewiston, Maine.

55. Ibid.

56. Interview, November 23, 2004, Lewiston, Maine.

57. Ibid.

58. Ibid.

59. Roger D. McGrath, "Coming to America: The Great Somali Welfare Hunt," *American Conservative,* November 18, 2002.

60. Interview, November 23, 2004, Lewiston, Maine.

61. Ibid.

62. D. G. Solorzano and T. J. Yosso, "Critical Race Methodology: Counter-Storytelling as an Analytical Framework for Education Research," *Qualitative Inquiry* 8, no. 1 (2002): 36.

63. Thandeka K. Chapman, "Expressions of 'Voice' in Portraiture," *Qualitative Inquiry* 11 (2005): 48.

64. Dolores Delgado Bernal, "Critical Race Theory, Latino Critical Theory, and Critical Raced-Gendered Epistemologies: Recognizing Students of Color as Holders and Creators of Knowledge," *Qualitative Inquiry* 8 (2002): 116.

65. J. C. Turner et al., *Rediscovering the Social Group: A Self-Categorization Theory* (Oxford: Basil Blackwell, 1987), 34.

66. In his work on young people navigating becoming adults amid violence and war in Guinea-Bissau, Henrik Vigh describes this kind of navigation, as the "complex political praxis of moving toward a goal while at the same time being moved

by a socio-political environment." Henrik Vigh, *Navigating Terrains of War: Youth and Soldiering in Guinea-Bissau*, Methodology and History in Anthropology (New York: Berghahn, 2006), 236.

67. Interview, February 8, 2019.

68. Fieldnotes, April 10, 2003.

69. From UNHCR-Kampala, "Refugee Statistics as End of December 2002" (Kampala: UNHCR, 2003).

70. In 2002, a United Nations report to the secretary-general identified five Canadian companies involved in illegal mining in DRC. United Nations Security Council, "Final Report of the Panel of Experts on the Illegal Exploitation of Natural Resources and Other Forms of Wealth of the Democratic Republic of the Congo" (New York: United Nations, 2002).

71. This took place on December 4, 2015.

72. C. Michael Lanphier, "Host Program Evaluation: Overview" (Toronto: York University and Settlement Directorate, Immigration Section, Ontario Region, Immigration Canada, 1993).

73. Citizenship and Immigration Canada, "Evaluation of the Host Program" (Ottawa: Citizenship and Immigration Canada, 2010); Government of Canada, "Immigration and Refugee Protection Act" (Ottawa: Government of Canada, 2001 [last amended on June 21, 2019]), 2.

74. Interview, December 4, 2005, Beirut, Lebanon. This interview was conducted by Vidur Chopra and Joumana Talhoul for a collaborative project.

75. Interview, December 3, 2005, Toronto, Canada.

76. Interview, December 5, 2005, Toronto, Canada.

77. Interview, December 2, 2005, Toronto, Canada.

78. Interview, December 3, 2005, Toronto, Canada.

79. Interview, December 4, 2005, Toronto, Canada.

80. Interview, June 20, 2006, Toronto, Canada.

81. Interview, June 16, 2006, Toronto, Canada.

82. Ibid.

83. Ibid.

Epilogue

1. Poem by Adbi, given to me in hard copy, dated March 28, 2003, time 3:07 a.m.

2. UNHCR, "Global Trends: Forced Displacement in 2020," (Geneva: UNHCR, 2021), 2.

3. Fieldnotes, April 10, 2003, Kyaka II refugee settlement, Uganda.

4. Email to me, dated March 6, 2012.

5. "Reading the world" is from Paulo Freire, *Pedagogy of the Oppressed* (New York: Continuum, 2000).

6. Langston Hughes, "Montage of a Dream Deferred," in *The Collected Poems Of Langston Hughes*, ed. David Roessel and Arnold Rampersad (New York: A.A. Knopf, 1995), 387–388.

7. Gerald E. Wickens, *The Baobabs: Pachycauls of Africa, Madagascar and Australia* (Dordrecht: Springer Netherlands, 2007).

8. Conversation with Siyabulela, March 21, 2004.

Appendix

1. Some of the details of this day were corroborated through a conversation with Igor Kuperman on January 14, 2019 and Zheyna Stekovic on June 21, 2021.

2. See also Steve Springer, "The NHL: To Keep His Job, He Had to Censor Himself," *Los Angeles Times*, March 13, 1991.

3. "Exclusive Interview: Gorbachev Says He'll Fight on, but He's Already a Man without a Country," *Time*, December 23, 1991.

4. Ken Dryden, *The Game*, 20th anniversary ed. (New York: Wiley, 2003), 208–209.

5. See also work on the concept of "listening" as a political act and as a way of sharing power, both in academic work and in the public sphere, including Astra Taylor, "The Right to Listen: As Citizens of a Democracy, We Need to Hear One Another. Why Can't We?," *New Yorker*, January 27, 2020; and Leah Bassel, *The Politics of Listening: Possibilities and Challenges for Democratic Life* (London: Palgrave Macmillan, 2017).

6. For more on the critical intersection between who one is, ways of knowing, and, ultimately, what is knowable, see Pierre Bourdieu and Loïc J. D. Wacquant, *An Invitation to Reflexive Sociology* (Chicago: University of Chicago Press, 1992); John D. Brewer, *Ethnography*, Understanding Social Research (Philadelphia, PA: Open University Press, 2000); Michael Burawoy, "The Extended Case Method," *Sociological Theory* 16, no. 1 (1998); Anselm Strauss and Juliet Corbin, *Basics of Qualitative Research: Techniques and Procedures for Developing Grounded Theory* (Thousand Oaks, CA: SAGE, 1998).

7. Sara Lawrence-Lightfoot and Jessica Hoffmann Davis, *The Art and Science of Portraiture* (San Francisco: Jossey-Bass, 1997), 41.

8. Conversation, March 24, 2003, documented in fieldnotes, Kyaka II refugee settlement, Uganda.

9. Daniel Bertaux, "From the Life-History Approach to the Transformation of Sociological Practice," in *Biography and Society: The Life History Approach in the Social Sciences*, ed. Daniel Bertaux (Beverly Hills, CA: SAGE, 1981), 39.

10. Conversation, March 28, 2003, documented in fieldnotes, Kyaka II refugee settlement, Uganda.

11. Lesley Bartlett and Frances Vavrus, *Rethinking Case Study Research: A Comparative Approach* (New York: Routledge, 2017), 1. See also ideas connected to transnational social fields, traveling resources, transnational social protection, relational ethnography, and multisited ethnography including, for example, Anna Lowenhaupt Tsing, *Friction: An Ethnography of Global Connection* (Princeton, NJ: Princeton University Press, 2005); Peggy Levitt et al., "Transnational Social Protection: Setting the Agenda," *Oxford Development Studies* 45, no. 1 (2017); Matthew Desmond, "Relational Ethnography," *Theory and Society* 43, no. 5 (2014); and George E. Marcus, *Ethnography through Thick and Thin* (Princeton, NJ: Princeton University Press, 1998).

12. These other studies include a set of interviews designed to understand experiences of language among Burundian refugees returning to Tanzania (with Vidur Chopra, 2013); a research and training project in collaboration with the University of Nairobi and the International Rescue Committee that looked at content and pedagogy of refugee education in the Kakuma refugee camp and Nairobi, Kenya (with Mary Mendenhall, Lesley Bartlett, Caroline Ndirangu, Rosemary Imonje, Daniel Gakunga, Loise Gichuhu, Grace Nyagah, Ursulla Okoth, and Mary Tangelder, 2013–2015); and archival research at the Library and Archives of the United Nations Office of Geneva, the Archives of UNHCR, and within the Education Unit at UNHCR, including education reports, strategies, policies, and internal documents from 1951 to the present (n = 214).

13. This approach sees the empirical substance of the research as driving the choice of methods. See also Michèle Lamont and Ann Swidler, "Methodological Pluralism and the Possibilities and Limits of Interviewing," *Qualitative Sociology* (2014). They contend that "each technique has its own limitations and advantages and that a technique does not have agency: all depends on what one does with it, what it is used for. In other words, there are no good and bad techniques of data collection; there are only good and bad questions, and stronger and weaker ways of using each method" (2).

14. For more on the methods of this study, see Sarah Dryden-Peterson, *Education of Refugees in Uganda: Relationships between Setting and Access* (Refugee Law

Project, 2003); Sarah Dryden-Peterson and Lucy Hovil, "A Remaining Hope for Durable Solutions: Local Integration of Refugees and Their Hosts in the Case of Uganda," *Refuge* 22 (2004); Sarah Dryden-Peterson, "'I Find Myself as Someone Who Is in the Forest': Urban Refugees as Agents of Social Change in Kampala, Uganda," *Journal of Refugee Studies* 19 (2006); Sarah Dryden-Peterson, "The Present Is Local, the Future Is Global? Reconciling Current and Future Livelihood Strategies in the Education of Congolese Refugees in Uganda," *Refugee Survey Quarterly* 25 (2006); Sarah Dryden-Peterson, "Refugee Children Aspiring toward the Future: Linking Education and Livelihoods," in *Educating Children in Conflict Zones: Research, Policy, and Practice for Systemic Change (a Tribute to Jackie Kirk)*, ed. Karen Mundy and Sarah Dryden-Peterson (New York: Teachers College Press, 2011); and Sarah Dryden-Peterson, "Refugee Education: Education for an Unknowable Future," *Curriculum Inquiry* 47, no. 1 (2017).

15. Lamont and Swidler, "Methodological Pluralism and the Possibilities and Limits of Interviewing," 8.

16. For more on the methods of this study, see Sarah Dryden-Peterson, "Bridging Home: Building Relationships between Immigrant and Long-Time Resident Youth," *Teachers College Record* 112, no. 9 (2010).

17. For more on the methods of this study, see Sarah Dryden-Peterson, "Social Networks and the Hidden Job Market: The Role of Bridging Social Capital in the Integration of Highly-Skilled Newcomers in Canada" (qualifying paper, Harvard Graduate School of Education, 2006).

18. For more on the methods of this study, in both the article and the online methodological appendix, see Sarah Dryden-Peterson et al., "The Purposes of Refugee Education: Policy and Practice of Including Refugees in National Education Systems," *Sociology of Education* (2019).

19. For more on the methods of this study, in both the article and the online methodological appendix, see Sarah Dryden-Peterson, Negin Dahya, and Elizabeth Adelman, "Pathways to Educational Success among Refugees: Connecting Local and Global Resources," *American Educational Research Journal* 54, no. 6 (2017).

20. For more on asset-based and desire-based approaches to research in education, see Eve Tuck, "Suspending Damage: A Letter to Communities," *Harvard Educational Review* 79, no. 3 (2009).

21. For more on the methods of this study, see Sarah Dryden-Peterson and Celia Reddick, "'What I Believe Can Rescue That Nation': Diaspora Working Transnationally to Transform Education in Fragility and Conflict," *Comparative Education Review* (2019).

22. For more on the methods of this study, see Sarah Dryden, "Mirror of a Nation in Transition: Teachers and Students in Cape Town Schools" (MPhil diss.,

University of Cape Town, 1999); and Sarah Dryden-Peterson and Rob Siebörger, "Teachers as Memory Makers: Testimony in the Making of a New History in South Africa," *International Journal of Educational Development* 26, no. 4 (2006).

23. For more on the methods of this study, see Sarah Dryden-Peterson, "Transitions: Researchers' Positionality and Malleability of Site and Self over Time," *Harvard Educational Review* 90, no. 1 (2020).

24. For more on the methods of this set of studies, see Sarah Dryden-Peterson and Bethany Mulimbi, "Pathways toward Peace? Negotiating National Unity and Ethnic Diversity through Education in Botswana," *Comparative Education Review* 61, no. 1 (2017); Bethany Mulimbi and Sarah Dryden-Peterson, "Responses to Cultural Diversity in Botswana's Schools: Links between National Policy, School Actions and Students' Civic Equality," *Journal of Curriculum Studies* (2017); Bethany Mulimbi and Sarah Dryden-Peterson, "'There Is Still Peace. There Are No Wars': Prioritizing Unity over Diversity in Botswana's Social Studies Policies and Practices and the Implications for Positive Peace," *International Journal of Educational Development* 61 (2018); and Bethany Mulimbi and Sarah Dryden-Peterson, "Experiences of (Dis)Unity: Students' Negotiation of Ethnic and National Identities in Botswana Schools," *Anthropology and Education Quarterly* 50, no. 4 (2019).

25. Irving Seidman, *Interviewing as Qualitative Research*, 3rd ed. (New York: Teachers College Press, 2006).

26. Beth Harry, Keith M. Sturges, and Janette K. Klingner, "Mapping the Process: An Exemplar of Process and Challenge in Grounded Theory Analysis," *Educational Researcher* 34, no. 2 (2005).

27. See, for example, J. Gerring, "What Is a Case Study and What Is It Good For?," *American Political Science Review* 98, no. 2 (2004); Alexander L. George and Andrew Bennett, *Case Studies and Theory Development in the Social Sciences*, BCSIA Studies in International Security (Cambridge, MA: MIT Press, 2005); Peter Hedström and Petri Ylikoski, "Causal Mechanisms in the Social Sciences," *Annual Review of Sociology* 36 (2010); Charles C. Ragin, *Fuzzy-Set Social Science* (Chicago: University of Chicago Press, 2000); Bartlett and Vavrus, *Rethinking Case Study Research*.

28. Bruno Latour, *Reassembling the Social: An Introduction to Actor-Network-Theory*, Clarendon Lectures in Management Studies (Oxford: Oxford University Press, 2005).

29. John McPhee, "Elicitation," *New Yorker*, April 7, 2014.

30. Email to me, dated February 16, 2018.

31. Conversation, July 2, 2011, by telephone, documented in fieldnotes.

32. Letter to me, dated March 22, 2005.

33. Skype message to me, April 21, 2020; WhatsApp message to me, December 3, 2019.

34. Listening notes, July 24, 2013, done collaboratively with Bethany Mulimbi.

35. Listening notes, March 3, 2016, done collaboratively with Elizabeth Adelman.

36. WhatsApp message to me, April 4, 2019.

37. WhatsApp message to me, May 14, 2019.

38. James E. Ryan, *Wait, What?: And Life's Other Essential Questions* (New York: HarperOne, 2017).

39. Email to me, dated October 7, 2020.

40. Email to me, dated October 26, 2020.

41. Email to me, dated July 17, 2016.

Acknowledgments

Bringing a book to life requires communities of learning and belonging who listen, nurture, share, resist, and love. I am grateful to these communities who have shaped me, my thinking, and this book. It is an arc of thanks, one that stretches from the small and intimate spaces of family and home to classrooms and schools close by and far away where I met strangers who I came to know as teachers, students, parents, and visionaries. Many of these people are visibly present in the pages of the book, as I sought to make more transparent how research happens, how ideas take shape, and the kind of collective learning that develops in time spent together. Even when unnamed for reasons of confidentiality, you can, I hope, see yourselves embedded.

Thank you to each person who participated in this research. Thank you for your trust in me, to use the privileges that I have to navigate across spaces, to help in weaving together among places and time the strands of your powerful local conversations and actions. Your courage, generosity, engagement, and commitment are not only daily inspiration but also the impetus to build more just and peaceful education and futures through each and every relationship and action.

Conversations sustained over many years have nurtured the thinking in this book, and me. While swimming, around office tables, on FaceTime, in cafés, on long drives, or while we bounced our own and each other's babies, thank you Mehana Blaich Vaughn, Nicole Shepardson, Lori Chodos,

Ryhna Thompson, Cathy Oh, Bethany Good, Karen Mundy, Lesley Bartlett, Mary Mendenhall, Negin Dahya; and for taking these conversations into shared work now and in the future, thank you Elizabeth Adelman, Michelle J. Bellino, Vidur Chopra, Cindy Horst, Francine Menashy, Bethany Mulimbi, Benjamin Piper, Celia Reddick, Natasha Robinson, Hiba Salem. I so admire the capacious teachers, discerning writers, engaged scholars, and good love-filled people you are.

Thank you to my colleagues at the Harvard Graduate School of Education (HGSE), who have supported me with deep intellectual community and who have, together, embraced linking research, teaching, and practice in ways I know we collectively hope inspire our students and the field. Thank you Gretchen Brion-Meisels, Irene Liefshitz, Dana McCoy, Jal Mehta, Matt Miller, Nonie Lesaux, Meira Levinson, Bridget Terry Long, Felipe Barrera-Osorio, Fernando Reimers, Julie Reuben, Jim Ryan, Catherine Snow, Paola Uccelli. Thank you, Sara Lawrence-Lightfoot, for being steadfast and full of grace in your teaching and mentoring throughout. Thank you, Wendy Angus, for being as up for a conversation about the kids we love who play hockey as for inclusive choice of words as for supporting our students.

Thank you also to colleagues who have shown me that cross-institution and transnational academic community is possible, and wonderful: at the University of Botswana, Nkobi Owen Pansiri; at the University of Nairobi (Kenya), the late Caroline Ndirangu; at Makerere University (Uganda) and the Refugee Law Project, Lucy Hovil, Zachary Lomo, Kyohairwe Sylvia, and Silas Oluka; at the American University of Beirut (Lebanon), Carmen Geha and Joumana Talhouk; and Kathy Bickmore, Dana Burde, Don Dippo, Marion Fresia, Wenona Giles, Mario Novelli, Rebecca Winthrop.

Thank you to the many students who have brought their minds and their passions to this work and to conversations about it; I hope to have contributed to your learning as much as you each have to mine: students in Education in Armed Conflict and Education in Uncertainty at HGSE over the past decade; research assistant Katy Bullard; students working with the Refugee REACH Team, including Dagan Rossini, Hellen Zziwa, Bethany Dill, Aybahar Qarqeen, Sarzah Yeasmin; teaching team members Elizabeth Adelman, Alysha Banerji, Ranya Brooks, Michelle J. Bellino, Shelby Carvalho, Vidur Chopra, Amy Cheung, Bibi-Zuhra Faizi, Jessica Fei, Orelia Jonathan, Hania Mariën, Eva Flavia Martinez Orbegozo, Celia Reddick, Deepa Vasudevan, Eleanor (Nell) O'Donnell Weber; and all of the members of our Mowana Lab community, past and present, Maya Alkateb-Chami, Elizabeth Adelman, Michelle J. Bellino, Shelby Carvalho, Alexandra Chen, Amy Cheung, Vidur Chopra, Pierre de Galbert, Bibi-Zuhra Faizi, Martha Franco, Orelia Jonathan, Hania Mariën, Bethany Mulimbi, Celia Reddick, Natasha Robinson, Hiba Salem, Timothy Williams, Eleanor (Nell) O'Donnell Weber, Deepa Vasudevan, and the sixteen children we have among us to teach and love collectively.

Thank you to those who work daily in policy and practice to expand opportunities in refugee education who have shared with me your hopes, your questions, your dilemmas, and have trusted me to work alongside you: Jeff Crisp, Ita Sheehy, Ann Scowcroft, Margaret Sinclair, Chris Talbot, Jackie Strecker, Fadi Yarak, Suha Tutunji, Mary Winters, Adam Turney, Maysa Jalbout, Mialy Dermish, Manos Antoninis, and others at the United Nations High Commissioner for Refugees, UNICEF, UNESCO, the Windle Trust, the International Rescue Committee, and Save the Children.

For invitations to share and receive the gift of critical feedback and dialogue on parts of this work, I thank: at Harvard University, the Weatherhead Center for International Affairs, the Center for African Studies, the FXB Center for Health and Human Rights, the Harvard Humanitarian Initiative, and the Harvard Graduate School of Education; the Brookings Institution, particularly Rebecca Winthrop; the University of Minnesota, particularly Fran Vavrus; the National Academy of Education and the Spencer Foundation; the Peace Research Institute of Oslo (PRIO), particularly Cindy Horst; the University of Wisconsin-Madison, particularly Lesley Bartlett; the Oxford University Department of Education, particularly David Mills; the Center for Lebanese Studies, particularly Maha Shuayb; the University of Pennsylvania, particularly Dan Wagner; University College London Institute of Education, particularly Tejendra Pherali; the American University of Beirut, particularly Carmen Geha; the Georg Arnhold Symposium on Education and Sustainable Peace, particularly Jennifer Riggan; the Migration Policy Institute, particularly Randy Capps; the Migration Lab of the Princeton Institute for International and Regional Studies and the Study Group for Language and the United Nations.

Thank you to the many colleagues and friends who read sections of, or all of, the manuscript. The book is stronger and truer to its purposes with your ideas and suggestions as well as those of three anonymous reviewers; Jacques; and the most thought-provoking book conference group I could hope for, Jacqueline Bhabha, Kathy Bickmore, Zachary Lomo, Noah Sobe, Hiro Yoshikawa. At Harvard University Press, I am grateful to Andrew Kinney, my editor, who listened deeply, probed wisely and then, like great teachers, trusted me to apply the new thinking. Thank you to the HUP team, including Mihaela Pacurar, Stephanie Vyce, and Lisa Roberts; and mapmaker Isabelle Lewis, and compass artist Jaclyn Reyes. Thanks also to production editor Angela Piliouras at Westchester Publishing Services.

Thank you to the institutions that have taken their time and lent their guidance to approvals of research, including: Harvard University, the University of Botswana, the University of Cape Town, the University of Toronto; the United Nations High Commissioner for Refugees; the Uganda National Council of Science and Technology; the National Council for Science and Technology of Kenya; the Republic of Botswana and the Permanent Secretary Ministry of Education; the Western Cape (South Africa) Education Department; the Ministry of Education and Higher Education of Lebanon; and schools and community organizations in each site of work.

Thank you to the funders who have believed in this work: the Fulbright Commission; the Mellon Foundation Migration and Urbanization

Node of the University of the Witwatersrand; the Rotary Foundation; the Research Council of Norway (No.274650); the National Academy of Education and Spencer Foundation; the Social Sciences and Humanities Research Council of Canada; the United Nations High Commissioner for Refugees (UNHCR) under a Research-Practice Project Partnership Agreement; the Cheng Yu Tung Education Innovation Research Fund; the Harvard Research Enabling Grant; the Harvard University William F. Milton Fund; the Harvard Weatherhead Center for International Affairs; the Harvard University Center for African Studies; and the Harvard Graduate School of Education.

Thank you to my own teachers who with their listening, probing, and shared commitments to good work that makes a difference have made me a better teacher, scholar, and parent: Grandpa Dryden and Grandpa Curran, who gave me stamps and told me stories that opened a wider world; my uncle and school principal, Dave, who trusted me to translate his school motto into Latin when I was thirteen and is the kind of teacher kids flock to like geese; my parents-in-love, Sheila and Pete, my aunt, Jill, and my cousin, Deb, who bring to family meals stories of their delight at being teachers and their love for their students; my brother Michael and siblings-in-love Tammy, Heather, and Kirk, with whom we have grown as the most intimate of teachers—as parents—in our fierce love and endless hope for these five and the ways they will help create the future; and those who, in classrooms, have taught me, who I taught with, and who have taught our children: Mrs. Marr, Mr. Baker, Ms. Smythe, Dr. Mann, Rob Siebörger, Bertram Qobo, Steve Cohen, Soo Hong, Mark Warren, John Willett, Tricia Morrow, Tracy Pimentel.

Linking past, present, and future, so core to the arguments of this book, has been nurtured in me by my family. Mom and Dad, you created the table and world map around which you two, Mikey, and I sat to listen, to ask questions, to engage in conversations about what is and what could be. You have been my first readers, always, from beaver projects to books, never too tired for one more read, for making sure I know what makes you excited and what can stretch further, always ready to make me feel like I can take a risk, can go where I end up, surrounded by safety, love, purpose, belonging. Scott, your gift of a map helped to link my history to our present and future, shaping our building of a new table around which we sit as a family to talk and make sense of the world and our roles in it. In Toronto and Taku Harbor, in Kalimantan and Kampala, in Cape Town and Gaborone, in Boston and Birch Pond, it is always home, wherever we are together. Our delight is home together with you, Khaya and Mara, whose names in languages of places we love echo home, love, sanctuary, and belonging. You live into those names more and more each day and are our best teachers for the future. Together, Scott, Khaya, and Mara, you typed the t-h-e and the e-n-d of this book and then we raced outside together to play in the newly fallen snow. The end is, quite wonderfully, always a new beginning, for, as Jacques continues to remind me, we are never done here.

Publication Credits

Portions of Chapter 1 were first published as "Refugee Education: Education for an Unknowable Future," *Curriculum Inquiry*, 47:1 (2017): 14–24 and Chapter 2 builds on ideas first presented in this article. Chapter 2 continues discussions first made in and Chapter 3 reprints portions of text first published as "Refugee Education: The Crossroads of Globalization," *Educational Researcher*, 45:9 (2016): 473–482. Chapters 2 and 6 advance work presented in "Bridging Home: Building Relationships between Immigrant and Long-Time Resident Youth," *Teachers College Record*, 112:9 (2010): 2320–2351. The article I wrote with Negin Dahya and Elizabeth Adelman, "Pathways to Educational Success among Refugees: Connecting Locally and Globally Situated Resources," *American Educational Research Journal*, 54:6 (2017): 1011–1047, is the jumping-off place for Chapter 6. The two articles that inform Chapter 4 are "Civic Education and the Education of Refugees," *Intercultural Education*, 31:5 (2020): 592–606 and "The Purpose of Refugee Education: Policy and Practice of Including Refugees in National Education Systems," *Sociology of Education*, 92:4 (2019): 346–366, which I wrote with Elizabeth Adelman, Michelle J. Bellino, and Vidur Chopra.

Index